Lecture Notes in Computer Science 536

Edited by G. Goos and J. Hartmanis

Advisory Board: W. Brauer D. Gries J. Stoer

J. E. Tomayko (Ed.)

Software Engineering Education

SEI Conference 1991
Pittsburgh, Pennsylvania, USA, October 7-8, 1991
Proceedings

Springer-Verlag
Berlin Heidelberg New York
London Paris Tokyo
Hong Kong Barcelona
Budapest

Series Editors

Gerhard Goos
GMD Forschungsstelle
Universität Karlsruhe
Vincenz-Priessnitz-Straße 1
W-7500 Karlsruhe, FRG

Juris Hartmanis
Department of Computer Science
Cornell University
Upson Hall
Ithaca, NY 14853, USA

Volume Editor

James E. Tomayko
Software Engineering Institute, Carnegie Mellon University
Pittsburgh, PA 15213, USA

Carnegie Mellon University
Software Engineering Institute

CR Subject Classification (1991): D.2, K.3.2

ISBN 3-540-54502-6 Springer-Verlag Berlin Heidelberg New York
ISBN 0-387-54502-6 Springer-Verlag New York Berlin Heidelberg

Typesetting: Camera ready by author
Printing and binding: Druckhaus Beltz, Hemsbach/Bergstr.
45/3140-543210 - Printed on acid-free paper

Preface

The Fifth SEI Conference on Software Engineering was held in Pittsburgh, Pennsylvania on October 7 and 8, 1991. This annual conference is sponsored by the Education Program of the Software Engineering Institute, a federally-funded research and development center of the U.S. Department of Defense. For the first time, it was also held in conjunction with the Association for Computing Machinery and the IEEE Computer Society. The conference is a forum for discussion of software engineering education and training among members of the academic, industry, and government communities.

The 18 papers were selected for the conference by a SEI program committee consisting of:

> Mark Ardis
> Maribeth Carpenter
> Lionel Deimel
> Gary Ford
> Norm Gibbs
> Nancy Mead

In addition to the above people, the following were referees:

> Daniel Berry, *SEI and Technion*
> David Bustard, *University of Ulster*
> James Collofello, *Arizona State University*
> Neal Coulter, *Florida Atlantic University*
> Verlynda Dobbs, *Wright State University*
> Theodore Elbert, *University of West Florida*
> Charles Engle Jr., *Florida Institute of Technology*
> Frank Friedman, *Temple University*
> Richard Hamlet, *Portland State University*
> James Howatt, *U.S. Air Force Institute of Technology*
> Lawrence Jones, *U.S. Air Force Academy*
> John Knight, *University of Virginia*
> David Lamb, *University of Maryland*
> Jeffrey Lasky, *Rochester Institute of Technology*
> J. L. Mate, *Universidad Politecnica de Madrid*
> Everald Mills, *Seattle University*
> Robert Noonan, *College of William and Mary*
> R. Perrott, *The Queen's University of Belfast*
> Raclav Rajlich, *Wayne State University*
> Mahesh Rathi, *The Wichita State University*
> John Robinson, *U.S. Air Force Institute of Technology*

Dieter Rombach, *University of Maryland*
Walter Scacchi, *University of Southern California*
Joseph Turner, *Clemson University*
Edward Stabler, *Syracuse University*
Judith Vernick, *SEI*

As is usual with an undertaking of this size and scope, nothing would have been accomplished without an excellent support staff. The level of success is due to the efforts of Barbara Mattis more than anyone else for her tireless tracking of papers, referees, and final manuscripts. Mary Rose Serafini once again devised the schedule and kept the budget, tasks too onerous for program chairs to handle. My sincere thanks to them, the program committee, and the reviewers.

Pittsburgh, Pennsylvania   James E. Tomayko
July, 1991   Conference Chair, CSEE'91

Contents

KEYNOTE ADDRESS:

Soft Ware for Hard Physics

Steve Shafer
School of Computer Science
Carnegie Mellon University
Pittsburgh PA 15213

Abstract. All that we know about software design and reliability comes from the study of programming languages and discrete logic. We really know little or nothing about modeling the continuous, complicated world of nature. Yet, more and more, software systems are called upon to act in or make decisions about the physical world. If the world were discrete and lent itself to "black-box" abstractions, we could directly apply what we know about software engineering to produce competent and reliable systems. However, we have problems in world modeling that begin long before we actually write control and data structure code -- they begin as soon as we parameterize or model the structure of the world. Every time we make a decision about how to represent the world, we necessarily partition the world states into equivalence classes of states with identical representations. We therefore lose the ability to reason about the differences among the states within each equivalence class. I call this "model aliasing", since it's a symbolic version of the "aliasing" phenomenon of signal processing. As a result of model aliasing, we can write programs that are provably "correct" by traditional measures, yet fail because their internal representations of the world are not faithful. Model aliasing actually pervades all of computer science, although it has only become painfully evident in the domains that model the physical world. In real system-building, the problem is exacerbated by our dependence on measurements to calibrate input devices; such measurements induce additional aliasing that we also need to understand and reason about. The usual vocabulary and curriculum in programming and software engineering doesn't even begin to address these issues, and as a result, most programmers and researchers are caught absolutely unprepared to acknowledge, understand, and cope with these problems. In this talk, I will illustrate these issues and present some very fundamental formalisms that, while not anywhere near a useful "theory" of representation, nevertheless help to illustrate the problems that arise when software meets the hard physics of the world.

"A Family Album of Software Project Courses"

Moderator: James E. Tomayko,
Software Engineering Institute, Carnegie Mellon University

Medium Size Project Model: Variations on a Theme
Peter J. Knoke, University of Alaska Fairbanks

A Controlled Software Maintenance Project
Frank W. Calliss and Debra L. Trantina
Arizona State University

Models for Undergraduate Project Courses in Software Engineering
Mary Shaw and James E. Tomayko
Software Engineering Institute, Carnegie Mellon University

MEDIUM SIZE PROJECT MODEL:

VARIATIONS ON A THEME

Peter J. Knoke

University of Alaska Fairbanks

Abstract. *This paper describes some recent variations on a tested theme for teaching Software Engineering in an undergraduate Computer Science program. This theme is referred to here as the Medium-Size Project Model. It has been used as the basis for an introductory Software Engineering course which has been evolving for the last 7+ years at the University of Alaska Fairbanks. The course features 3-way reality in that it uses real software development projects supplied by real customers, and the projects are conducted under realistic schedule and cost constraints in a simulated computer industry environment. Small teams of students acting as a software development company develop a software product for a customer in one semester. The scope of the software development effort is from proposal through software test and customer sell-off. Complete documentation is required, including everything from the proposal through to the customer sell-off document. A short project history is also required. The software product is expected to be developed at a "profit". Project status is monitored by frequent team presentations which cover cost and schedule as well as technical issues. Software engineering lectures are synchronized and interleaved with project reviews. Customer, student, and other feedback indicates that the course has been very successful. The 3-way reality feature is a basic reason for this success. The theme is readily portable to other educational environments, and it allows many interesting implementation variations. Current variations in the six areas of project generation, project selection, instructor roles, student team and role assignments, technical documentation, and grading bases are described.*

1. INTRODUCTION

There is an apocryphal story of an IBM Product Planner who, when asked why IBM tended to have major product announcements at 7 year intervals, reportedly answered "because 8 years is too long and 6 years is too short". The general benefits of using a project-intensive approach to the teaching of an introductory software engineering course are well recognized. However, the particular question arises "what kinds of project should be used, and how big should they be?" At University of Alaska Fairbanks (UAF) we have been using a medium-size projects model for introductory software engineering education with good success for more than 7 years. If asked the question "why use a medium-size project model (and not a large size project model or a small size project model)?", we could give an answer similar to the IBM answer above. Such an answer is correct but not very helpful. Some reasons for it are given below.

Tomayko has prepared a Software Engineering Institute Technical Report about project-intensive courses (Tomayko, 1987) which sings the praises of such courses and provides good rationale for them.

In his report Tomayko identifies four models for an "Introduction to Software Engineering" course, namely:

* The "Software Engineering as Artifact" Model

  All talk, no projects. Major concepts of Software Engineering covered by lecture.

* The "Topical Approach" Model

  All talk, no projects. Major concepts of Software Engineering, plus in-depth coverage of selected areas covered by lectures and student presentations.

* The "Small Group Project" Model

  Half talk, half small group project. Typically 3-5 students on a team. Usually uses instructor-invented projects, fictitious customers, and unrealistic software development environment.

* The "Large Project Team" Model

  Mostly project, little talk. One large real project, with a real customer. Project team of 15-30 students.

The course at UAF which uses the Medium Size Project Model (MSPM) was originally called CS 401 (Software Engineering) and was recently renamed CS 402 (Senior Project and Professional Practice). For convenience we refer to it here as CS 40X. This course fits between Tomayko's "small group project" model and his "large project team" model. It is very similar to the latter except for a smaller team size and a "medium" size project. The basic reasons for the choice of project size are time constraints, the desire for 3-way reality, the desire for full scope, and manpower constraints. The time constraint arises because this introductory Software Engineering course must fit into one 15 week semester. It is a required undergraduate course for Computer Science seniors, and the UAF undergraduate Computer Science program is already fully packed leaving no room for an additional required Software Engineering course. The desire for 3-way reality approach (real project, real customer, and realistic software development environment) and the desire for a "soup-to nuts" scope (proposal to customer sell-off) are also significant constraints. A final constraint is manpower limitations, because a CS 40X class size is typically 15 students and sometimes less. Given all these constraints, it is clear that a "large" size project is not feasible at UAF. On the other hand, to get maximum benefits as large a project as possible is desirable, and it is feasible to do larger projects than those called "small" by Tomayko. Thus we use the descriptor "medium". At UAF a medium-size project is typically about 3500 lines of code and it is carried out by a 5 person team consisting of Computer Science seniors.

This paper summarizes the CS 40X course which implements the basic MSPM theme, and describes some variations that are being explored in the current course implementation.

2. RELATED WORK

CS 40X is described in some detail in an as yet unpublished paper (Knoke, 1990). Copies of this paper are available upon request to Knoke at UAF.

CS 40X is also briefly described in the Software Engineering Institute's Software Engineering Education Directory (McSteen et al., 1989 and 1990). This directory provides a place to search for existing CS-40X-similar courses. Two Software Engineering Institute Software Engineering Education Directories (McSteen et al., 1989 and 1990) were recently examined in search for CS 40X-similar courses. This search revealed only one course (Software Systems Development 544 at Western Michigan University in Kalamazoo) which was strikingly similar. Coordinator Mark Kerstetter recently confirmed this similarity and the fact of the course success (Kerstetter, 1990). The low count of similar courses is a little surprising. However it's possible that a number of other courses described in those directories are also very similar, but with similarities concealed by the standard form of description used.

3. COURSE SUMMARY

CS 40X is briefly described below in terms of goals, design and implementation, results and portability.

3.1 GOALS

At present, CS 40X has four main goals:

* provide realistic project experience

* develop software engineering skills

* address computer ethics issues

* improve written and oral communications skills

The first two goals are briefly treated below. The last two are beyond the scope of this paper.

REALISTIC PROJECT EXPERIENCE

A major goal of CS 40X is to instill in students some sense of software development realities by means of a realistic project. Some major realism subgoals are the following:

* cost and schedule awareness

* teamwork consciousness

* "true requirements" skepticism

* software maintenance issues awareness

* "ornery customers" discovery and recognition

  e.g., the discovery of the existence of customers who may actually:

  - insist on changing requirements in mid-project

  - insist on the use of COBOL or Fortran or even BASIC instead of Pascal or C.

  - insist on the use of a new database package that isn't yet fully debugged.

  - insist on the use of a new computer that isn't yet fully debugged.

  - decline to hold every meeting at the students'

convenience.

- deny access to promised hardware needed for software development, test, or demonstration.

- insist on the use of special purpose hardware for which documentation has been long since lost.

SOFTWARE ENGINEERING SKILLS

Much of the body of knowledge and skills that comprises Software Engineering deals with methods for coping with problems of software development realism. A second major goal of CS 40X is to acquaint students with key parts of this body.

CS 40X can be efficient in imparting Software Engineering knowledge and skills if during the software development period lectures on Software Engineering concepts and knowledge are provided concurrently with the need for them. Thus, when the proposal is being written students can be introduced to methods for determining and documenting the "true" software requirements. Also, when the development schedule is being prepared the students can be shown some methods for estimating project cost and schedule even though some requirements are uncertain. And so on.

Efficiency in imparting Software Engineering knowledge and skills is also enhanced because the MSPM allows multiple concurrent projects. Students on one team can and do learn much by observing the progress and struggles of other teams. They are often surprised to discover that their particular problems are not unique. Furthermore, the teams tend to help each other in structured walkthroughs, by sharing problem solutions, and in other ways.

3.2 DESIGN AND IMPLEMENTATION

A typical recent syllabus and recent schedule for CS 40X are given in Tables 1 and 2 respectively. At the end of the semester project, each team must assemble and submit a Project Notebook wich is typically a 150-200 page document with a table of contents like that shown in Table 3. A typical set of projects with team and functional assignments is provided in Table 4.

TABLE 1

CS 40X   SOFTWARE ENGINEERING

SYLLABUS

CATALOG   DESCRIPTION:

Software design as an engineering discipline. Project planning, proposal writing, and management. Program design, verification, and documentation. Additional topics from security, legal aspects of software, and validation. Students will work on group projects and produce appropriate reports and a project history. (Prerequisites: CS 311, CS 321, and senior standing).

COURSE OBJECTIVES:

Learn-by-doing on a realistic software development team project. Become familiar with emerging software engineering concepts, methods, and tools (e.g. CASE). Become familiar with emerging concepts in computer ethics and law.

COURSE STRUCTURE:

15 lectures, 10 project-related meetings (requirements reviews, design reviews, test results reviews, etc.). Two exams covering Software Engineering concepts and methods, computer ethics, etc. Both exams open book and open notes.

GRADE BASIS:

Project grade (including customer evaluation)   – 75%
(Same grade received by all on the project team)
Exam grade (received on an individual basis)   – 25%

COURSE TEXT:

"Software Engineering - A Practitioner's Approach 2nd ed", Roger S. Pressman, McGraw-Hill, New York, 1987.

REFERENCES:

* "Software Engineering", S. R. Schah, Aksen Assoc., 1990
* "Concise Notes on Software Engineering", de Marco
* "Guide to Effective Software Technical Writing", Browning
* "The Mythical Man-Month", Brooks
* "Urgency of ethical standards intensifies in the computer community", McFarland, IEEE Computer, March '90

TABLE 2

CS 40X   SOFTWARE ENGINEERING

SCHEDULE   SPRING 1990

W#	M#	L#	DAY	DATE	SUBJECT
1	1	1	TH	18 JAN	INTRODUCTION
2	2	2	TU	23 JAN	PROJECT DESCRIPTIONS, SW ENG
	3	3	TH	25 JAN	ATT BUG, TEAM FORM, SW ENG
3	4	-	TU	30 JAN	PROJ B, C REVIEW 30
	5	4	TH	1 FEB	PROJ A REVIEW #0, COMP SYS ENG
4	6	-	TU	6 FEB	PROJECT REVIEWS #1 (A,B,C)
	7	5	TH	8 FEB	SW PROJ PLANNING-1
5	8	6	TU	13 FEB	SW PROJ PLANNING-2
	9	-	TH	15 FEB	PROJECT REVIEWS #2 (A,B,C)
6	10	7	TU	20 FEB	REQ ANAL FUND/METHODS
	11	-	TH	22 FEB	EXAM 1
7	12	8	TU	27 FEB	EXAM #1 REVIEW, SW DESIGN FUND
	13	-	TH	1 MAR	PROJECT REVIEWS #3 (A,B,C)
8	14	9	TU	6 MAR	DATA FLOW ORIENTED DESIGN
	15	-	TH	8 MAR	PROJECT REVIEWS #4 (A,B,C)
*	*	*	TU	13 MAR	SPRING BREAK
*	*	*	TH	15 MAR	SPRING BREAK
9	16	10	TU	20 MAR	CAREER PLANNING (BOB EGAN)
	17	-	TH	22 MAR	PROJ REV #5 (A,B,C) - VIDEO
10	18	11	TU	27 MAR	COMPUTER ETHICS/LAW-1 (KNOKE)
	19	-	TH	29 MAR	PROJECT REVIEWS #6 (A,B,C)
11	20	12	TU	3 APR	COMPUTER ETHICS/LAW-2 (HASSLER)
	21	-	TH	5 APR	PROJECT REVIEWS #7 (A,B,C)
12	22	13	TU	10 APR	DFOD/DSOD
	23	-	TH	12 APR	PROJECT REVIEWS #8 (A,B,C)
13	24	14	TU	17 APR	OOD/REAL TIME DESIGN
	25	-	TH	19 APR	EXAM #2
14	26	15	TU	24 APR	REVIEW OF EXAM #2
	27	-	TH	26 APR	PROJ REV #9 (LAST CLASS)

TABLE 3

PROJECT NOTEBOOK TABLE OF CONTENTS

		Approx size (pg)
1)	Proposal	12
2)	Project Plan	9
3)	Requirements (User's Manual)	27
4)	Design	16
5)	Source Code/Implementation Details	87
6)	Test Plan/Results	11
7)	Customer Acceptance Document	3
8)	Project History/Evaluation	3
		168

TABLE 4

CS 40X SW DEV PROJECT TEAMS

SPRING 1990

	TEAM A	TEAM B	TEAM C
PROJ NAME.	STRIKE	411	PARADOX
SW DESC	PC-BASED SYS FOR LIGHTNING STRIKE LOCATION	HP RISC-BASED SYSTEM FOR UAF TELEPHONE # AND RELATED INFORMATION.	PC-BASED BIDDERS LIST SYSTEM FOR FNSB PROCUREMENT
USERS	BLM FIRE FIGHTERS	TELEPHONE SYSTEM USERS	FNSB PROCUREMENT PEOPLE
ORGAN	BLM	UAF	FNSB
CUSTOMER	JOHN PALMER	DAN LAROE	S. SNEDDEN
CUST PH #	356-5660	474-5341	542-4761
PROJ LDR	JOHN MCCRANIE	ART ORR	VALDA MCMAHAN
DESIGN	EARL VOORHIS	B. KIRKPATRICK	PAT TILSWORTH
IMPLEM	DON LEVINSON	DAVE BRAUN	ANDY WELCH
TEST	TOM STRAUGH	PETER PARKER	DAN GRAHEK
DOCUMENT	STEVE BARRETT	MISTRA MOAZAMI	KARY MCFADDEN

NOTES: On the organization row:

* "BLM" stands for United States Department of the Interior, Bureau of Land Management, Alaska Fire Service.
* "UAF" stands for University of Alaska Fairbanks

Administrative Computing Department
* "FNSB" stands for Fairbanks North Star Borough.

IMPLEMENTATION QUESTIONS AND ANSWERS

A question and answer format is used below to cover some of
the major course design and implementation issues.

3.2.1   Where do the "real" projects come from?

We "beat the bushes" and solicit projects afresh for each
course offering. The telephone is the main instrument used
for this. We also receive and consider unsolicited proposals
from customers who have learned of the course by word of
mouth or from occasional local newspaper articles. This
marketing job is simplified because we have a set of
"regular" customers who from past experience like both the
product and price ($0).

3.2.2   How do we select project from among those proposed?

Some considerations in project selection are the following:

*   Is the project able to be done in 15 weeks by the
    available set of students?

    We seek a realistic challenge for the students, but not
    a Quixotic adventure.

*   Does the customer really want the software end product?

    If so, he has probably had it "on the back burner" for
    awhile. If not, then this project might not be a good
    candidate.

*   Is the project technically interesting?

*   Is the customer a "regular"?

    Regulars get priority. Customers are really partners
    with the school in the educational process, and it
    helps to have partners who understand the rules of the
    game.

*   Does the customer understand the nature of the CS 40X
    paradigm, and is he willing to play his role properly?

    We are not interested in using students as low cost
    programming fodder. The customer must be willing to act
    like a real customer by meeting with students
    periodically, discussing requirements, treating the
    student as a contractor and not as an employee, etc.

3.2.3   What is the nature of the contract between the customer and the UAF software development team?

UAF

1) Agrees to make a strong effort to deliver the software per customer requirements, on time, and tested, with complete documentation.

2) Agrees to try to make student teams behave like "good" software development companies.

3) Does not guarantee that the developed software will be satisfactory functionally, or bug free, or that the documentation will be fully satisfactory.

4) Will not maintain the software after it has been developed and delivered.

CUSTOMER

1) Agrees to try to be a "good" and a "real" customer (i.e., will meet with the students reasonably frequently, will show a real interest in the project status, and will try to refrain from excessively outrageous behavior).

2) Agrees to assist the educational process by providing feedback on team performance to be used for team project grade purposes.

3) Agrees to provide student access to the customer's target hardware and software for software development, test, and demo purposes.

3.2.4   How are students assigned to projects?

In a typical UAF class there are about 15 students and 3 preselected projects. What is the best way to assign these 15 students to the 3 projects? One method is let the students self-assign. Students are given the project descriptions, and indicate their first, second, and third choices. This method (with some adjustments) is very easy to use. Another method is instructor-assign, wherein the instructor makes the assignments on the basis of his knowledge of the students, the projects, and certain assignment goals (such as a uniform distribution of the best students among the projects). Both of these methods have been used with success. One important consideration is that, however done, the assignment should be made quickly because time is very limited and a fast start on the project work is essential.

3.2.5 How are students assigned to functional slots within projects?

As in the question above, two options are modified self-assign and instructor-assign. For either, descriptions of the functional slots must be provided to the students. Both methods have been tried, and both have worked well. Lengthy arguments could be provided in favor of each alternative. Whatever method is used, this assignment must also be made quickly. Adjustments can easily be made later to correct outstandingly bad initial assignments.

3.2.6 What is the size of a reasonable project?

The last half-dozen projects have averaged about 3500 lines of source code, and this size seems to be about right. For planning purposes, we assume about 10 hours per student per week for the CS 40X project, or about $14 \times 10 \times 5 = 700$ hours for a typical project labor budget. Dividing 3500 by 700, we get a baseline productivity measure of 5 lines of implemented, tested, and documented code per man-hour, a respectable figure by current industry standards. At an assumed labor rate of $10/hr, this yields a direct labor cost estimate of about $7000 per 5-man project. With an assumed overhead cost of 35%, we get an estimate of $10,500 as the value of the typical CS 40X software development effort that is donated to the customer by the student team. This is an approximate dollar size for a reasonable project.

3.2.7 What is the role of the instructor in the course?

As a minimum, the instructor must provide initial project descriptions, assistance in assignments (students to projects and students to functional slots), guidance during project executions, lectures on software engineering topics and ethics, and grading services. Additional roles vary depending on instructors, projects, and students. Sometimes instructor intervention is needed to "save" projects. For example, the project leader may be unable to handle his job, or there may be serious dissension among project team members or between a project team and a customer. To minimize risk of disaster, it is desirable for an instructor to have significant actual software development experience or its equivalent. Difficult situations requiring some kind of instructor intervention are the rule rather than the exception. In fact, these situations provide an important aspect of the desired project realism. It is predictable that the difficult situations will arise, but unfortunately for the instructor their exact nature is not predictable.

3.2.8   How are the grades assigned?

Table 1 shows a possible grading basis. However, the actual grading basis can vary with the instructor's preferences. Assuming the Table 1 basis, the overall grade for a student is a mix of team project grade and individual grade.

The project grade can be based on several criteria, but it tends to be dominated by customer feedback. If the customer says that the project grade should be 100, and gives each team member a free dinner at a leading local restaurant, and provides a glowing letter of commendation together with a favorable press release to the local newspaper, then it is hard for an instructor to avoid assigning a project grade of A. On the other hand, if a customer is quite unhappy then the instructor may have to exercise independent judgement to avoid injustice to graduating seniors. This is particularly true at UAF where CS 40X is a required course for Computer Science majors, normally taken in the last semester before graduation.

3.2.9   How does the project grade take into consideration the 80/20 rule (which states that 20% of the students tend to do 80% of the work on a team project)?

This difficult question is applicable to any graded team activity. It is desirable for the instructor to ensure the existence of some individual accountability measures. Such measures help the instructor to perceive who is in the 80% group and who is in the 20% group; however it isn't always clear how best to use this information. So far it has always been the practice in CS 40X to assign the same project grade to every team member. However the overall course grade assigned to a student can be better or worse than his team project grade.

3.2.10   How can the instructor ensure that all projects get off to a fast start?

A fast start is essential to get a substantial project done in one semester. Unfortunately an instructor can't ensure that a fast start will occur for every project because there is always the chance that some unforeseen event will foul things up. To minimize chances of a startup delay the instructor should have all preselected project descriptions and other materials ready for the first class, and he should be prepared to give considerable assistance (push) to all teams in the key first steps of the project. Specifically, those steps are proposal preparation, requirements determination, and project planning. The push is necessary because students usually have no experience in carrying out a project of this kind.

3.3 RESULTS

Customer reports, student reports, and other indicators suggest that CS 40X has worked well over time.

When a customer is very happy with a project, positive indicators are numerous. These indicators include post-project parties given by the customer for the team of students and their instructor, free dinner certificates for team members, letters of appreciation and commendation and favorable press releases. Customer hirings of students who were on their project team are another form of positive success indicator. All the foregoing are quite common for CS 40X projects.

Formal student-generated CS 40X success indicators are routinely available at UAF. They are part of a standard Instructional Assessment System now in use. This system feeds back two items to instructors and administrators, the first a standardized Student Evaluation of Teaching form and the second an Individual Student Comment Sheet. In the most recent issue of the former, the highest student ratings for CS 40X were the "relevance and usefulness of course content". In the most recent issue of the latter, a representative comment was "conceptually the course is great, giving students exposure to real world problems in Software Engineering".

Instructor observation of increasing team enthusiasm as the semester wears on is an example of another success indicator. It is easy for an instructor to tell when a team is "getting into it" - by quality of presentations, by demonstrated creativity in solving difficult problems, etc. Other indicators of course success include student reports of job interviews where they've found recruiters especially interested in their CS 40X team project; what it was, what their roles were, and how it worked out. Students are also pleased that recruiters will consider CS 40X as "experience" in an otherwise experience-devoid resume.

3.4 PORTABILITY

The MSPM-based CS 40X works well at UAF and in Fairbanks Alaska, but is it readily portable to other educational environments? After all, UAF and Fairbanks constitute an atypical educational environment.

There are three main environmental requirements for the success of the CS 40X approach. It is portable to any educational environment that satisfies them. They are:

1) a supportive and receptive local industrial/government community (needed as a continuing source of good projects and customers).

2)   a stable supply of senior-level Computer Science
     students in appropriate numbers (needed to allow a
     course to start and acquire some momentum and reputation
     in its host community).

3)   a supply of suitable Computer Science instructors
     (preferably with industrial/government software
     development experience) to direct the projects in a
     realistic manner.

Since these requirements are not difficult to satisfy, we
conclude that the basic CS 40X approach is readily portable
to many different academic environments.

4.   VARIATIONS ON A THEME

The following features remain constant from one course
offering to the next, and thus constitute its main theme:

*   The "real projects, real customers" feature.

*   The Software Development Company paradigm, with the
     simulated computer industry software development
     environment and the "soup to nuts" scope.

*   The main elements of the instructor's role.

*   The Project Notebook requirement and outline.

The course is continually evolving. The basis for the
evolution is mainly experimentation with variations on the
main theme. We tend to keep the variations that work and
discard those that don't, but the evolution process is not
highly formalized. Items that have been varied in the past
include methods of personnel resource allocation (students
to teams, and team members to functional slots) the coverage
of   particular   software   engineering   and   computer
professionalism topics, details of the instructor's role,
and the grade basis.

A notable problem with the most recently completed version
of CS 40X was the classical one of trying to stuff 10 pounds
of material into a 5 pound bag. To execute a medium-size
software development project from proposal through customer
selloff in a one semester while providing full documentation
is in itself a challenging task. To also include coverage of
many key software engineering concepts and techniques plus
professionalism issues is to flirt with student overload.
The 5 pound bag problem has been recently solved by the
addition of a new course which handles important Software
Engineering material that won't fit into a 3 credit hour CS

40X implementation (this is the reason for the CS 40X naming problem). That new course is presently being designed. It will be offered for the first time in Fall semester 1991.

In the version of CS 40X now underway, six variations are being explored. The areas of variation are listed below, with short discussions following. Brief preliminary assessments on how well the variations worked out are given in Section 5.

SIX AREAS OF VARIATION

* method of project generation

* method of project selection

* details of instructor role

* methods of student team and role assignment

* approach to technical documentation

* basis for grade

4.1 Method of project generation

In his discussion of the project generation issue, Tomayko implies that the requirement for a source of suitable projects is not difficult to satisfy. He makes the following statement:

> "So where are these fascinating projects? Everywhere. Non-profit agencies need all kinds of help; many engineering and science research groups on campus could use computational tools, and there are at least 432 football teams out there using manual scouting analysis methods......" (Tomayko, 1987, pg. 7).

He is certainly correct. This year at UAF we tried to generate projects by placing a small article in the local newspaper (the Fairbanks Daily News-Miner). The article was the following (exact language used was not under the direct control of UAF):

> Students offer software help
>
> If your business or organization needs help getting started, students at the University of Alaska Fairbanks may be able to help.

Students in a senior software engineering course hope to gain experience by designing computer software programs for actual businesses.

If you think the class could design a program for you, submit a brief description of what you need to Ron Gatterdam, a professor in the Math Sciences Department. Gatterdam will choose three or four projects, and the class will design, test and install the program for the business.

In most cases, the customer will be charged only $10 to $20 to cover photocopying charges.

In the past, the class has designed programs for the Bureau of Land Management, the Fairbanks Running Club, and the Fairbanks North Star Borough.

For more information, contact Gatterdam at 474-6174.

That little article ran in the Fairbanks Daily News-Miner on Sunday, 13 Jan 91. On the following Monday, Gatterdam's phone began ringing off the hook, and by the following Friday 15 promising projects had been identified. Previously tried methods had all worked quite well, but the speed, quantity and quality of responses for this method were surprisingly good.

4.2 Method of project selection

In past versions of the course, project selections were made by the instructor without student input. This year we experimented with student input into the selection process by describing the available project descriptions to the students and having them vote their preferences. Approval voting was used. The student selections correlated highly with instructor preferences (could this be because the instructor provided biased project descriptions initially?).

4.3 Details of the instructor's role

Anomalies and dynamics of teacher assignments in the UAF Computer Science program this Spring semester gave rise to a problem for which team teaching of CS 40X seemed to be a good solution. Also, the CS 40X class was unusually small (only 7 students). Therefore, it was decided to select only two projects, and to use a different instructor as the coach/monitor of each of the two project teams. Lecture duties were split between the two instructors.

4.4 Methods of student team and role assignment

Two projects were selected, and there were two instructors to handle them. The method of assigning students to projects was vintage sandlot baseball style. That is:

There was a starting pool of 7 "players"

1. Instructor 1 made his first choice from the pool

2. Instructor 2 made his first choice from the pool

3. Instructor 1 made his second choice from the pool

4. etc.

This left 4 students on one project, and 3 on the other. The assignment of students to specific roles on the projects remained to be made. One instructor made the assignment himself according to his views of what would be best for the students and the project. The other instructor defined the roles and allowed the students to self-assign.

4.5 Approach to technical documentation

This year a new approach is being taken by having a graduate student in English serve as a technical editor for both project teams. By prior arrangement with the English department, this student receives course credit for his technical editing efforts on behalf of the two projects.

4.6 Basis for grade

In the last two course offerings, the student grade was based 75% on team project performance and 25% on individual performance on exams. In the current course offering, the student grades are entirely based on team performance on the projects. The premise is that peer pressure is more than sufficient to minimize or eliminate the 80/20 problem (see question 3.2.9).

Another promising idea for a CS 40X course variation is to to place greater emphasis on marketing aspects of computer software product planning (Gatterdam, 1990). This could be done by attempting to generalize some CS 40X-developed software product to make it more broadly useful. Collaboration with the UAF Business Administration Department could be appropriate in the implementation of this idea. At least one of the two current CS 40X projects is a promising candidate for this treatment. One of the best-received lectures in this Spring 1991 course offering was given by a local software development entrepreneur speaking on the software marketing problem.

In summary, the CS 40X approach to teaching undergraduate Software Engineering is still evolving at UAF. Content growth has caused the original course associated with the approach to be split into two courses. Six variations are being tried in the current implementation, and some promising new ideas await testing in possible future course implementations.

5. SUMMARY AND CONCLUSIONS

An introductory Software Engineering course based on the Medium Size Project Model has been described. The main features of the course model define a theme which has been used successfully at UAF for more than 7 years. The current version of a course based on this proven theme contains six variations which are now being tested. Ideas for other variations await test in future course implementations.

The general merits of a project-intensive introductory Software Engineering course are not in doubt. The particular merits of the Medium-Size Projects Model for such a course are not in doubt either. However, the benefits of specific (seemingly) promising variations on the theme of this model need to be determined by testing.

Six variations have been under test in the current Spring 1991 course implementation. Since this version of the course has not yet ended at this writing, a full report on how these variations worked out can't be given. However, preliminary indications are as follows:

5.1 Method of project generation

Tried a small article in the local newspaper. Worked very well. Many good potential projects identified in a short time.

5.2 Method of project selection

Tried to allow student into the selection of projects from available alternatives. Benefits hard to determine. Tended to interfere with the objective of fast project startups.

5.3 Details of instructors' role

Tried team teaching, one instructor for each of two teams. Problems included confusion for students and coordination problems for the instructors. Not a disaster, but definitely not a great idea (too many cooks spoil the broth).

5.4 Methods of student team and role assignment

The "choose up sides" approach seems to have worked all right for assigning students to projects, but the results of the projects aren't yet in. For student role assignments, one team used self-assign and the other used instructor-assign. No obvious disasters have occurred so far, but again the final results aren't yet in.

5.5 Approach to technical documentation

Tried the use of a graduate student in English to act as a technical editor for both teams. This was done in cooperation with the English Department, with the graduate student receiving course credits for his efforts. At this point this variation doesn't appear to be a great success, but the final results aren't in and an analysis of what actually happened and of what might be improved hasn't yet been done.

5.6 Basis for grade

All students will receive a grade based entirely on the team project grades. One instructor favors this concept, while the other (the writer) doesn't like it. Discussions between the two instructors are planned following the completion of the course to see if a consensus position can be developed.

6. ACKNOWLEDGEMENTS

I thank the four anonymous referees for their careful reading of this paper, and for their suggestions for improvements. I've tried to make the indicated changes wherever possible.

7. REFERENCES

[1] R.Gatterdam. CS 40X private communication at UAF. 11 December 1990.

[2] M.Kerstetter. Answers to questions on Software Systems Development 544. E-mail correspondence on 30 Oct 1990 (kerstetter@gw.wmich.edu)

[3] P.Knoke. Teaching Undergraduate Software Engineering. Computer Science Education (submitted December 1990)

[4] B.McSteen, B.Gottier, and M.Schmick. Software Engineering Education Directory. Technical Report CMU/SEI-90-TR-4, Software Engineering Institute, Carnegie Mellon University, April 1990.

[5] B.McSteen and M.Schmick. Software Engineering
    Education Directory. Technical Report CMU/SEI-89-TR-10,
    Software Engineering Institute, Carnegie Mellon
    University, February 1989.

[6] J.Tomayko. Teaching a Project-Intensive Introduction
    to Software Engineering. Technical Report CMU/SEI-87-R
    -171, Software Engineering Institute, Carnegie Mellon
    University, August 1987.

A Controlled Software Maintenance Project

Frank W. Calliss and Debra L. Trantina
Department of Computer Science and Engineering
College of Engineering and Applied Sciences
Arizona State University
Tempe, AZ 85287–5406, U.S.A.

Abstract. *A group project is presented that introduces students to the need for inter-group communication and controlled work on an evolving program. The project concentrates on the maintenance phase of the software lifecycle and gives students experience in configuration management, version control and software management.*

1 Introduction

Group projects are an important part of many software engineering courses. Factors, such as group dynamics, egoless programming and team organisation, that affect the way programmers work together cannot be taught effectively in a classroom setting. Students have to experience the problems of working in a group in order to understand them. Exposing students to these problems by having the students work in groups is an important step towards the students' appreciation of the solutions to these problems.

Unfortunately, traditional group projects suffer from several weaknesses. As most projects are offered in general software engineering courses, the projects have to encompass aspects from each of the main stages of software development. Some more focused projects have been developed, such as the University of Durham's Software Maintenance Workshop [1] and the SEI's Software Maintenance Exercises [2]. Another weakness is the organisation of the students in the classes. Usual models either use the class as a whole or divide the class into multiple groups. The single group acts as one development team while the multiple groups either work on the same project in parallel or work on different projects. The groups do not depend upon inter-group communication for the completion of their projects.

A group project was designed that would require groups to communicate with each other as they worked on an evolving program. The project was incorporated into the workload of a graduate level course on software maintenance.

This paper covers the project in detail. Section 2 presents the software maintenance course and described the students who worked on the project. Section 3 discusses a proposed model for the maintenance process used to control the work on the project. Section 4 then discusses the project and the students' work. Finally, Section 5 gives an evaluation of the project.

2 Course Description

Arizona State University offers several courses in software engineering. The basic software engineering concepts are introduced in a senior level undergraduate course which serves as a prerequisite for all graduate software engineering courses. The graduate courses specialise in each of the software lifecycle stages: requirements and specifications, design, verification and maintenance, as well as special subject courses such as software metrics and software engineering environments. These courses complement each other so students taking multiple graduate software engineering courses will encounter little repeated material.

The software maintenance course is a one semester class. Students can take this class by either attending the lectures or by using the instructional television service provided by Arizona State University. The students taking this course were spread over many sites at distances of over 35 miles from the main campus. Eight students attended lectures on campus, while twelve students attended through instructional television. The twelve students were located at five off-campus sites, with some sites having only one student and others having two or four students.

The background of the students varied. Some were Masters students taking their first graduate level course in computer science, while others were Ph.D. students completing their course requirements. The computing experience of these students also varied considerably. Some were or had been in industry, while others had received all of their computing experience in academic settings.

The workload for the software maintenance course included term exams, papers and the group project. The project accounted for 30% of the total grade for the class and was the most important assignment of the course. As with many project assignments, the project was aimed at supplementing the material covered in the lectures by giving students personal experience of the subjects. Four important topics covered in the class were: configuration management, version control, software maintenance management, and software maintenance models.

Configuration management is the process of managing the evolution of a system. An important part of configuration management is version control. With version control, different versions of a program are recorded along with information such as creation date, programmers responsible for the version, etc. RCS [5] is a version control system that executes under Unix*. With RCS, it is possible for a programmer to restrict access to a program to prevent two programmers from simultaneously performing different modifications to the same code. RCS also allows a manager to restrict access to a given program to a limited set of named programmers. The students were instructed how to use RCS and were required to use this

---

*Unix is a trademark of AT&T

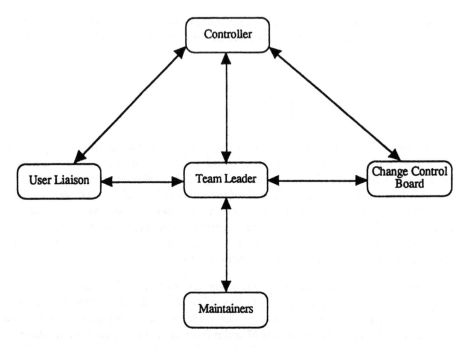

Figure 1: Subset of the Gamalel-Din and Osterweil Maintenance Model

version control system during the project.

In order to properly control a process, it is important that a model of the process be created. A manager can then use this model to control the progress of a task or delegate responsibility to a group or individual. A model of software maintenance should show the activities and personnel involved in the maintenance process. The interactions between the activities or personnel should be marked. Several such models were studied. A subset of the model proposed by Gamalel-Din and Osterweil [3] was adopted for the maintenance project

3 The Gamalel-Din and Osterweil Maintenance Model

Gamalel-Din and Osterweil [3] propose a model of the maintenance process that resembles a business model. The personnel and their interaction are described in this model. Management can use the maintenance model to monitor the progress of a given maintenance request. Each group of programmers has a distinct role in the maintenance process. Figure 1 gives a subset of the model that was used in the group project.

The students and the instructor played various roles in this model. The Maintainers and Team Leader were roles played by the students. Work had to be allocated to different members of the groups to ensure that each member contributed

Player	Roles
Student	Maintainer
	Team Leader
Instructor	Controller
	User Liaison
	Change Control Board

Figure 2: Maintenance Roles and Players

his fair share. How the workload was distributed was left to the students within the group, with the instructor having final approval. The work distribution within a group was explicitly stated and passed on to the Controller. The Controller, played by the instructor, is the person responsible for scheduling the maintenance work and allocating the work assignments to the different groups of programmers (students). The instructor also played the roles of the Change Control Board and the User Liaison. The roles and players are summarised in Figure 2.

The Change Control Board is the means by which configuration management is enforced. All modifications to a program must be approved by the Change Control Board *before* the programmers can implement the change. Similarly, after a modification has been made to the program, the Change Control Board has to approve the new version for release. The User Liaison is the person through which the programmers can communicate with the person requesting the modification. This role was necessary in the class project because the requested modifications were deliberately vague and needed clarification. The Change Control Board was another means by which the user's request was enforced. Any assumptions the Maintainers made that had *not* been approved by the User Liaison would be detected by the Change Control Board.

4   The Project

4.1   The Maintenance Task

The maintenance task was similar to that used by the University of Durham in its Software Maintenance Workshop [1]. Each group of students had to implement a change to the Pascal-S compiler. The program is a non-trivial program with 4,000 lines of Pascal. It was assumed that the students had no previous background in compiler construction.

The four modifications to the Pascal-S compiler are of varying complexity and are described below.

Modification One Pascal-S requires that the program to be compiled reside in a file called *source*. The modification requires the file name be given through the command line.

Modification Two A new looping construct allows an exit from a loop statement in Pascal-S.

Modification Three The modified case statement allows ranges in the tag part and allows a default action section.

Modification Four The symbol table currently uses a sequential search. A hash function is to be used.

4.2 Group Organisation

Four duplicate versions of the Pascal-S compiler were needed. Each version had two or three groups modifying it. Each group was making a different modification, but each modification was affected by the other groups' work. Therefore it was important that the groups communicate with each other so that they would be aware of the other groups' work that could affect their own.

In organising students into groups, it was important the students be able to meet with each other in order to work on the maintenance requirements. Because of distances involved, each of the off-campus sites represented different maintenance teams. The eight students on campus were then split into four groups of two students each. The students were assigned to groups on the basis of their previous work in the class. These students were ranked by grades and paired by (highest, lowest), (second highest, second lowest), etc.

The nine groups of students were then distributed over the four programs. All groups working on the same version were physically separated and no group knew which other groups were working on their version of the code. The only means of communication was through the Controller or the Change Control Board.

4.3 Work Method

The project lasted six weeks and was done in two phases. In the first phase, a design of the modification was developed. The second phase was the implementation of the modification. Each phase is discussed below.

4.3.1 Phase One

The students received a maintenance request and were given three weeks to design the modification. At the end of this time, the students submitted the design documents to the Change Control Board for evaluation. The design documents had to contain each of the following: a description of the maintenance requirements, design of the modification, and a description of the sections of code that may be affected by the modification.

In order to design the modification, many of the groups found it necessary to consult with the User Liaison to clarify what the user actually wanted. Examples of these types of questions are "what keyword did the user want to denote the default action in the new case statement?" and "Did the introduction of an exit statement mean the user would allow an exit from a while or a for loop?" All consultations were record by the instructor in the role as the User Liaison. When the instructor was acting as the Change Control Board and reviewing the design documents, the additional information given to particular groups was available.

In order to design the modification, it was necessary for the students to examine the program and establish which sections of code would be affected and how they were to be altered. Students were not given on-line access to the code. Instead, they were given access to an executable version of the code and a hard copy of a structured cross reference. A listing and description of the program were also given in a required text for the class [4].

4.3.2 Phase Two

The second phase of the project began with the return of the design documents to the groups. The Change Control Board returned the design documents with comments to notify the teams of other teams' changes to the code that could affect their work. For example, the group re-implementing the symbol table as a hash would need to know that new keywords were being added. For this project, the Change Control Board did not report any errors or omissions in the design documents. The students had been told that if they needed to update the design documents during the second phase, an errata or addendum sheet could be submitted to the Change Control Board for evaluation.

During Phase Two, the groups still had contact with the User Liaison although this contact was not likely to be needed. The main contacts for the Maintainers (students) were the Controller and Change Control Board.

The Controller needed to schedule the work of the groups for each version of the compiler. Each group was given a one week window to implement its modification. For the class, it was important the maintenance requirements were serviced in an order that would affect the greatest number of students. For example, changing the name of the input file would be the first change as this would affect all subsequent groups.

A total of three weeks was given for all the groups to modify a particular version of the Pascal-S compiler. In this three week period, it was important that the Controller allowed some overflow time so that a group that did not complete its modification could go back and finish the work.

It was only when Phase Two started that the students were given access to the source of the Pascal-S compiler. The source code was provided in RCS format and the students were required to use RCS during their modifications of the compiler.

The deliverables for Phase Two included the modified source code and several support documents. One document was the updated RCS file with check-in messages. The groups were required to enter a message each time they checked in a version of the compiler to RCS. Other deliverables for Phase Two included the errata and addendum to the design documents that were created in Phase One. The final deliverable was a document that described the actual modification that was performed. An important part of this document was the section describing how the modifications had been tested.

4.4 Grading

The work of the students was graded in terms of how well the code had been modified and tested, and the quality and accuracy of the documentation submitted to the Change Control Board. These documents included the design documents, the modification description documents and the RCS file.

The students were informed that when grading the design documents, they would not be penalised for failing to indicate a change that would be needed, or failure to indicate a potential ripple effect resulting from the modification *if* in a subsequent errata or addendum sheet, the error or omission from the design document was corrected. If the students did not identify the error they would be penalised. And, if the students did notice the error but failed to submit the errata or addendum sheet to the Change Control Board for approval, they would be penalized twice: once for having an incorrect design document and once for performing the modification phase incorrectly. Therefore, if a student failed to follow the chosen maintenance model, they would be penalised.

4.5 Results

Only one group failed to successfully implement the change. The use of RCS meant that other groups were not affected and were able to implement their maintenance requirements because they could retrieve the version of the program that preceded the incorrect version. The remaining groups completed their tasks correctly and on schedule.

5 Evaluation of the Project

The project gave students experience of working on an evolving program where all work was required to be controlled. No modification to the code could be done without first being approved by the "management". The times when students could work on the code were also restricted.

The instructor plays several key roles in this project organisation. If students were to play these roles in the class, they would gain even more of an appreciation of controlled software maintenance. Since many of the students in the class were at different locations, it was not possible to allow the students to experience all the roles in the maintenance model.

A possible criticism of this project is that the maintenance model used is unrealistic. In industry, different groups of programmers communicate informally as well as through a formal system such as the one described in the model. However, this project was not aimed at simulating industry work practices. Instead, the students were given an appreciation for how the maintenance process could be controlled and why this control is needed.

Acknowledgements

I would like to thank David Robson for providing the source code and the structured cross reference listing of the Pascal-S compiler.

References

[1] Cornelius, B.J., Munro, M., and Robson, D.J., "An Approach to Software Maintenance Education," *Software Engineering Journal*, vol. 4, pp. 233–236, July, 1989.

[2] Engle, C.B., Ford, G., and Korson, T., *Software Maintenance Exercises for a Software Engineering Project Course*, Software Engineering Institute, Carnegie Mellon University, CMU/SEI-89-EM-1.

[3] Gamalel-Din, S.A. and Osterweil, L.J., "New Perspectives on Software Maintenance Processes," in *Conference on Software Maintenance — 1989*, IEEE Computer Society Press, pp. 14–22, 1989.

[4] Rees, M.J. and Robson, D.J., *Practical Compiling with Pascal-S*, Addison-Wesley, Reading, Massachusets, 1988.

[5] Tichy, W.F., "RCS — A System for Version Control," *Software — Practice and Experience*, vol. 18, no. 7, pp. 637–654, July 1985.

Models for Undergraduate Project Courses in Software Engineering

Mary Shaw

School of Computer Science
&
Software Engineering Institute
Carnegie Mellon University

and

James E. Tomayko

Software Engineering Institute
Carnegie Mellon University

Abstract

The software engineering course provides undergraduates with an opportunity to learn something about real-world software development. Since software engineering is far from being a mature engineering discipline, it is not possible to define a completely satisfactory syllabus. Content with a sound basis is in short supply, and the material most often taught is at high risk of becoming obsolete within a few years.

Undergraduate software engineering courses are now offered in more than 100 universities. Although three textbooks dominate the market, there is not yet consensus on the scope and form of the course. The two major decisions an instructor faces are the balance between technical and management topics and the relation between the lecture and project components. We discuss these two decisions, with support from sample syllabi and survey data on course offerings in the US and Canada. We also offer some advice on the management of a project-oriented course.

For most undergraduate students, an upper-level software engineering course provides their best opportunity to learn about "real-world" software development: group projects, large-scale design, integration of software with larger systems, applying theory in practical settings, understanding clients' requirements, models of the development life cycle, configuration management, quality assurance, maintenance, and so on. In many universities it is our last and best chance to show students that developing a real software system is not at all the same thing as writing a programming assignment that will be graded and thrown away. The course is most often taken by students about to enter the work force as programmers; our experience is that corporate recruiters are *very* enthusiastic about the things students learn in these courses.

A great deal of material is available—much more than can be covered in a quarter or a semester—so the course design problem is one of selecting the subset to present and the viewpoint from which to present it. Versions of this course have been offered for nearly 20 years, but despite that extended history the course is far from standard in either content or format.

Any curriculum design task is in part a resource allocation task. The scarce resource is course content, measured indirectly by class time, student energy, and testing attention, among other factors. The evaluation criterion for the use of this resource is benefit to the student through his or her career, and we often describe as "fundamental" course content with this durable value. Software engineering includes both fundamental material and techniques (often management strategies) that are currently useful but are likely to be superseded as fundamental material emerges. As a result, the challenge to the software engineering instructor is to find meaty, substantive material that will continue to be significant to the student over many years.

An instructor faces two major decisions in selecting a strategy for the software engineering course. The first is what balance to strike between technical issues of software design and development on the one hand and project management topics on the other. Section 1 discusses the considerations that affect this decision. The instructor's second decision is how to allocate class effort between project work and lectures—and how to coordinate the two. Section 2 describes several course models that make different tradeoffs on this dimension, and Section 3 discusses the *kinds* of projects used in undergraduate courses.

In doing this analysis we had the benefit of the Software Engineering Institute's annual survey of Software Engineering Courses [83] and personal contact with some two dozen instructors. Section 4 and the Appendix present some objective data from the spring 1990 survey, including the position of the courses in the curriculum and the textbooks in use.

To put flesh on the bones of this overview, Sections 5.1 through 5.5 present the plans of several versions of the course, including syllabi of actual offerings, outlines of textbooks, and curriculum designs.

Finally, no matter which decision the instructor makes on the two major questions of content and organization, any course with a significant group-project component presents several special problems. Section 6 notes some of these and suggests ways to deal with them.

Software engineering education has regularly been singled out for special attention. An early workshop was held in 1976 [129]. An annual series of workshops on software engineering education has been sponsored since 1986 by the Software Engineering Institute [56, 47, 49, 55, 38]. Papers on particular topics also appear regularly in the ACM *SIGCSE Bulletin* and in special issues of other professional journals.

1. Content Balance: Technical vs. Management

Traditionally, engineering is defined as "creating cost-effective solutions to practical problems by applying scientific knowledge to building things in the services of mankind" [113]. Against that standard, the phrase "software engineering" is a statement of aspiration, not a description of accomplishment. Nevertheless, we face a crying need to get better control over the software development task, and to do so in the short term.

Engineering disciplines have historically emerged from ad hoc practice in two stages. They are rooted in the exploitation of a technology by individual craftsmen. As the technology becomes more significant, management and uniform production techniques are developed to support a stable market. Problems with production in this commercial setting stimulate the development of a supporting science. As the science matures, it merges with established practice to enable a professional engineering practice rooted in the science [113]. Figure 1-1 depicts this evolution.

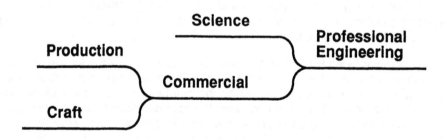

Figure 1-1: Evolution of an Engineering Discipline

Certainly the software development task is appropriately an engineering problem: it involves "creating cost-effective solutions to practical problems". What's currently lacking is widespread routine application of scientific knowledge to a wide range of practical design tasks. Some science is mature, most notably algorithms, data structures, and compiler construction theory. However, the current demands are far ahead of the scientific base. In other words, the field of software engineering is still immature, but the situation is improving, albeit more slowly than need requires.

Absent a mature science base, developers of large software systems resort to establishing routine practices which, even if ad hoc, will nevertheless guide programmers to relatively predictable outcomes. As a result, the "software engineering" label is being applied to a set of management topics such as project planning, cost/schedule estimation, and team organization.

These topics may represent best current practice, but
- the pipeline of scientific results with practical utility is filling, particularly in specific application areas,
- course energy will have the highest payoff if invested in the most durable content, and
- use of the "engineering" label for what are essentially management topics may preempt its use for real engineering techniques—and may even divert attention from the cultivation of those techniques.

Here lies the source of the instructor's dilemma: whether to emphasize the mature science or the current practice. The former is less applicable at present but has been refined enough to retain its value for years to come. The latter represents useful skills that may become obsolete—and may further be inefficient in course time per unit of content. The decision is complicated by the need to present material that is simply required in order to carry out a sizeable group project.[1] For concreteness, we list here typical technical and management topics. It is difficult to fully separate the two, for a given subject can sometimes be approached with either emphasis. For example, "configuration management" has both technical content (formal methods of system description) and management aspects (composition and activities of a configuration control board). This dichotomy exists for several other areas within the scope of software engineering: life cycle models, quality assurance, maintenance topics, etc.

Technical engineering topics
- abstraction and specification, and their proper use in design
- formal methods of requirements specification and of verification
- large-scale data, including scientific, commercial database, and AI issues
- security and reliability
- distributed systems, including synchronization/atomicity and network communication
- real-time systems
- concepts of prototyping
- development of metrics for measuring quality factors
- system description languages
- techniques for software reuse

---

[1]An additional argument for including management topics arises from employers' needs: it has been our experience that students with a solid background in software engineering currently advance quite rapidly after graduation to team leadership positions in which they need to know those skills. In one instance, a Carnegie Mellon graduate found himself leading a small independent research and development team in a major aerospace company within four months of leaving school. He reported that his supervisors chose him for the lead because he had a better understanding of the overall software development process than the more experienced computer science graduates who had not studied software engineering and also had not as yet gained an appreciation for the "big picture."

- automated development environments and their characteristics
- configuration management
- structuring software for maintenance

Management topics

- life cycle models as a framework for development planning
- requirements analysis
- estimation and tracking
- nature and use of development standards
- configuration management
- development team organization, structured design methods (e.g., Yourdon, Jackson, SADT)
- tracking progress through internal documents
- the use of quality assurance
- reviews and walkthroughs
- maintenance

In general, the course plans that we have reviewed show a strong management emphasis both in the topics discussed in class and in the project work. The most often-used textbooks, whose outlines are presented in Section 5.1 certainly show that emphasis. For comparison, an example of a course based on a technical theme, in this case abstraction, is given in Section 5.2. We can suggest several reasons for the predominance of courses with a management emphasis:

- The most popular texts spend a considerable percentages of their content discussing life cycle models, management issues relating to organizing software teams, quality assurance and configuration management from the standpoint of their organizational impact rather than their technical activity, etc.; this textual emphasis creeps into the syllabi of inexperienced instructors.

- Instructors with industrial experience recognize that the chief failings of software projects in the commercial world are poor effort and resource estimates, poor communication, lack of configuration management and quality assurance, and the like rather than technical problems.

- A certain amount of management material is needed to keep a group project running well. Since this material is qualitatively different from the topics students are used to seeing in computer science courses, it is likely to be more time-consuming to teach.

- Most of the students plan to go directly into industry after graduation, and this is the only place in the undergraduate computer science curriculum where these topics can be adequately taught.

Alas, these reasons put vocational considerations ahead of the traditional criteria of curriculum design.

Until very recently the technical issues associated with software engineering fit quite well within the course alongside the management issues in that there was so little to discuss there was plenty of class time for both. The students usually enter the course with a solid grounding in program construction, so the challenge appeared to be meshing the management techniques with the software development techniques. Software engineering as a technical discipline has hardly stood still, and formal methods, new design paradigms, and other technical topics are squeezing the syllabus from one end, while process maturity models, post-development management issues, and other management topics are squeezing it from the other. There is now a very real need to make decisions on content different from the decisions early in the last decade.

Many different decisions about the balance of technical and management topics can be supported for different institutional settings and variations on the basic objective of learning about "real-world" software. But to justify the title "software engineering", the course must convey to students the engineering point of view: that engineering of software involves generating alternative designs and selecting—for good reasons—the ones that best resolve conflicting constraints and requirements of the ultimate customer.

2. Models of the Undergraduate Software Engineering Course

Beginning software engineering courses have been taught with content that crosses a range from no project work at all to highly-intensive project work. Figure 2-1 is an illustration of the spectrum of courses. These models are drawn from extensive discussions with instructors of these courses over seven years, augmented by the literature.

An underlying assumption of these models is that students enter the course with the technical background of program construction gained in the prerequisite courses, and the purpose of the software engineering course is to demonstrate how this technical material is applied in the context of large scale software development. Students are expected to have knowledge and skills in the application of high level programming languages, especially those that emphasize structure and abstraction, knowledge of machine organization, perhaps demonstrated by facility with assembly language, and grounding in the fundamental principles and algorithms of computer science. Further, students ought to be good writers and also to have senior standing. This last requirement is to ensure that the students have had some upper-division courses such as theory, compiler design, survey of programming languages, and the like, and also so that they have some maturity in both their academic and personal lives. Jon Bentley once said that a useful prerequisite for the study of software engineering is that the student "should have been married at least once." This is not strictly enforced(!), but the students should have some ability to communicate and work together somewhat harmoniously.

2.1. The "Software Engineering as Artifact" Model

The leftmost model illustrates the subject taught mostly by lecture, with some interaction among the instructor and students, mostly relating to questions and difficult points. There are two advantages of this approach: there is easily enough time in either a 10-week quarter or 16-week semester to present the major concepts of software engineering; and the absence of a project means that the students can concentrate on the issues the instructor wants to discuss rather than the "crisis of the week." The major disadvantage is that teaching software engineering without doing it is as bad as teaching piano playing by the lecture method. Many issues in software engineering, particularly in communication and configuration control, simply can not be appreciated in the absence of experience. Since most projects that fail do so because of deficiencies in those two areas, we would be doing our students an injustice by not exposing them to the problems inherent in actually working on software products. Due to the nature of these courses (and for reasons discussed in Section 1, they often follow the plan described in Section 5.1.

2.2. The "Topical Approach" Model

Although this is another of the all-talk, no-action models, it has the advantage of in-depth exploration of some aspects of the subject. Usually used at the graduate level, the lecture part of the course is roughly the same as the previous model, but it is supplemented by weekly presentations by the students. Each student is assigned a topic (object-oriented design, automated specification tools, verification of real-time software, etc.) and asked to read two or three papers on it and conduct a seminar for the other students. Here a succinctly written text such as one by Fairley [46] or Sommerville [118] can be used to back up the main lectures, while the students provide their own reading material for the discussion sessions. Alternatively, essay collections such as Brooks [23] or Mills [88] can feed the discussions. Yourdon's publishing arm has also produced a pair of collections of outstanding papers in software engineering [134, 135], although some are becoming dated. Again, these courses often follow the Section 5.1 plan, even though they have additional readings.

2.3. The "Small Group Project" Model

This model includes a project as part of the course, for the positive reasons discussed above. Currently the most common model of this course, it makes a fairly even division between project work and class work. The projects chosen are often familiar to the students and can be done in a single term. However, the limited course effort dedicated to the project necessarily limits its size and scope.

In Kant's presentation of this model [68], she lists some suggestions: a string-handling package for standard Pascal, a reservation system for the computer center's terminal room, and an interactive text editor, among others. Typically, from three to five students are included in each team. This model provides the students with some of the experience needed to apply the software engineering concepts discussed in class. However, it is deficient in its ability to enable the students to experience the critical difficulties inherent in doing "programming-in-the-large."

The use of a small project, small teams, and often fictitious customers may simply extend the "programming-in-the-small" experience normally gained in computer science course work. However, adequate attention to configuration management and quality assurance issues can bring in larger project issues. One way of taking advantage of the manageability of small teams while still teaching something about programming-in-the-large is to use the course organization described in Section 5.5. Another reason that small teams are used is that the start of the project is delayed until about the middle of the term due to the desire to teach some prerequisite technical material. [62] This often happens when using the course plan described Section 5.2.

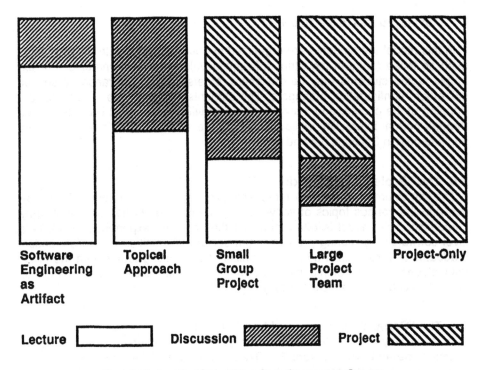

Figure 2-1: Models of the One-Semester Course

2.4. The "Large Project Team" Model

This model posits that the best way to learn techniques for dealing with programming-in-the-large (which often means dealing with programming-in-the-many) is to conduct a large team project within the class. Quite simply, there is one project, usually one piece of deliverable software; often there is also a real customer, who provides a form of motivation different from grades. If we accept that a central objective of the course is to immerse the student in a practical, real-life software product development process, then this is how to do it. The figure indicates, quite correctly, that the majority of the work the students do is on the project. Many instructors object to this model because they feel that it is too difficult to manage. Not so. If it is too difficult to manage a project team of 15 to 30 students, then how is it possible to manage a real-life corporate development team of 15 to 30 software engineers? The authors have run introductory courses using this model at least 10 times, in general quite successfully. Even with partial failure, the students learn more about real software engineering than with any other model. The key for the instructors using this model is to remember the following:

> *The students are doing the project. You are not. You are managing the project, which means that you are delegating nearly all aspects*

of the process to the students.[2].

In this model the students are organized in one large team with different roles such as those found in industrial software development environments. For example, some students may be designers, others quality assurance personnel, still others configuration managers. The students remain in these roles for the duration of the course, and learn about the activities associated with other roles through normal interaction while developing the software. This model is shown implemented in Sections 5.4 and 5.5.

2.5. The "Project Only" Model
The fifth column in Figure 2-1 represents this model: the entire course is a project, and the various topics of software engineering are learned and applied by immersion. This model is often found as the capstone experience of master's level software engineering programs, but several universities also allow undergraduates to take such a course, organizing the resulting teams with the graduate students in leadership positions and the undergraduates subordinate to them. The undergraduates learn by doing.

2.6. The "Separate Lecture and Lab" Model
In many ways, this model is a combination of the courses represented by columns one and five of Figure 2-1. Though nominally linked by related course numbering, software engineering lecture courses with separate labs have coordination reminiscent of freshman physics courses of twenty years ago. The amount of coordination is strongly related to whether or not the course instructor is also the lab instructor.

3. Project Styles
Independent of the organization that connects the lecture and project components of the course, several styles of projects are available. They differ primarily in the degree to which they stretch the student beyond traditional programming assignments, and in the degree of interaction with other students in the course. They also differ in emphasis and in the amount of instructor effort required.

Virtually all project courses organize the students into teams. The major parameters in the project decision are:

- Is the project standalone, or does it involve integrating hardware or software components from other sources?

- Is the project specified by the instructor, by the class (as the first task of the course), or by an external client? How detailed is this specification (and how much work must the students do to make the requirements precise)?

- Do all teams complete the same assignment, or do the teams develop separate components and integrate them?

---

[2]Examples of other instructors successfully managing this sort of course are described in [93] and [109]

- Does each student play all roles in the project team, or is there specialization of individuals or teams?

- Is the emphasis on the technical development of software, on the organization and management of the team, on the interaction with the client (e.g., for requirements and delivery), or on something else?

Some of the common points in the space defined by these parameters are described below.[3]

3.1. Toy Project

The class is divided into teams of 3-5 students; each team gets the same task, pre-specified by instructor. In a variant, each team creates its own specification, perhaps within a given scope such as "create a computer game using this interface/library."

The advantages of this style are that it teaches teamwork in a small group and it results in a large-ish program, but it rarely addresses requirements or integration. It is probably the simplest to manage from the instructor's viewpoint, and teaching assistants can be effectively used as advisors to groups. Also, where there is a mix of graduate and undergraduate students in a course, the graduate students often lead these small teams. However, this style fails to transcend the development methods effective for most smaller programs, and often ignores configuration management and other issues important to programming-in-the-large. Despite these disadvantages, Leventhal and Mynatt [77] report that 40 per cent of all software engineering courses use this style.

3.2. Mix-and-match Components

In this style, the project's software product requires several components. Small teams develop each one (to precise specification) and several versions of the final software result from integrating different collections.

One instantiation of this style is Horning's *Software Hut* [63]. The project requires half to a third as many components as there are teams. In first stage, each team develops one component, then "buys" components from other teams and "sells" its own so each team gets a complete set. In second stage, each team integrates components to produce complete system. A third stage, requiring another round of sales and a modification task, may follow.

This project style teaches many of the same topics as the "Large Programming Assignment"; additionally it gives the students some experience with rigidly-defined interface specifications and integration techniques on a larger scale. Additionally, the concept of software reuse can be vividly demonstrated. Management of this style is nearly the same as for "Toy Project."

---

[3]Two other studies of undergraduate software engineering courses also have taxonomies of project styles. Thayer and Endres [122] specify 11 examples of courses and projects, while Leventhal and Mynatt [77] derived only three. These two analyses make roughly the same distinctions as we have, but they do not clearly distinguish the separate concerns about project size (Section 2) and project style (this section).

3.3. External Client

The student teams work on components of a product for an external client, integrate results, and then pass an acceptance test set by the client. This style teaches teamwork, project organization, requirements extraction and representation, integration, and client relations. From the course management perspective, this style potentially requires much work from the instructor, especially on "customer relations." Whereas a simulated economy such as Software Hut is designed to be competitive, this style is intended to be cooperative—the success of all depends on successful delivery.

As described in Sections 5.4 and 5.5, either a group of small teams or a single large team can be used to implement the project. Experience shows that the motivation of the students is significantly higher with an external client, most probably due to the prospect of seeing their software in actual use, perhaps by their peers.

3.4. Individual Projects

Projects are individually arranged for each team in this style. Often these have clients outside the course, for example, the campus computing facility or departmental research projects. For this reason, the course may be chaotic from a management standpoint, especially if it is essentially an independent-study course for groups of students rather than individuals. Otherwise, it has many of the same features as the other small-team approaches.

4. Survey of Software Engineering Courses

The Software Engineering Institute annually conducts a survey of software engineering degree programs and courses [83]. The most recent survey, reported in April 1990, included 12 degree programs and courses at 165 schools in the US and Canada. The degree programs all lead to a Masters degree and are not considered here. The survey originally queried schools with graduate programs in computing and information systems and has been extended to include schools with undergraduate offerings in those areas.

The reporting from school to school was not uniform: some included software-related courses that do not appear to be at all like the course of interest here. After deleting a variety of courses in subjects such as data structures, artificial intelligence, security, and networking, we summarized the reported data on the remainder. Details are provided in the Appendix (Section 8). After this pruning, the survey found 472 courses at the 165 institutions.

A total of 126 schools reported 205 software engineering courses explicitly open to undergraduates. Of these, 144 were reported to be undergraduate courses and 61 were open to both graduates and undergraduates. Since the survey pool is biased in favor of schools with strong computing programs, it is reasonable to expect that the survey will find more undergraduate offerings than the college and university population at large. Thus the availability of software engineering courses to undergraduates in only 75% of those schools suggests a substantially weaker market penetration overall. We speculate that the reasons might include resource constraints, shortage of faculty prepared to teach the course, or the fact that it is listed only as an elective in Curriculum '78 [2], the most recent recommendation from the professional organizations. Note, however, that over half of the purely undergraduate courses are reported in the survey as required.

The most common course titles among the undergraduate courses are shown in Table 4-1. We also grouped the titles into rough categories, finding 87 software engineering courses (42%), 41 courses concerned with particular stages of the life cycle (20%), 28 project courses (14%), and assorted others.

Number	Course Name
30	Software Engineering (one term)
17	Software Design and Development, SW Design, SW Development, etc
13	Systems Analysis and Design, Systems Analysis, Structured System Design, etc.
9	Introduction to Software Engineering
9	Software Engineering Project, Senior Project
8	Software Methodology, Programming Methodology
7	Software Engineering I and II (two terms)

Table 4-1: Most Common Undergraduate Software Engineering Course Titles

Leventhal and Mynatt [77] surveyed software engineering courses in 240 of the 820 undergraduate computer science programs listed in ACM's 1984 administrative directory. With a 25% response rate, they found 35 courses that match the portion of the SEI survey reported here. The most commonly-used course title was "Software Engineering" or some variant(19 of 35); an additional 9 course titles referred to specific stages in the life cycle; the remaining 7 course titles were related to software development.

Well over a hundred textbooks are mentioned in the SEI survey; the vast majority are used by only one or two courses. Even when a textbook is assigned for a course, the course does not necessarily follow the text closely. However the text and the course title are the best indicators of content provided by the survey. Table 4-2 shows the dozen or so of most frequently-used textbooks for all the courses surveyed together with the number of courses open to undergraduates that use each. These account for about 60% of the courses. The Appendix extends the list and compares graduate to undergraduate text selection.

5. Course Plans: Examples

These models have been realized in a variety of ways. This section surveys five rather different forms. In each case we have described the general flavor of the course and provided citations to more detail. The details are brought together in an expanded version of this paper [114].

5.1. Life Cycle Emphasis

College courses often use textbooks as resources rather than following them strictly. However, the textbooks certainly show how their authors intended the courses to be structured. When an instructor is not fully confident of the subject matter, the text organization often prevails. In the case of the three dominant texts, this means that the waterfall life cycle model drives the course organization, with the emphasis heavily on the six stages of project planning, require-

# Cites		Textbook
All	Open to UGs	
60	38	Pressman, *Software Engineering: A Practitioner's Approach* [103]
46	31	Sommerville, *Software Engineering* [118]
46	29	Fairley, *Software Engineering Concepts* [46]
32	20	manuals on languages and tools
32	5	selected readings
26	18	Booch, *Software Engineering with Ada* [20]
20	12	Brooks, *Mythical Man-Month* [23]
15	1	Shooman, *Software Engineering: Design, Reliability, and Management* [116]
10	4	Yourdon, *Modern Structured Analysis* [136]
10	2	Conte, *Software Engineering Metrics and Models* [34]
9	5	Liskov, *Abstraction and Specification in Program Development* [79]
9	5	Myers, *The Art of Software Testing* [91]
9	5	Page-Jones, *The Practical Guide to Structured Systems Design* [97]
8	8	Lamb, *Software Engineering: Planning for Change* [76]

Table 4-2: Commonly-Used Software Engineering Texts

ments analysis and specification, design, implementation, validation, and maintenance. Other topics are discussed, but often in an order that actually precludes good software development practice. For example, material on configuration management is relegated to the back of the texts, giving the impression that it either comes into play at that point in a software project, or that it is so unimportant as to be a candidate for exclusion if the other topics fill the semester.

The life cycle emphasis is clearest in Fairley's text [46]. It is also visible in Pressman [103] and Sommerville [118].

5.2. Abstraction Emphasis

One example of a text that breaks the waterfall organizational paradigm is the one by Liskov and Guttag which concentrates on abstraction as a tool and method for software development [79]. In this organization, the technical basis for abstraction and a suitable language are introduced prior to the presentation of a model of the software development process. The authors are careful to provide explicit examples of design based on abstraction in this latter section. In many ways this text is a good statement of the fact that there is some available technical underpinning for software engineering practice.

5.3. Technical Emphasis

In the early 1980s, Carnegie Mellon proposed a plan for a complete undergraduate curriculum; the curriculum was published in 1985 [112]. That plan included *both* a project-based software engineering course and a follow-on project-only course that allowed for extended experience.

- *Software Engineering:* The student studies the nature of the program development task when many people, many modules, many versions, or many years are involved in designing, developing, and maintaining the system. The issues are both technical (e.g. design, specification, version control) and administrative (e.g., cost estimation and elementary management). The course will consist primarily of working in small teams on the cooperative creation and modification of software systems.

- *Software Engineering Lab:* This course is intended to provide a vehicle for real-world software engineering experience. Students will work on existing software that is or will soon be in service. In a work environment, a student will experience first-hand the pragmatic arguments for proper design, documentation, and other software practices that often seem to have hollow rationalizations when applied to code that a student writes for an assignment and then never uses again. Projects and supervision will be individually arranged.

5.4. Large Project Management Emphasis

During the last decade, one of the authors (Tomayko) has frequently taught the introductory software engineering course organized in a highly project-intensive manner. One such offering, in 1986, was captured in a technical report of the SEI Software Engineering Curriculum Project [123]. The course was revised for the Fall 1990 offering [124]. It is interesting to compare the two offerings, which are four years apart, to note changes in topics and emphasis. For example, the concept of software process assessment is absent in 1986, and although risk reduction activity was practiced in the earlier course, it was not highlighted as in the later course.

5.5. Even Balance of Management, Engineering, Tools

This version of the introductory software engineering course was taught in fall 1989 by one of the authors (Shaw) around a project with a real deliverable for a real client. This case study describes the background and organization of the course and sketches the project. The description is drawn from a complete report on the course, including the supplemental materials and course handouts, prepared for the SEI Software Engineering Curriculum Project [24].

We decided that we could make these characteristics of software systems more vivid by choosing a project whose result could benefit some group on campus, preferably the campus computing community at large. We polled the local community for suggestions, and chose a proposal from the Information Technology Center (the group that developed Andrew, the campus-wide computing system). They suggested combining various existing software facilities to provide a bridge between electronic mail and facsimile transmission provided by a special fax board running in a personal computer. The students succeeded in developing a running prototype, which they demonstrated in a formal presentation and acceptance test at the client's site.

In planning the lecture component of the course, we examined most of the popular textbooks. None of them suited our conviction that the course should emphasize the technical substance that should lie behind design decisions. We decided that our students should be able to read material at the level of *IEEE Software* and *IEEE Computer* and further that the material would be more vivid in the words of the original authors that after digestion into a textbook. We therefore decided to teach the course from a collection of readings instead of a textbook. We had to allow lecture time for enough material on project planning, organization, and management to run the course project and also for tools and technical information in support of the project. After making these allowances, we wound up with a roughly even balance of technical, management, and tool topics, with a few lectures left to address the character of the profession.

6. Administering a Project Course

A first course in software engineering is a daunting experience for both student *and* teacher. The students must work in cooperation with one another on a project that uses almost all their computer science skills and illustrates the techniques taught in the class portion of the course. Since this is often the most interesting single course they take, students tend to throw themselves into it at the expense of other courses. Even when they do not want to live solely for the course, the new experience of having to cooperate with their peers instead of competing with them uses unforeseen amounts of energy in communication and compromise. The instructor is also involved more heavily in this course than in most others he or she will teach. The demands of providing a sensible project or guiding students' choices, acquiring resources, giving advice and guidance, sitting in on reviews, walkthroughs, and other meetings, all contribute to a higher-than-normal time investment. However, for both student and teacher, the rewards of this course are so great as to quickly erase any bad memories of the workload. The feeling of accomplishment, the experience of learning to work together as a team, the actual use of skills previously only exercised in limited situations, all contribute to an exceptionally positive learning experience. Our former students often tell us that the only college friends they keep in touch with are their teammates from the software engineering course. Their positive feelings also are reflected in significantly higher teaching ratings for the instructor.

Despite the expected positive outcomes, the beginning teacher of this course has a thousand questions and fears. How do you find a reasonable project? Should you use a "real" customer or make something up? How do you organize students into teams? What do they do? How do you keep the class meetings closely related to the project work? How should the project documents look? How do you grade teams? Will I see my spouse and children again before Christmas?

6.1. Preliminary Preparation

Getting ready to teach this course begins several months in advance. The instructor needs to determine class size, choose a project, select the development environment (including tools), and develop the syllabus. It is critical that these factors be decided *before* the first day of class, because efficient launching of the project is critical to the overall success of the course.

6.1.1. Class Size

A class of 15 to 20 students is enough critical mass to cause the communications and configuration control explosion that the instructor is trying to engineer. Actually, any number over that helps you because it increases the entropy. However, to be realistic in terms of helping students, grading papers, and general management, 30 to 35 ought to be the absolute upper limit. Any more than that compromises the instructor's ability to do the job. Using assistants often backfires since they also require management. Frankly, the main reason for keeping the class to 20 or so is that is all the people needed to successfully do a project that has a four-month development period. In one case, the actual number of students that showed up the first day was 38. By the next class, eight had disappeared, presumably because they had read the syllabus (a good reason for handing one out right away). The remaining 30 were too many for the actual project, so the instructor decided to develop a single set of requirements, then do a dual implementation in Pascal and Ada. This meant that some roles would be duplicated (coders are needed for both languages, for example), thus using up some manpower.

6.1.2. Choosing a Project

In a project-intensive course, it is very important to come up with an interesting project. The requirement for "interesting" immediately eliminates the commonplace stuff like text editors, parts of operating systems, text editors, reservation systems, and text editors. Software engineering, though often tremendously exciting, has long stretches of tedium associated with it. A gripping project sustains and motivates the students. However, if the project is for a real customer, then that factor compensates somewhat for a little tedium. For example, some of our more recent project choices include an automated scouting analysis system for an NCAA Division I football team, a choreographer's assistant, a simulation of the Gemini spacecraft onboard guidance computer (including applications software), software to send a fax directly from a workstation, a mission planning simulator for a manned research station on Mars, and an orbital rendezvous simulator as a teaching exhibit for a science museum. The weakest project of these in terms of general interest was the choreographer's assistant, but the constant interaction with computer-naive dancers dependent totally on the students for technical expertise balanced things out. Also note that each of these projects were unlikely to have "experts" in the class that outshine the other students in requirements analysis. Choosing a project area in which students do not have much experience creates a situation where the students have to interact with the user very intensely during the requirements definition stage, thus developing a bond that can be used for motivation throughout the project.

So where are these fascinating projects? Everywhere. Non-profit agencies need all kinds of help; many engineering and science research groups on campus could use computational tools, and there are at least 432 football teams out there using manual scouting analysis methods. Many of these projects can be repeated after a suitable interval. When coaches are fired, the new coach almost always has a different offensive and defensive philosophy, which calls for a totally new scouting system. Research projects run out of funds and are replaced by new ones with similar requirements. There is nothing wrong with repeating a similar experience, just as long as it is new to the students students. Some instructors have created continuing projects based on this principle. Walt Scacchi of the University of Southern California had many undergraduate and graduate students in software engineering courses participate in creating programming tools. This class of projects survived for many years.

6.1.3. Choosing the Development Environment

After the project and class size are determined, the next preliminary step is choosing the development environment. Sometimes this is a trivial matter, since only one environment exists. If PCs or mainframe systems are all that are available, then the project may have to be adapted. If PCs are available but the class size dictates that they will be overused, then the class might have to stay on the mainframes. Sometimes the customer will have a specific target machine. For instance, the football team we did the scouting system for had a booster donate an IBM System 23 with only BASIC. Our classes have used PCs, mainframes, MicroVax workstations, Macintosh IIs, and superminis, all without having to abandon good software engineering practice. Furthermore, remember that only a very small percentage of the class will actually be coding. During the choreographer's assistant project, we were limited to developing code on two graphics-equipped PCs, which was no problem. Project documentation, however, had to be maintained on a central mainframe system.

A more influential consideration is the availability of tools. Needed, at least, are an editor, an appropriate compiler, version control tools, and electronic mail and/or bulletin board facility. The first two are familiar to everyone and need no elaboration, although the availability of a particular compiler might limit the choice of machines. Configuration management and version control tools such as RCS under UNIX, CMS under VMS, and Softool's CCC under VM/CMS, provide most of what is needed. Without these or similar tools, configuration management must be done manually. The e-mail or electronic bulletin board is extremely useful. The main difficulty in keeping this course realistic is that the students are not in the same general area all day as they would be in a software development company. Bulletin boards and e-mail help overcome that problem. As a result, most of the development information and out-of-class instruction is conducted by electronic mail. One of the authors handled about 1,400 messages relating to the course during a recent semester. Fortunately, most mainframe and minicomputer systems now come with some sort of communications. However, non-networked PCs are obviously not capable of being used for mail. That is another reason to keep documentation and mail on some central system even if the target is a PC.

6.2. Staffing

A project-intensive course in software engineering requires considerable time and attention to detail on the part of the course staff. A list of things to be done by the instructor include:

- Preparing and presenting lectures
- Preparing and grading quizzes
- Preparing and grading homeworks
- Designing the project and anticipating where it can go astray
- Writing and revising project documents
- Setting up common procedures (version control, document templates)
- Acquiring tools, components and associated documentation

- Coordination with client

- Trouble shooting the lab

If a department provides teaching assistants, they can handle many of these tasks. If not, the instructor may be able to get graduate students to volunteer as group leaders and mentors; if the course enrollment includes graduate students with more experience than the undergraduates, they can take on these roles. Another potential source of assistance is university staff, particularly if the project will yield a system of general utility. Programming staff are sometimes delighted to have the opportunity to get some teaching experience.

6.3. Coordination between Lectures and Project

In a course organized around a project, synchronization between the class lectures and the project phases is very important. If done well, the student can instantiate class concepts almost immediately in the project and the project experience can be used in class.

The bulk of the coordination takes place in pre-course planning, when lecture topics are scheduled. Lectures on activities most directly related to the project need to be scheduled at the times they will be most helpful, and any remaining lectures can then be arranged in the best available approximation to a coherent thread. Unfortunately, this plan requires about half of the lectures to be given in the first three weeks of the course.

Especially in the early phases of the project, synchronization is hard to achieve. The students are not yet familiar with certain concepts which are already needed for the project. Conversely, it is not possible to have the students apply all the concepts taught in class. One solution to this problem would be to teach the course in two semesters. In the first semester, all the software engineering concepts are taught, and then they are applied to the project. However, we believe it is better to teach the course in one semester and cope with the synchronization problems as best you can. Whenever the project demanded some knowledge from the students before it was taught, we found that the students were much more motivated when we covered the material in the lecture!

We also tried to keep the lectures coordinated with the project by assigning homework questions in which the student had to apply lecture material to the project. In more than one case we then incorporated their answers into our next lecture!

6.4. Credit and Grading Policy

A course of this kind presents several special problems, including

- grading team efforts,

- fostering cooperation rather than competition,

- keeping lectures relevant, and

- getting the readings read.

We will address each in turn. The common thread of the solutions is to be explicit about our objectives and align the incentives (primarily grades) with the behaviors we wish to encourage. This does, of course, force us to grade what's important rather than what's easy.

6.4.1. Grading team efforts

Grading a team of students is different from grading students individually. With group grades there is the danger that very active students might carry the load while others get a "free ride". Careful project management is the best way to avert this problem. Part of learning to work in a team is learning how to share the load. It's always possible that a problem student will require special handling, but a good policy is to assume that groups can work together until a problem arises.

Another alternative is to assign individuals tasks that are specific enough to assign individual, rather than group, grades.

6.4.2. Fostering cooperation rather than competition

Like many students, ours are competitive. This competition is often grade-directed, and students can get distracted from learning by uncertainties about their class standing. Even worse, they are accustomed (or claim to be) to courses graded "on a curve"—with a limit on the number of "A" and "B" grades awarded. This inhibits cooperation and even leads to counterproductive behavior that would lower some other student's grade.

Since a project course depends critically on cooperation among students, we addressed this directly: we defused the uncertainty of the grading curve by publishing the grading scale at the beginning of the semester and declaring that there would not be a curve. In addition to assigning group grades (which promotes cooperation within groups), we provided a completion incentive: if the project passed the acceptance test through the efforts of the class as a whole, every student would receive at least 55 of the 60 project points.

6.4.3. Keeping lectures relevant

When the grade in a course depends primarily on project work, students tend to spend their time on the project instead of the lecture and associated readings. (This is true in programming courses in general; in extreme cases we've seen students so focussed on making progress on a project with brute force that they wouldn't pay attention to the lectures telling them how to solve the problems easily).

We addressed the problem of convincing students the lectures were relevant in several ways. First, we committed 40% of the course grade to individual performance in the lecture portion of the course. This is commensurate with our assessment of the appropriate balance of time and content; happily it also helps reduce apprehension about the vulnerability of one's own grade to the vagaries of other students. Second, we scheduled the material for presentation as nearly as possible at the time students would need it for the project. Finally, we usually wrote the homework assignment to require students to explain a connection between the lecture and the project.

6.4.4. Getting the readings read

In any course, assigned readings are often postponed—usually until the night before they will be tested. We have been daunted by the prospect of students trying to do the reading in this way.

Instead, we gave a 5-minute quiz at the beginning of every class with assigned reading (about 22 of the 28 classes). The quiz was easy and intended to determine whether the students had captured the main point of the reading. For the most part, the quizzes showed the students to be doing the reading. An added benefit was that the lectures could then assume the reading as shared context between the instructor and the students—so the lectures could provide motivation, context, and evaluation rather than just repeating the substance of the reading.

7. Acknowledgements

This analysis relies heavily on our prior work. Tomayko's comparison of formats [123] supplied the bulk of Section 2, much of Section 6, and the case study of Section 5.4. Bruegge, Cheng, and Shaw's description of another offering provided much of Section 6 and the case study of Section 5.5 [24]. Section 5.3 was taken from Shaw's earlier curriculum design effort [112]. Objective survey data was taken from the Software Engineering Institute's annual survey of software engineering programs [83]; the more informal survey of organizations has been done over a period of seven years by Tomayko during visits to computer science departments as an ACM Distinguished National Lecturer and as part of the SEI Software Engineering Curriculum Project.

8. Appendix: Survey Details

This appendix includes summary material on software engineering courses reported in the Software Engineering Institute's annual survey [83]. It gives summary statistics on the courses, analyzes the textbooks reported in that survey, and lists the courses represented.

As noted in Section 4, the reporting from surveyed schools was not uniform. In order to concentrate on software engineering courses, we deleted from our analysis courses whose titles or textbooks suggested that the main emphasis was in areas other than software engineering. We eliminated courses that appeared to be primarily about such topics as

> Information systems, database management systems
> Programming-in-the-small, programming skills, data structures
> Formal methods, specifications
> User interface design, human factors, graphics
> Artificial intelligence
> Compilers, operating systems
> Networking, communications
> Real-time systems
> Security, privacy
> Procurement and contracting
> Technical writing, communication

Table 8-1 summarizes some basic information about these courses. Since graduate courses are often unofficially open to undergraduates, we have included them in the overall summary. Because of incomplete data, the totals are not consistent.

As noted in Section 4, only 126 of the 165 institutions provide courses explicitly open to undergraduates. Of those 205 courses, 51 (about 25%) are not necessarily offered every year. Most of the undergraduate courses require prerequisites, suggesting that they can synthesize lower-level software development skills. In contrast, nearly a quarter of the graduate courses do not have prerequisites. Some of the prerequisite function might be served by the admissions process of the graduate program, but some of the graduate courses appear to be "re-tread" or conversion courses for software developers with original education in another discipline.

	Undergraduate	Both Grad and Undergrad	Graduate	Total
Number				
Courses	144	61	263	472
Schools	100	42	116	165
Prerequisites?				
yes	138	59	193	391
no	6	2	60	68
Status				
required	74	7	99	181
elective	60	41	144	245
both	3	7	11	21
other	3	3	4	10
Frequency				
biennial	3	9	25	37
once a year	75	30	154	260
once a term	33	7	27	67
alternate terms	4	2	8	14
on demand	4	4	14	22
other	24	7	22	53
Number of Years Taught				
average	4.6	4.7	3.9	4.2
Textbooks				
# distinct texts	44	26	91	116
Total # texts assigned	176	72	266	515
Mean # uses each text	4.0	2.8	2.9	4.4

Table 8-1: Statistics on Software Engineering Courses

Of the 472 courses, 135 do not assign textbooks, 224 use one text, 84 use two texts, and 29 use three or more.

Undergraduate and graduate courses show a slightly different pattern of textbook preferences; these are compared in Table 8-2. The most notable result of this comparison is the heavy reliance on selected readings in graduate courses but their near-absence in undergraduate courses. Pressman's *Practitioner's Approach* [103] dominates all categories, usually followed by Fairley [46] and Sommerville [118]. Pressman's *Beginner's Guide* [104] and Gane's *Structured System Analysis* are predominantly undergraduate texts, whereas Shooman

[116] is predominantly a graduate text. The popularity of Booch's *Software Engineering with Ada* is somewhat surprising in light of the fact that it is essentially an Ada programming text that emphasizes object-oriented development (abstract data types).

Undergraduate	Both Grad & Undergrad	Graduate	Total
Pressman(Pract) [103]	Pressman(Pract) [103]	Selected readings	Pressman(Pract) [103]
Fairley [46]	Booch(SE/Ada) [20]	Pressman(Pract) [103]	Fairley [46]
Sommerville [118]	Sommerville [118]	Fairley [46]	Sommerville [118]
Manuals	Manuals	Sommerville [118]	Manuals
Booch(SE/Ada) [20]	Lamb [76]	Shooman [116]	Selected readings
Brooks [23]	Fairley [46]	Manuals	Booch(SE/Ada) [20]
DeMarco(Str Anal) [39]	Liskov [79]	Booch(SE/Ada) [20]	Brooks [23]
Page-Jones(Design) [97]	Selected Readings	Brooks [23]	Shooman [116]
Pressman(Beginner) [104]	Brooks [23]	Conte [34]	Conte [34]
Yourdon(Str Anal) [136]	DeMillo87 [42]	Boehm [19]	Yourdon(Str Anal) [136]
Gane(Str Anal) [53]	Hausen [60]	Yourdon(Str Anal) [136]	Liskov [79]
Lamb [76]	Myers [91]	Connor [33]	Myers [91]
Myers [91]	(14-way tie for next slot)	DeMarco(Projects) [41]	Page-Jones(Design) [97]
Wiener [133]		Myers [91]	Lamb [76]
(7-way tie for next slot)		Page-Jones(Design) [97]	Boehm [19]

Table 8-2: Comparison of Text Selections by Course Level

The textbooks, in order of overall popularity, are shown in Table 8-3. Note that, as is common with such data, the top 10% of the texts account for about 60% of the usage. Accordingly, we show the title in the table only for the 20% of the texts most often selected. All of the full citations are in the bibliography. Table 8-3 reports overall textbook usage.

 # Cites   Textbook

60	Pressman, *Software Engineering: A Practitioner's Approach* [103]
46	Fairley, *Software Engineering Concepts* [46]
46	Sommerville, *Software Engineering* [118]
32	manuals on languages and tools
32	selected readings
26	Booch, *Software Engineering with Ada* [20]
20	Brooks, *Mythical Man-Month* [23]
15	Shooman, *Software Engineering: Design, Reliability, and Management* [116]
10	Conte, *Software Engineering Metrics and Models* [34]
10	Yourdon, *Modern Structured Analysis* [136]
9	Liskov, *Abstraction and Specification in Program Development* [79]
9	Myers, *The Art of Software Testing* [91]
9	Page-Jones, *The Practical Guide to Structured Systems Design* [97]
8	Lamb, *Software Engineering: Planning for Change* [76]
7	Boehm, *Software Engineering Economics* [19]
6	Pressman, *Software Engineering: A Beginner's Guide* [104]
6	DeMarco, *Structured Analysis and System Specification* [39]
5	Wiener, *Software Engineering with Modula-2 and Ada* [133]
4	Beizer, *Software Testing Techniques* [12]
4	Connor, *Information System Specification and Design Road Map* [33]
4	DeMarco, *Controlling Software Projects: Management, Measurement, and Estimation* [41]
4	Fisher, *CASE (Computer Aided Software Engineering): Using the Newest Tools* [48]
4	Freeman, *IEEE Tutorial on Software Design Techniques* [52]
4	Gane, *Structured Systems Analysis: Tools and Techniques* [53]

Used three times: Babich [5], DeMarco [40], Gilbert [59], K.&J. Kendall [70], Metzger [85], Pfleeger [101], Yourdon (Classics) [134], Yourdon (Structured Design) [137]

Used twice: Aron [3], Barstow [7], Bauer [9], Beck [10], Bentley (Efficient Programs) [14], Booch (Components) [21], Brockmann [22], Cohen [32], Davis (Str Anal) [36], DeMillo [42], Freedman [50], Gehani [54], Gilb [58], Hausen [60], King [73], Kopetz [74], Meredith [84], Metzger [86], Miller [87], Peters [99], Peters [100], Radice [106], Shneiderman [115], Teague [120], Thayer [121], Weinberg [130], Whitten [132]

Used once: Abbott [1], Arthur [4], Backhouse [6], Basili [8], Beizer (Test & QA) [11], Bell [13], Bentley (Pearls) [15], Bergland [16], Bersoff [17], Birrell [18], Bryan (Config Mgt) [25], Bryan (Product Assurance) [26], Buckley [27], Budde [28], Chandrasekaran [29], Charette [30], Chow [31], Darnell [35], Davis (Requirements) [37], Deutsch (V&V) [43], Deutsch (Quality) [44], Eliason [45], Freeman (Reuse) [51], Gilb (Metrics) [57], Hetzel [61], Humphrey [64], Hunke [65], Jones (SW Dev) [66], Jones (Productivity) [67], P. Kendall [69] Kernighan [71], Kezsbom [72], Kowal [75], Lewis [78], Londeix [80], Marca [81], Martin [82], Mills [89], Musa [90], Mynatt [92], Orr [94], Ould [95], Page-Jones (Proj Mgt) [96], Parikh [98], Powers [102], Putnam [105], Reifer [107], Sage [108], Semprevivo [110], Senn [111], Simpson [117], Steward [119], Turner [125], Vick [126], Wallace [127], Ward [128], Wetherbe [131]

Table 8-3: Textbooks Cited By All Courses in SEI Survey of SE Courses

The table on the following pages lists the undergraduate courses that remained after eliminating courses in the subjects list. The table includes courses designated in the SEI survey as open to undergraduates only and courses designated as open to both graduates and undergraduates. While we realize that undergraduates are often admitted to graduate courses, those courses were not designed with undergraduates in mind. Thus the list presented here contains courses *intended* for undergraduates.

Key to Table:

School	Name of college or university
ST	State
Course	Name of course
Level	Level of offering
	u: undergraduate
	b: both graduate and undergraduate
Prer	Prerequisites
	p: course has at least one prerequisite
	n: no prerequisites
	x: no information supplied
Stat	Status in requirements
	r: required
	e: elective
	b: both
	o: other
	x: no information supplied
Freq	Frequency of offering
	b: biennial
	y: once a year
	t: once a term
	a: alternate terms
	d: on demand
	o: other
	x: no information supplied
Yrs	Number of years the course has been taught
#txts	Number of textbooks used in the course
next 7 columns	Most popular texts; mark in a column indicates the course used indicated text
other text	Reference to any other text used in course

School	ST	Course	Level	Prereqs?	Status	Freq	Yrs	#texts	Pressman87	Sommerville89	Fairley85	Manuals	Booch87a	Brooks82	Lamb88	Other texts
U of AK Fairbanks	AK	Software Engineering	u	n	r	y	6	1		1						
Auburn U	AL	Software Engineering I	b	p	e	y	4	1		1						
Auburn U	AL	Intro to SW Engr	u	p	r	a	4	1		1						
Arizona St U	AZ	SW Design	b	p	r	t	5	1								Liskov86
Arizona St U	AZ	Sw Proj Mgt, Dev I	u	p	r	t	9	1		1						
U of Arizona	AZ	SW Design	b	p	r	t	5	2				1				Liskov86
Cal Tech	CA	Concurrency in Computation	b	p	e	o	5	0								
Cal Tech	CA	Programming Lab	b	p	e	o	5	0								
Cal Poly, San Louis Obispo	CA	Software Engineering I	u	p	r	o	9	1		1						
Cal Poly, San Louis Obispo	CA	Software Engineering II	u	p	r	o	1	1		1						
Cal Poly, Pomona	CA	Software Engineering	u	p	r	o	2	1					1			
Cal St Chico	CA	Software Engineering	u	p	e	t	3	2						1		
Cal St Chico	CA	Sys Design	u	p	r	t	11	1			1					Wetherbe84
Cal St Northridge	CA	SW Engr Economics	b	p	e	y	4	1								Boehm81
Cal St Northridge	CA	SW Engr with Ada	b	p	r	y	3	1								
Cal St Northridge	CA	Prog Design Tech	b	p	e	t	9	2						1		DeMarco79a, Gilbert83
Cal St Northridge	CA	SW Sys Dev & Lab	u	p	r	t	11	1								Gilbert83
Cal St Sacramento	CA	Cmptr SW Engr	u	p	e	t	5	1								Steward87
Cal St Sacramento	CA	Cmptr Sys Anlys	u	p	e	t	13	1								Kendall87
Cal St Sacramento	CA	SW Engr Proj Mgt	u	p	e	y	11	2						1		Meredith89
Cal St Sacramento	CA	Intro to Sys Eng	u	p	e	y	3	1								Sage77
Northrop U	CA	Software Engineering I	u	p	e	o	3	1								Pfleeger87
Northrop U	CA	Software Engineering II	u	p	e	y	1	0								
Northrop U	CA	Adv SW Design	u	p	e	y	3	1								
Santa Clara U	CA	Intro to SW Engr	b	p	b	y	4	1		1						Gane82
Stanford U	CA	SW Engr Lab	u	p	o	y	1	0								
U Cal Irvine	CA	Proj in Sys Design	u	c	o	t	4	1								
U Cal Santa Cruz	CA	SE Methodology	u	p	e	y	1	1	1							
U Southern Cal	CA	Intro to SW Engr	u	p	r	t	1	2				1				Page-Jones88
U Southern Cal	CA	Design&Cnstr of Lg SW Sys	u	p	e	y	1	2				1				
U of CO, CO Springs	CO	Sys Eng Mgt	b	n	e	y	1	0								
U of CO, CO Springs	CO	SW Engr Lab	b	c	e	a	1	0								
U of CO, CO Springs	CO	Intro to SW Engr	u	c	r	t	1	1								Wiener84

School	ST	Course	Level	Prereqs?	Freq	Yrs	#texts	Pressman87	Sommerville89	Fairley85	Manuals	Booch87a	Brooks82	Lamb88	Other texts
USAF Academy	CO	Sys A&D I	u	p	r y	7	2	1							Gane82
USAF Academy	CO	Sys A&D II	u	p	r y	7	1								Page-Jones88
USAF Academy	CO	RT Sys	u	p	r y	1	0								
Central CT St U	CT	Intro to SW Engr	u	p	e y	5	1								Wiener84
American U	DC	Software Engineering	u	p	e y	2	1		1						
George Washington U	DC	Sys SW & SW Engr	u	p	e t	5	1		1						
FL Atlantic U	FL	Prin of SW Design	u	p	r t	2	2				1				Bell87
U of Central FL	FL	Software Engineering I	b	p	b y	1	2			1	1				
U of Hawaii, Hilo	HI	Compiler Th	u	p	e y	4	0								
U of Hawaii, Hilo	HI	CS Applications	u	p	e d	1	0								
U of Hawaii, Hilo	HI	SW Engr Meth	u	p	e y	3	3	1	1						Yourdon89
U of Hawaii, Hilo	HI	Sys A&D	u	p	r y	5	7	1	1						Kendall88, Pressman88, Radice88, Yourdon89, Sel rdgs, Shooman83
Iowa St U	IA	Software Engineering	u	n	e o	6	1	1							
U of Idaho	ID	Software Engineering	b	p	e y	7	1	1							
U of Idaho	ID	SW QA & Test	b	p	e b	4	2								Beizer90 Deutsch88
U of Idaho	ID	Empirical Studies In Progg	b	p	e b		0								
U of Idaho	ID	CS Design I	u	p	r t	7	1	1							
U of Idaho	ID	CS Design II	u	p	r t	7	1	1							
Bradley U	IL	SysAnly&Design(SS&D)	u	p	e o	8	1								DeMarco79a
Bradley U	IL	Intro to SW Engr	u	p	e y	2	0								
DePaul U	IL	SW Projs	u	p	r o	6	0								
DePaul U	IL	Software Engineering	u	p	e y	6	1	1							
DePaul U	IL	SW Meas & Quality	u	p	e y	2	1								Conte86
DePaul U	IL	Programming in Ada	u	n	r y	3	1					1			
So IL U, Edwardsville	IL	SW Design & Dev	b	p	e y	5	1							1	
Sangamon St U	IL	Intro to SW Engr	u	p	e y	1	0								
U of IL Chicago	IL	Intro to SW Engr	u	p	r o	8	1	1							
UI, Urbana-Champaign	IL	Software Engineering	b	p	e y	6	2	1		1					
Ball St U	IN	SE I (Sys Anlys)	u	p	r o	11	3				1				DeMarco79a Semprevivo82
Ball St U	IN	SE II (Design & Dev)	u	p	r o	5	3				1				DeMarco79a Yourdon79b
Purdue U	IN	Software Engineering	u	p	e e	1	1	1							
Rose-Hulman IofT	IN	Software Engineering	u	p	r y	5	2	1					1		

School	ST	Course	Level	Status	Prereqs?	Freq	Yrs	#texts	Sommerville89	Pressman87	Fairley85	Manuals	Booch87a	Brooks82	Lamb88	Other texts
Rose-Hulman IofT	IN	Senior CS Proj I & II	u	r	p	y	2	0								
U of Evansville	IN	Software Engineering	u	r	p	o	1	0								
U of Evansville	IN	SW Engr Proj	u	r	p	t	1	0								
Wichita St U	KS	Intro to SW Engr	b	e	p	t	8	1	1							
Northern KY U	KY	Software Engineering	u	r	p	t	5	1								Pressman88
U of Louisville	KY	Anlys&Design of InfoSys	u	r	p	y	4	2								Martin88 Whitten89
U of Louisville	KY	SpecTopics: Prog in the Lg	u	e	p	b	2	3								Booch87b
Western KY U	KY	Structured Sys Anlys	b	e	p	y	5	0				1				
Western KY U	KY	Intro to CS: Ada	u	r	p	t	3	1					1			
LA St U Shreveport	LA	SW Engr Proj	u	r	p	y	5	1								
Louisiana Tech U	LA	Structured Design	u	r	p	o	4	1	1							Pfleeger87
Louisiana Tech U	LA	SW Methodology	u	e	p	y	5	1	1							
Northeast LA U	LA	Software Engineering	u	r	p	y	4	1			1					
UofSouthwesternLA	LA	Intro to SW Meth	b	e	p	y	4	2		1						Kernighan78
Boston U	MA	SW Sys Design	u	r	p	y	4	1		1						Liskov86
MIT	MA	Lab in SW Engr	u	r	p	a	6	1								
Northeastern U	MA	SW Design & Dev	u	r	p	a	6	1			1					
U Mass, Amherst	MA	Software Engineering	b	x	p	y	5	2								Select readings Wiener84
U Mass, Amherst	MA	Programming Meth	u	x	p	o	10	1								Wiener84
Worcester Poly Inst	MA	Software Engineering	u	o	p	y	5	1		1						
U of Maryland	MD	SW Design & Dev	b	e	p	t	6	2							1	Bryan88
Andrews U	MI	Sys Anlys I	b	r	p	y	5	1								Whitten89
Andrews U	MI	Sys Anlys II	b	r	p	y	5	0								
Michigan St U	MI	Sys SW Dev	u	r	p	t	2	2								Beck90
Michigan Tech U	MI	Software Engineering	u	e	p	y	3	1			1					
Michigan Tech U	MI	Sys SW Proj	u	r	p	y	1	1								
Western MI U	MI	SW Sys Dev	b	b	p	o	8	2		1				1		Pressman88
St. Cloud St U	MN	Software Engineering I	b	e	p	b	1	3					1		1	Selected readings
St. Cloud St U	MN	Software Engineering II	b	e	p	b	1	2					1			Selected readings
St. Cloud St U	MN	Software Engineering III	b	o	p	b	1	3					1		1	Selected readings
St. Cloud St U	MN	SW Engr Proj	b	b	p	b	1	1				1				
U of Minnesota	MN	Software Engineering I	b	e	p	y	6	1								Liskov86
U of Minnesota	MN	Software Engineering II	b	e	p	y	3	1					1			

School	ST	Course	Level	Prereqs?	Status Freq	Yrs	#texts	Pressman87	Sommerville89	Fairley85	Manuals	Booch87a	Brooks82	Lamb88	Other texts
U of Minnesota	MN	Software Engineering III	b	p	e y	3	4						1		Demillo87 Hausen84 Myers79
U of Minnesota	MN	SW Rqt, Design & Maint	b	p	e b	3	2								Bergland81 Vick84
U of Minnesota	MN	SW Ver & Val, Met	b	p	e b	3	5								Conte86, DeMillo87, Hausen84, Miller81, Myers79
U of Minnesota	MN	SW Engr with Ada	b	p	e y	3	1					1			
Washington U	MO	SW Engr Workshop	b	p	r o	11	1				1				
Lenoir-Rhyne Col	NC	SW Sys A&D	u	p	r y	4	1		1						
Lenoir-Rhyne Col	NC	SeniorProj-SE Option	u	p	r y	1	2			1					
North Carolina St U	NC	SW Engr Proj	u	p	e y	4	0	1							
North Carolina St U	NC	Intro to Programming Envts	u	p	e y	4	0								
North Carolina St U	NC	SW Engr with Ada	u	p	e y	4	1					1			
U of NC Chapel Hill	NC	SW Engr Lab	b	p	b y	53	3			1			1		Freeman83
North Dakota St U	ND	Sys Anlys	u	p	x y	1	0								
North Dakota St U	ND	Sys Test & Maint	u	p	r y	1	1								Myers79
North Dakota St U	ND	RT SW Design	u	p	r y	1	0								
Dartmouth Col	NH	SW Design & Imp	u	p	r o	2	2			1		1			Bentley86
Fairleigh Dickinson U	NJ	APLCUA	u	p	e d	1	1				1	1			
Stockton St Col	NJ	SW Engr with Ada	u	p	e y	1	2								
NM Inst ofMining&Tech	NM	SW Cnstr	u	p	r o	6	1		1					1	
New Mexico St U	NM	SW Dev	u	p	r t	5	2					1			
U of New Mexico	NM	Intro to SW Engr	u	n	r y	2	1	1	1						
Clarkson U	NY	SW Design & Dev	u	p	e y	6	1			1					
Clarkson U	NY	SW Tools	u	p	r y	2	0								
Columbia U	NY	Software Engineering	b	p	b b	5	1		1						
Columbia U	NY	Sp Proj in CS	b	p	e d	5	0								
Columbia U	NY	SW Design Lab	u	p	r t	5	0								
Iona College	NY	Software Engineering	u	p	e y	4	1	1							
Poly U Brooklyn	NY	SW Design & Eng	u	p	e y	1	0								
RensselaerPolyInst	NY	SW Design & Dev	u	p	o y	2	3							1	1 Brockmann86
St U of NY Col Brockport	NY	SW Sys Dev	u	p	r y	4	2								
St U of NY Binghamton	NY	Software Engineering I	u	p	e b	5	2			1	1		1		
Union College	NY	Software Engineering	u	p	x y	1	1								
BowlingGreen St U	OH	SW Dev	b	p	e y	8	1								Mynatt90

School	ST	Course	Level Prereqs?	Status Freq		Yrs	#texts	Pressman87	Sommerville89	Fairley85	Manuals	Booch87a	Brooks82	Lamb88	Other texts
Cleveland St U	OH	Structured Sys Anlys	u	p	e / o	6	1								Teague85
Cleveland St U	OH	Structured Sys Design	u	p	e / o	6	1								Page-Jones88
Kent St U	OH	SW Engr Proj	u	p	e / d	3	1			1					
Ohio St U	OH	Software Engineering	b	p	e / o	5	1		1						
Ohio St U	OH	SW Engr Proj	b	p	e / o	5	0								
Ohio St U	OH	Sys Programming	u	p	r / t	5	1								Beck90
Wright St U	OH	Intro to SW Engr	b	p	r / t	1	2			1		1			
Oregon St U	OR	SW Design	u	p	r / t	1	1			1					
Portland St U	OR	Software Engineering	b	p	e / y	4	0								
U of Oregon	OR	SW Methodology I	u	p	r / t	5	1		1						
U of Oregon	OR	SW Methodology II	u	p	e / o	51	3			1					Bentley82 Page-Jones88
Carnegie Mellon U	PA	Software Engineering	u	p	e / t	6	1		1						
Cheyney U	PA	SW Engr Using Ada	b	p	e / d	2	1				1				
Drexel U	PA	Software Engineering I	u	p	r / y	6	1								1
Drexel U	PA	Software Engineering II	u	p	e / y	6	1								1
Lehigh U	PA	Software Engineering	u	p	r / y	6	1			1					
PA St U	PA	SW Design Meth	b	p	e / y	4	2				1				
Shippensburg U	PA	SW Design for Info Sys	u	p	e / y	4	1		1	1					
Temple U	PA	SW Design	u	p	e / y	1	3		1						Meyers79 Yourdon79d
Villanova U	PA	Software Engineering	u	p	r / y	4	2			1			1		
Clemson U	SC	SW Dev Methodology	b	p	b / y	5	1			1					
Clemson U	SC	Intro to SW Dev	u	p	r / t		1		1						
East Tenn St U	TN	Software Engineering	u	p	r / a	4	1								Pressman88
East Tenn St U	TN	Adv Programming Tech	u	p	r / a		2								Page-Jones88 Yourdon89
Fisk U	TN	Sp Top: Intro to SW Engr	u	p	e / d		3					1			Booch87b
U of TN Chattanooga	TN	Software Engineering I	u	p	r / y	10	1								Eliason90
U of TN Chattanooga	TN	Software Engineering II	u	p	r / y	6	2			1		1			Hetzel88
Vanderbilt U	TN	Software Engineering	b	p	e / y	1	1		1						
Baylor U	TX	Intro to SW Engr	b	p	b / y	4	2	1							
Southwest TX St U	TX	Software Engineering	u	p	e / y	5	2	1					1		
St. Edward's U	TX	Software Engineering	u	p	e / y	1	1	1							
TX Christian U	TX	Object Oriented Progg	b	p	e / d		0								
Texas Tech U	TX	Senior Proj Design	u	p	r / y	3	2			1					Fisher88

School	ST	Course	Level Prereqs?	Status	Freq	Yrs	#texts	Pressman87	Sommerville89	Fairley85	Manuals	Booch87a	Brooks82	Lamb88	Other texts
Texas Tech U	TX	Senior Proj Imp Lab	u	p	r	y	3	2								Fisher88
U Texas, Arlington	TX	Meth in SW Engr	u	p	e	y	6	2						1		
U Texas, Austin	TX	Software Engineering	u	p	e	t	7	1	1							
U Texas, El Paso	TX	Software Engineering I	u	p	r	y	4	1	1							
U Texas, El Paso	TX	SW Engr II (Proj Course)	u	p	r	y	4	0								
U Texas San Antonic	TX	Programming Meth	u	p	r	o	1	2	1		1					
UofHouston,ClearLake	TX	SW Design Meth	u	p	e	y	3	1								Wallace87
Brigham Young U	UT	Intro to SW Design	u	p	e	o	10	2		1						Myers79
Brigham Young U	UT	SW Test	u	p	e	o	10	1								Beizer90
Brigham Young U	UT	Sys Anlys	u	p	e	o	10	2								DeMarco79s Gane82
U of Utah	UT	Software Engineering	b	p	x	x		0								
U of Utah	UT	Software Engineering	b	p	x	x		1	1							Liskov86
U of Utah	UT	SW Engr Lab	u	p	x	x		0								
Utah St U	UT	SW Sys	u	p	r	o	8	1								Turner84
Col of William & Mary	VA	Software Engineering	b	p	e	y	1	1	1		1					
U of Virginia	VA	SW Engr Lab	u	p	e	y	6	1			1					
VA Commonwealth U	VA	Software Engineering	b	p	e	d	1	1		1	1					
Eastern WA U	WA	Senior Sem	u	p	r	y	4	1	1		1			1		
Washington St U	WA	SW Dev	u	p	e	y	1	3				1				
Washington St U	WA	SW Dev Lab	u	p	e	y	1	1	1			1				
U Wisc, Milwaukee	WI	Intro to SW Engr	b	p	r	o	8	2	1							Darnell88
U Wisc, Milwaukee	WI	SW Engr Lab	b	p	e	y	1	0								
U Wisc, Stout	WI	Software Engineering	u	p	e	t	6	2		1			1			
West Virginia U	WV	Ada with SW Engr	b	p	e	y	3	1					1			
West Virginia U	WV	Software Engineering	u	p	e	y	2	1		1						
West Virginia U	WV	Prin of SW Dev	u	p	e	y	5	0								
West Virginia U	WV	Sys Anlys	u	p	e	y	1	1	1							'Yourdon89
U of Wyoming	WY	Software Engineering	b	p	o	b	1	1								
U of Wyoming	WY	SW Engr Lab	b	p	o	b	1	0								
U of Aalberta	AB	Software Engineering	u	p	r	t	4	1			1					
U of Victoria	BC	Software Engineering	u	p	r	t	6	1						1		
U of Victoria	BC	Imp of SW Engr Meth	b	p	e	y	3	0								
Acadia U	NS	Software Engineering	u	p	b	y	4	1	1							

School	ST	Course	Level	Prereqs?	Status	Freq	Yrs	#texts	Pressman87	Sommerville89	Fairley85	Manuals	Booch87a	Brooks82	Lamb88	Other texts
Queen's U	ON	Modules and Spec	u	p	e	y	2	0								
Queen's U	ON	Software Engineering	b	p	e	y	4	1								1
U of Ottawa	ON	Software Engineering I	u	p	r	y	4	2		1	1					
U of Ottawa	ON	Software Engineering II	u	p	r	y	6	2		1	1					
U of Waterloo	ON	Applications SW Engr	u	p	e	y	1	1		1						
U of Waterloo	ON	SW Sys Design & Imp	b	p	e	t	1	1		1						
Concordia U	PQ	Software Engineering	u	p	r	t	2	1			1					
UofQuebecMontreal	PQ	Software Engineering	u	p	r	b	5	1	1							
U of Regina	SK	Adv Sys A&D	u	p	e	y	4	1								Kendall87
Totals							4.64	1.21	38	31	29	20	18	12	8	

9. References

1. Russell J. Abbott. *An Integrated Approach to Software Development.* John Wiley & Sons, Inc., New York, New York, 1986.

2. ACM Curriculum Committee on Computer Science. "Curriculum 78: Recommendations for the Undergraduate Program in Computer Science." *Communications of the ACM 22,* 3 (March 1979), 147-166.

3. Joel D. Aron. *The Program Development Process.* Addison-Wesley Publishing Company, Reading, Massachusetts, 1974.

4. Lowell Jay Arthur. *Software Evolution: The Software Maintenance Challenge.* John Wiley & Sons, Inc., New York, New York, 1988.

5. Wayne A. Babich. *Software Configuration Management: Coordination for Team Productivity* . Addison-Wesley Publishing Company, Reading, Massachusetts, 1986.

6. Roland C. Backhouse. *Program Construction and Verification.* Prentice-Hall International, Englewood Cliffs, New Jersey, 1986.

7. David R. Barstow, Howard E. Shrobe, and Erik Sandewell, editors. *Interactive Programming Environments.* McGraw-Hill, New York, New York, 1984.

8. Victor R. Basili, editor. *Tutorial on Models and Metrics for Software Management and Engineering.* IEEE Computer Society, New York, New York, 1980.

9. Friedrich Ludwig Bauer, editor. *Advanced Course on Software Engineering.* Springer-Verlag, Berlin, Germany and New York, New York, 1973.

10. Leland L. Beck. *System Software: An Introduction to Systems Programming 2nd edition.* Addison-Wesley Publishing Company, Reading, Massachusetts, 1990.

11. Boris Beizer. *Software System Testing and Quality Assurance* . Van Nostrand Reinhold, New York, New York, 1984.

12. Boris Beizer. *Software Testing Techniques 2nd edition.* Van Nostrand Reinhold, New York, New York, 1990.

13. Doug Bell, Ian Morrey, and John Pugh. *Software Engineering: A Programming Approach.* Prentice-Hall International, Englewood Cliffs, New Jersey, 1987.

14. Jon Louis Bentley. *Writing Efficient Programs.* Prentice-Hall International, Englewood Cliffs, New Jersey, 1982.

15. Jon Louis Bentley. *Programming Pearls.* Addison-Wesley Publishing Company, Reading, Massachusetts, 1986.

16. Glenn D. Bergland, Ronald D. Gordon, editors. *Tutorial: Software Design Strategies 2nd edition.* IEEE Computer Society, Institute of Electrical and Electronics Engineers, Los Angeles, California; New York, New York , 1981.

17. Edward H. Bersoff, Vilas D. Henderson, and Stanley G. Siegel. *Software Configuration Management: An Investment in Product Integrity.* Prentice-Hall International, Englewood Cliffs, New Jersey, 1980.

18. N. D. Birrell and Martyn A. Ould. *A Practical Handbook for Software Development.* Cambridge University Press, Cambridge [Cambridgeshire], England; New York, New York, 1985.

19. Barry W. Boehm. *Software Engineering Economics.* Prentice-Hall International, Englewood Cliffs, New Jersey, 1981.

20. Grady Booch. *Software Engineering with Ada 2nd edition.* Benjamin/Cummings Publishing Company, Menlo Park, California, 1987.

21. Grady Booch. *Software Components with Ada: Structures, Tools, and Subsystems.* Benjamin/Cummings Publishing Company, Menlo Park, California, 1987.

22. R. John Brockmann. *Writing Better Computer User Documentation: From Paper to Online.* John Wiley & Sons, Inc., New York, New York, 1986.

23. Frederick P. Brooks, Jr.. *The Mythical Man-Month: Essays on Software Engineering.* Addison-Wesley Publishing Company, Reading, Massachusetts, 1982.

24. Bernd Bruegge, John Cheng, Mary Shaw, A Software Engineering Project Course with a Real client. Tech. Rept. SEI-91-EM-4, Software Engineering Institute, Carnegie Mellon University, March, 1991.

25. William Bryan, Christopher Chadbourne, and Stan Siegel. *Tutorial: Software Configuration Management.* Computer Society Press, IEEE Computer Society, Institute of Electrical and Electronics Engineers, Los Alamitos, California, 1980.

26. William L. Bryan and Stanley G. Siegel. *Software Product Assurance: Techniques for Reducing Software Risk.* Elsevier, New York, New York, 1988.

27. Fletcher J. Buckley. *Implementing Software Engineering Practices.* John Wiley & Sons, Inc., New York, New York, 1989.

28. Reinhard Budde et al., editors. *Approaches to Prototyping.* Springer Verlag, Berlin, Germany; New York, New York, 1984.

29. B. Chandrasekaran and Sergio Radicchi. *Computer Program Testing.* North-Holland Publishing Company, Amsterdam, Netherlands; New York, New York, 1981.

30. Robert N. Charette. *Software Engineering Environments: Concepts and Technology.* Intertext Publications, New York, New York, 1986.

31. Tsun S. Chow, compiler. *Tutorial Software Quality Assurance: A Practical Approach.* IEEE Computer Society Press, Silver Spring, Maryland, 1985.

32. Bernard Cohen, William T. Harwood, and Melvyn I. Jackson. *The Specification of Complex Systems.* Addison-Wesley Publishing Company, Wokingham, England; Reading, Massachusetts, 1986.

33. Denis Connor. *Information System Specification and Design Road Map.* Prentice-Hall International, Englewood Cliffs, New Jersey, 1985.

34. Samuel Daniel Conte, H. E. Dunsmore, and V. Y. Shen. *Software Engineering Metrics and Models.* Benjamin/Cummings Publishing Company, Menlo Park, California, 1986.

35. Peter A. Darnell and Philip E. Margolis. *Software Engineering in C.* Springer-Verlag, New York, New York, 1988.

36. William S. Davis. *Tools and Techniques for Structured Systems Analysis and Design.* Addison-Wesley Publishing Company, Reading, Massachusetts, 1983.

37. Alan Michael Davis. *Software Requirements: Analysis and Specification.* Prentice-Hall International, Englewood Cliffs, New Jersey, 1990.

38. Lionel E. Deimel, editor. *Software Engineering Education.* Springer-Verlag, Berlin, 1990.

39. Tom DeMarco. *Structured Analysis and System Specification.* Yourdon Press, Englewood Cliffs, New Jersey, 1979.

40. Tom DeMarco. *Concise Notes on Software Engineering.* Yourdon Press, Englewood Cliffs, New Jersey, 1979.

41. Tom DeMarco. *Controlling Software Projects: Management, Measurement and Estimation.* Yourdon Press, New York, New York, 1982.

42. Richard A. DeMillo et al.. *Software Testing and Evaluation.* Benjamin/Cummings Publishing Company, Menlo Park, California, 1987.

43. Michael S. Deutsch. *Software Verification and Validation: Realistic Project Approaches.* Prentice-Hall International, Englewood Cliffs, New Jersey, 1982.

44. Michael S. Deutsch and Ronald R. Willis. *Software Quality Engineering: A Total Technical and Management Approach.* Englewood Cliffs, New Jersey, Prentice-Hall International, 1988.

45. Alan L. Eliason. *Systems Development: Analysis, Design, and Implementation 2nd edition.* Scott, Foresman/Little, Brown Higher Education, Glenview, Illinois, 1990.

46. Richard E. Fairley. *Software Engineering Concepts.* McGraw-Hill, New York, New York, 1985.

47. Richard Fairley and Peter Freeman, editors. *Issues in Software Engineering Education.* Springer-Verlag, New York, New York, 1989.

48. Allen Fisher. *CASE: Computer-Aided Software Engineering: Using the Newest Tools in Software Development.* John Wiley & Sons, Inc., New York, New York, 1988.

49. Gary A. Ford, editor. *Software Engineering Education.* Springer-Verlag, New York, New York, 1988.

50. Daniel P. Freedman and Gerald M. Weinberg. *Handbook of Walkthroughs, Inspections, and Technical Reviews: Evaluating Programs, Projects, and Products 3rd edition.* Little, Brown, Boston, Massachusetts, 1982.

51. Peter Freeman, editor. *Tutorial: Software Reusability.* Computer Society Press of the IEEE, Washington, DC, 1987.

52. Peter Freeman and Anthony I. Wasserman. *Tutorial on Software Design Techniques 4th edition.* IEEE Computer Society Press, Silver Spring, Maryland, 1983.

53. Chris Gane and Trish Sarson. *Structured Systems Analysis: Tools and Techniques.* McAuto, St. Louis, Missouri, 1982.

54. Narain Gehani and Andrew D. McGettrick, editors. *Software Specification Techniques.* Addison-Wesley Publishing Company, Wokingham, England; Reading, Massachusetts, 1986.

55. Norman E. Gibbs, editor. *Software Engineering Education.* Springer-Verlag, Berlin Heidelberg, Germany, 1989.

56. Norman E. Gibbs and Richard E. Fairley, editors. *Software Engineering Education: The Educational Needs of the Software Community.* Springer-Verlag, New York, New York, 1987.

57. Tom Gilb. *Software Metrics.* Winthrop Publishers, Cambridge, Massachusetts, 1977.

58. Tom Gilb. *Principles of Software Engineering Management.* Addison-Wesley Publishing Company, Wokingham, England; Reading, Massachusetts, 1988.

59. Philip Gilbert. *Software Design and Development.* Science Research Associates, Chicago, Ilinois, 1983.

60. Hans-Ludwig Hausen. *Software Validation: Inspection - Testing - Verification - Alternatives.* Elsevier Science Publishers B.V., Amsterdam, Netherlands; New York, New York, 1984.

61. William C. Hetzel. *The Complete Guide to Software Testing 2nd edition.* QED Information Sciences, Wellesley, Massachusetts, 1988.

62. Daniel Hoffman. An Undergraduate Course in Software Design. In Gary A. Ford, Ed., *Software Engineering Education, SEI Conference 1988, Fairfax, VA, USA, Proceedings,* Springer-Verlag, 1988, pp. 154-168.

63. James J. Horning. The Software Project as a Serious Game. In Anthony I. Wasserman and Peter Freeman, Ed., *Software Engineering Education Needs and Objectives Proceedings of an Interface Workshop,* Springer-Verlag, 1976, pp. 71-77.

64. Watts S. Humphrey. *Managing the Software Process.* Addison-Wesley Publishing Company, Reading, Massachusetts, 1989.

65. Horst Hunke, editor. *Software Engineering Environments.* North-Holland Publishing Company, Amsterdam, Netherlands; New York, New York, 1981.

66. Cliff B. Jones. *Software Development: A Rigorous Approach.* Prentice-Hall International, Englewood Cliffs, New Jersey, 1980.

67. Capers Jones. *Programming Productivity.* McGraw-Hill, New York, New York, 1986.

68. Elaine Kant. "A Semester Course in Software Engineering." *ACM Software Engineering Notes 6,* 4 (August 1981), .

69. Penny A. Kendall. *Introduction to Systems Analysis and Design: A Structured Approach.* Allyn and Bacon, Boston, Massachusetts, 1987.

70. Kenneth E. Kendall and Julie E. Kendall. *Systems Analysis and Design.* Prentice-Hall International, Englewood Cliffs, New Jersey, 1988.

71. Brian W. Kernighan and P. J. Plauger. *The Elements of Programming Style 2nd edition.* McGraw-Hill, New York, New York, 1978.

72. Deborah S. Kezsbom, Donald L. Schilling, and Katherine A. Edward. *Dynamic Project Management: A Practical Guide for Managers and Engineers.* John Wiley & Sons, Inc., New York, New York, 1989.

73. David King. *Current Practices in Software Development: A Guide to Successful Systems.* Yourdon Press, Englewood Cliffs, New Jersey, 1984.

74. Hermann Kopetz. *Software Reliability.* Springer-Verlag, New York, New York, 1979.

75. James A. Kowal. *Analyzing Systems.* Prentice-Hall International, Englewood Cliffs, New Jersey, 1988.

76. David Alex Lamb. *Software Engineering: Planning for Change.* Prentice-Hall International, Englewood Cliffs, New Jersey, 1988.

77. Laura Marie Leventhal and Barbee T. Mynatt. Stalking the Typical Undergraduate Software Engineering Course:Results from a Survey. In Richard Fairley and Peter Freeman, Ed., *Issues in Software Engineering Education,* Springer-Verlag, 1989, pp. 168-195.

78. Theodore Gyle Lewis. *Software Engineering: Analysis and Verification.* Reston Publishing Company, Reston, Virginia, 1982.

79. Barbara Liskov and John Guttag. *Abstraction and Specification in Program Development.* MIT Press; McGraw-Hill, Cambridge, Massachusetts; New York, New York, 1986.

80. Bernard Londeix. *Cost Estimation for Software Development.* Addison-Wesley Publishing Company, Wokingham, England; Reading, Massachusetts, 1987.

81. David Marca. *Applying Software Engineering Principles.* Little, Brown, Boston, Massachusetts, 1984.

82. James Martin and Carma L. McClure. *Structured Techniques: The Basis for CASE.* Prentice-Hall International, Englewood Cliffs, New Jersey, 1988.

83. Bill McSteen, Brian Gottier, and Mark Schmick, editors. Software Engineering Education Directory. Tech. Rept. CMU/SEI-90-TR-4 ESD-TR-90-206, Software Engineering Institute - Carnegie Mellon University, April, 1990.

84. Jack R. Meredith and Samuel J. Mantel, Jr.. *Project Management: A Managerial Approach 2nd edition.* John Wiley & Sons, Inc., New York, New York, 1989.

85. Philip W. Metzger. *Managing a Programming Project 2nd edition.* Prentice-Hall International, Englewood Cliffs, New Jersey, 1981.

86. Philip W. Metzger. *Managing Programming People: A Personal View.* Prentice-Hall International, Englewood Cliffs, New Jersey, 1987.

87. Edward Miller and William E. Howden. *Tutorial: Software Testing and Validation Techniques 2nd edition.* IEEE Computer Society Press, New York, New York; Los Alamitos, California; Piscataway, New Jersey, 1981.

88. Harlan D. Mills. *Software Productivity.* Little, Brown, and Company, Boston, Massachusetts, 1983.

89. Harlan D. Mills, Richard C. Linger, and Alan R. Hevner. *Principles of Information Systems Analysis and Design.* Academic Press, Orlando, Florida, 1986.

90. John D. Musa, Anthony Iannino, and Kazuhira Okumoto. *Software Reliability: Measurement, Prediction, Application.* McGraw-Hill, New York, New York, 1990.

91. Glenford J. Myers. *The Art of Software Testing.* John Wiley & Sons, Inc., New York, New York, 1979.

92. Barbee Teasley Mynatt. *Software Engineering with Student Project Guidance.* Prentice-Hall International, Englewood Cliffs, New Jersey, 1990.

93. Linda M. Northrop. "Success with the Project-Intensive Model for an Undergraduate Software Engineering Course." *SIGCSE Bulletin 21*, 1 (February 1989), 151-155.

94. Ken Orr. *Structured Requirements Definition.* K. Orr, Topeka, Kansas, 1981.

95. Martyn A. Ould and Charles Unwin, editors. *Testing in Software Development.* Cambridge University Press on behalf of the British Computer Society, Cambridge [Cambridgeshire], England; New York, New York, 1986.

96. Meilir Page-Jones. *Practical Project Management: Restoring Quality to DP Projects and Systems.* Dorset House Publishing, New York, New York, 1985.

97. Meilir Page-Jones. *The Practical Guide to Structured Systems Design 2nd edition.* Prentice-Hall International, Englewood Cliffs, New Jersey, 1988.

98. Girish Parikh and Nicholas Zvegintzov, compilers and editors. *Tutorial on Software Maintenance.* IEEE Computer Society Press, Silver Spring, Maryland, 1983.

99. Lawrence J. Peters. *Software Design: Methods and Techniques.* Yourdon Press, New York, New York, 1981.

100. Thomas J. Peters and Robert H. Waterman, Jr.. *In Search of Excellence: Lessons from America's Best-run Companies 1st edition.* Harper & Row, New York, New York, 1982.

101. Shari Lawrence Pfleeger. *Software Engineering: The Production of Quality Software.* Macmillan; Collier Macmillan, New York, New York; London, England, 1987.

102. Michael J. Powers, David Robert Adams, and Harlan D. Mills. *Computer Information Systems Development: Analysis and Design.* South-Western Publishing Company, Cincinnati, Ohio, 1984.

103. Roger S. Pressman. *Software Engineering: A Practitioner's Approach 2nd edition.* McGraw-Hill, New York, New York, 1987.

104. Roger S. Pressman. *Software Engineering: A Beginner's Guide.* McGraw-Hill, New York, New York, 1988.

105. Lawrence H. Putnam. *Tutorial: Software Cost Estimating and Life-cycle Control Microform: Getting the Software Numbers.* IEEE Computer Society Press, Los Alamitos, California, 1980.

106. Ronald A. Radice and Richard W. Phillips. *Software Engineering: An Industrial Approach.* Prentice-Hall International, Englewood Cliffs, New Jersey, 1988.

107. Donald J. Reifer, editor. *Tutorial: Software Management 3rd edition.* IEEE Computer Society Press, New York, New York; Los Angeles, California, 1986.

108. Andrew P. Sage, editor. *Systems Engineering: Methodology and Applications.* IEEE Press, New York, New York, 1977.

109. Sidney L. Sanders. "Teaching Load and the Quality of Education." *SIGCSE Bulletin 21,* 4 (December 1989), 27-30.

110. Philip C. Semprevivo. *Systems Analysis - Definition, Process, and Design 2nd edition.* Science Research Associates, Chicago, Illinois, 1982.

111. James A. Senn. *Analysis and Design of Information Systems.* McGraw-Hill, New York, New York, 1984.

112. Mary Shaw, editor. *The Carnegie-Mellon Curriculum for Undergraduate Computer Science.* Springer-Verlag, New York, New York, 1985.

113. Mary Shaw. "Prospects for an Engineering Discipline of Software." *IEEE Software 7,* 6 (November 1990), 15-24.

114. Mary Shaw and James E. Tomayko. Models for Undergraduate Project Courses in Software Engineering. Tech. Rept. CMU/SEI-91-TR-10 ESD-91-TR-10, Software Engineering Institute, Carnegie Mellon University, , 1991.

115. Ben Shneiderman. *Software Psychology: Human Factors in Computer and Information Systems.* Winthrop Publishers, Cambridge, Massachusetts, 1980.

116. Martin L. Shooman. *Software Engineering: Design, Reliability, and Management.* McGraw-Hill, New York, New York, 1983.

117. Henry Simpson and Steven M. Casey. *Developing Effective User Documentation.* McGraw-Hill, New York, New York, 1988.

118. Ian Sommerville. *Software Engineering 3rd edition.* Addison-Wesley Publishing Company, Wokingham, England; Reading, Massachusetts, 1989.

119. Donald V. Steward. *Software Engineering with Systems Analysis and Design.* Brooks/Cole Publishing Company, Monterey, California, 1987.

120. Lavette C. Teague, Jr. and Christopher W. Pidgeon. *Structured Analysis Methods for Computer Information Systems.* Science Research Associates, Chicago, Illinois, 1985.

121. Richard H. Thayer, compiler. *Tutorial: Software Engineering Project Management.* IEEE Computer Society Press, Washington, DC, 1988.

122. Richard H. Thayer and Leo A. Endres. Software Engineering Project Laboratory: The Bridge Between University and Industry. In Norman E. Gibbs and Richard E. Fairley, Ed., *Software Engineering Education: The Educational Needs of the Software Community,* Springer-Verlag, 1987, pp. 263-291.

123. James E. Tomayko. Teaching a Project-Intensive Introduction to Software Engineering. Tech. Rept. SEI-87-SR-1, Software Engineering Institute, Carnegie Mellon University, March, 1987.

124. James E. Tomayko. Teaching a Project-Intensive Introduction to Software Engineering: Course Plan and Materials. Tech. Rept. CMU/SEI-91-EM-6, Software Engineering Institute, Carnegie Mellon University, , 1991.

125. Ray Turner. *Software Engineering Methodology.* Reston Publishing Company, Reston, Virginia, 1984.

126. Charles Ralph Vick and Chittoor V. Ramamoorthy. *Handbook of Software Engineering.* Van Nostrand Reinhold Company, New York, New York, 1984.

127. Robert H. Wallace, John E. Stockenberg, and Robert N. Charette. *A Unified Methodology for Developing Systems.* Intertext Publications: McGraw-Hill, New York, New York, 1987.

128. Paul T. Ward and Stephen J. Mellor. *Structured Development for Real-time Systems.* Yourdon Press, New York, New York, 1986.

129. Anthony I. Wasserman and Peter Freeman, editors. *Software Engineering Education: Needs and Objectives, Proceedings of an Interface Workshop.* Springer-Verlag, New York, New York, 1976.

130. Gerald M. Weinberg. *The Psychology of Computer Programming.* Van Nostrand Reinhold, , 1971.

131. James C. Wetherbe. *Systems Analysis and Design: Traditional, Structured, and Advanced Concepts and Techniques 2nd edition.* West Publishing Company, St. Paul, Minnesota, 1984.

132. Jeffrey L. Whitten, Lonnie D. Bentley, and Victor M. Barlow. *Systems Analysis and Design Methods 2nd edition.* Irwin, Homewood, Illinois, 1989.

133. Richard Wiener and Richard Sincovec. *Software Engineering with Modula-2 and Ada.* John Wiley & Sons, Inc., New York, New York, 1984.

134. Edward Nash Yourdon editor. *Classics in Software Engineering.* Yourdon Press, New York, New York, 1979.

135. Edward Yourdon editor. *Writings of the Revolution: Selected Readings on Software Engineering.* Yourdon Press, New York, New York, 1982.

136. Edward Yourdon. *Modern Structured Analysis.* Prentice-Hall International, Englewood Cliffs, New Jersey, 1989.

137. Edward Yourdon and Larry L. Constantine. *Structured Design: Fundamentals of a Discipline of Computer Program and Systems Design.* Prentice-Hall International, Englewood Cliffs, New Jersey, 1979.

"Software Engineering Training in Government and Industry"

Moderator: *Maribeth Carpenter*
Software Engineering Institute

The Establishment of an Appropriate Software Engineering Training Program
R. D. Kelly, D. L. Lapay and F. S. Pitcairn
Westinghouse Electric Corporation

Industrial Training for Software Engineers
P. Mann, A. Mason and M. T. Norris
British Telecom Research Laboratories

Software Engineering: Graduate-Level Courses for AFIT Professional Continuing Education
Nancy R. Mead, SEI
Patricia K. Lawlis, AFIT

THE ESTABLISHMENT OF AN APPROPRIATE
SOFTWARE ENGINEERING TRAINING PROGRAM

BY

R. D. KELLY

D. L. LAPAY

F. S. PITCAIRN

WESTINGHOUSE ELECTRIC CORPORATION
NUCLEAR AND ADVANCED TECHNOLOGY DIVISION
WESTINGHOUSE SCIENCE AND TECHNOLOGY CENTER
P.O. BOX 2728
PITTSBURGH, PA 15230-2728
(412) 256-6705

INTRODUCTION

Software engineering is an emerging discipline which has captured the attention of numerous corporations and industries whose strategic products require the development and maintenance of software applications. Dissemination of the knowledge about software engineering processes and technologies is a challenging task, and must be given careful attention if the discipline is to be embraced in a favorable manner by the receiving organizations.

During the mid-to-late 1980's, the organizations now comprising the Nuclear and Advanced Technology Division, NATD, of the Westinghouse Electric Corporation, recognized the need to formalize the process by which software is developed and maintained. During that period, both business unit level standards and division level quality procedures were issued which defined required software engineering activities and responsibilities. However, formalization of the process through the issuance of standards and procedures did not result in the desired improvement. In many cases, the new "rules" were not effectively followed due to a lack of knowledge of their existence or the belief that they were unnecessary and counter-productive. They were often applied "after the fact", or inefficiently followed. Clearly, some additional effort would be required to effect a cultural change among the Division's software developers.

During 1989, a training program was developed by NATD to provide an overview of software engineering and existing software standards/procedures. An early decision was made to present the overview course from a software engineering standpoint rather than a procedural one; the benefits of applying software engineering to the software development process should be stressed. The resultant primary goal of the course was to familiarize personnel involved in the software development process with the basic elements of software engineering and how those elements should be addressed in a productive and high-quality manner. The development and execution of this training program will be described in the following sections.

The program so far has been successful. Both management commitment and student participation have been good. Plans to continue the existing program and to expand its scope are underway.

MOTIVATION

Several conditions contributed to the motivation for establishing a software engineering training program for the personnel in NATD. Nearly all the products and services provided by the Division are dependent either directly or indirectly on some form of software. In many cases, software is used to analyze, qualify, or help design our commercial products. In other cases, software is directly included as a part of the product. In terms of providing engineering services, software is universally employed to assist with calculations and various analyses.

During 1989, software engineering requirements were included as part of the NATD Quality Assurance Program. However, relatively few engineers and software practitioners were aware of their existence, let alone effective ways of addressing them. It had become critical that divisional personnel be trained in not only the official requirements, but also in meeting those requirements in both a high quality and productive manner.

Finally, as industry statistics have overwhelmingly proven, NATD was missing an opportunity to improve both the quality and productivity of the process used to generate and maintain software by not adhering to modern software engineering principles. Software practitioners had to become familiar with accepted techniques and methods to reap the benefits already realized by other industries applying software engineering processes. A formal training program was selected as the best approach to meet the Division's software engineering needs.

ORGANIZATION

The training program was sponsored by NATD and strategic funds were allocated for development and presentation of the course materials. Representatives from three departments were appointed to participate in the "working group" which was responsible for the preparation and presentation of the training program. A "training board", consisting of upper level representatives from several departments, was appointed to provide direction to the working group and to review materials developed for the training. Product Assurance also participated in the review of the training material and were available at each training session to answer questions.

SCOPE

The full training program was defined to address all aspects of the software engineering process from project inception through software "decommissioning". Development of the contents of the various phases of the training would include materials prepared in-house as well as those obtained from outside sources. Outside sources of training include software engineering experts such as Roger Pressman and Tom DeMarco, academic courses, and organizations such as the Software Engineering Institute. Of particular interest were video series which could aid in the training of multiple sessions at varied times and locations.

The first phase of training to be addressed was an overview of the entire process. This was selected because of the recognized need to familiarize a significant number of NATD personnel with the basic concepts of software engineering prior to addressing selected aspects in greater detail. During the planning stage for this overview training course, it was first decided that a customized in-house training program would be used rather than a totally vendor supplied program. This would provide better flexibility, availability, and repeatability, while allowing the convenience of using some commercially available training materials. Next, it was agreed that the overview session should last approximately two hours; sufficient time had to be allotted for presentation of the materials without losing student attentiveness.

The initial departments targeted for the overview training were those involved primarily in engineering applications of software, however, it was recognized that the eventual goal included education of all personnel involved in the application of software, regardless of their organizational "location". It was estimated that approximately three hundred people would be trained during the first phase of the program.

TARGET TRAINING AUDIENCE

The audience targeted for the training included those personnel directly involved in the specification, design, implementation, verification, configuration, or management of engineering software applications. As a result, the training was directed to address the concerns of engineers, managers, technicians, as well as software development personnel. Although it was recognized that some personnel attending the training would already have attended previous software engineering training, the course was designed to address primarily the needs of the software engineering "novice", with all basic elements receiving adequate coverage. Training participants were nominated by their management.

PROGRAM CURRICULUM

The overview training was designed to serve as a prerequisite for the other detailed sessions that are to follow. As a stand alone session, however, the overview training was expected to provide participants with an awareness of divisional requirements and the basic steps that should take place when developing software. A set of objectives for the overview training curriculum were identified:

1. Increase the student's knowledge of software engineering.
2. Familiarize the students with the Business Unit's and Division's standards and procedures and train them on their cost effective use.
3. Emphasize the correlation between the goals of software engineering and their implementation in the Division's standards and procedures.

4.   Provide motivation for complying with the standards/procedures. Stress that the Division's standards/procedures are in accordance with industry practice.

5.   Focus on overall software engineering process rather than methods.

From these objectives, a course agenda was developed. A copy of this training agenda is included in Figure 1.

The overview course was introduced in a formal manner by a member of upper management. In this introduction the "why" of participation in the training program was discussed, and management endorsement of the training and software engineering principles was clearly evident. Following the introduction, the first of the "Software Engineering Training Curriculum" [1] videotapes by Roger Pressman was presented to provide an introduction to software engineering principles. The video presentation was followed by a slide presentation of the NATD software standards and procedures which recapitulated Dr. Pressman's software development discussion within the Division's context. The fourth agenda item was an example, in which the software engineering steps were shown in practice. The example presented an opportunity to further customize the training; trainees from a given department attended the training as a unit, and the example was tailored to model the type of work that department typically encounters. Finally, a discussion of future training and a question and answer period concluded the session.

Once equipped with a working knowledge of the overall software engineering process provided by this training, personnel would attend appropriate detailed training based on the job functions they are typically expected to perform. Additional training would be attended in specific areas of the software lifecycle including the following:

    Project Management
    Functional Specification
    Software Design
    Implementation and Testing
    Verification and Validation
    Configuration Control

Most of this training would be accomplished via the use of commercially available course materials such as the SETC video tape series.

COURSE STRUCTURE

The overview training was conducted in a formal fashion, typical of a Quality Assurance training session; attendance lists were collected and sent to management for retention as formal training records. Training for each department was identical (except for the customized example), and make-up sessions were made available. The subsequent detailed training will be conducted in a less formal manner since their course content will focus less on divisional requirements and more on techniques and methods. In all cases, exams and evaluations were administered at the completion of the course to "measure" the training's success in conveying materials. Students were (and will continue to be) encouraged to enhance their learning by asking questions and interjecting comments during the sessions. Training session were held at various sites for the convenience of the trainees.

TIME FRAME

The development of the training program was initiated at the beginning of 1989 and by May, a preliminary set of materials for the overview course and general outline for the contents of the other sessions had been prepared and presented to the training board by the working group. Comments received from the training board were incorporated in the training materials. Both the working group and the training board recognized that the proposed training would require significant resources, so a meeting was scheduled with the NATD staff to obtain the management commitment needed to allocate the time associated with training the projected three hundred personnel. Following that meeting, plans were made to conduct a "beta" session to obtain feedback from a selected set of participants prior to presenting the course "en masse".

Following the beta session and subsequent minor revisions made to the course materials, the training was conducted approximately bi-weekly starting in January of 1990 and running through June. In all cases, course exams and evaluations were distributed for monitoring the reception and success of the training. Additional overview training is planned for the third and fourth quarters of 1990, targeted at one session per quarter. Development of the next training module, Software Requirements, is also planned to occur during this time with projected beta presentation towards the end of 1990.

While the overview training was being prepared and reviewed, the opportunity to participate in and obtain the Software Project Management video training series from the Software Engineering Institute became available. Since that time, the full series has been presented on a formal basis inside Westinghouse, and additional sessions have been scheduled. This training consists of 7 full days of videotape sessions interspersed with short examples and discussion periods. This series has been conducted one day per week for 7 weeks when it has been presented in its entirety, and has generally been targeted at experienced software professionals who could utilize the videotapes in local training of their own design.

COST

The costs associated with preparing and presenting software engineering training are non-trivial; it is necessary to allow sufficient time and resources to make the program successful. During 1989, approximately $20K of strategic funds was spent for the preparation and presentation of the overview materials. During 1990, approximately $14K was spent to conduct the sessions through June. It is projected that another $14K will be required to complete the remaining activities planned for 1990. These costs do not include the approximate 900 manhours of the personnel who attended the training.

RESULTS

The results of the overview training include those obtained from analyzing the replies to the course evaluation and exam. Copies of the evaluation and exam are shown in Figures 2 through 4.

Of the 319 personnel invited to the training, approximately 90%, or 284, attended. Of those 284 attendees, approximately 230 returned evaluations and exams. Responses from the evaluation questions are illustrated in the remaining Figures. Results from the exam question generally confirmed that our training objectives were achieved.

Overall, responses to the evaluation indicated a positive reception and reaction to the training. Most participants felt the material was useful, of good quality, and adequate for an overview presentation. The length of the class was also generally judged as about right. Almost 90% indicated that they would be able to apply the materials to their job duties.

In terms of familiarity with software engineering concepts, about 70% of the respondents indicated that they were already familiar with them; however, an equal percentage replied that they had not previously attended other software engineering training. Most attendees had some familiarity with the NATD software engineering Quality Assurance procedures prior to attending the training.

Although generally favorable replies were obtained for most evaluation questions, responses to some of the questions indicate that improvements should be made in the overview course as well as in the overall approach to software engineering training in NATD. Approximately 25% indicated that the example was NOT helpful and 30% of the personnel replied that they would NOT recommend the course to their colleagues. Also of concern, over 30% indicated that they did not believe that NATD is committed to good software engineering practices.

Additional results of the training were not indicated on the response forms. The training program provided an opportunity for cross-fertilization of ideas from different software organizations within the Division. The training facilitated an informal "Software Engineering Network", providing the names of contacts with which Software Engineering matters could be discussed. Anecdotal evidence of the cultural change, which was one of the desired results of this training, has been received through such contacts.

LESSONS LEARNED

Management commitment to and endorsement of training is essential for meaningful training to occur; the formal introduction by upper management at the beginning of each session appears to have been a key ingredient in the success of the training. Early meetings with division management to secure their endorsement, and the involvement of lower levels of management in the trainee nomination process were also key to building commitment.

By selecting trainers from focal points within the Division, responsibilities for various courseware development and course execution activities could be shared effectively. For example, the availability of three trained trainers facilitated advance scheduling of the course sessions; if the planned trainer became un-available, an alternate could be quickly appointed.

The ability to tailor the course and particularly the example to a specific audience was very important for the overview training; without the ability to relate the standards and procedures to day-to-day work experience, many of the trainees might have gained little from the session. The use of trainers from throughout the Division contributed to the ability to accomplish this tailoring. Some consideration was given to eventually videotaping this presentation, but the benefits of tailoring seem to outweigh the convenience of videotape for this course.

While there were various levels of software engineering expertise in the target audience, the realization that others shared their views kept the more advanced students connected with the class.

The decision to expend more than the minimum for the slides appears to have been well thought out. The feedback graded the slides as high quality, and the occasional cartoon inserted in the slides seems to have served to help sustain the audience through the middle of the session.

SUMMARY

In general, the training program proved successful in providing the students with a baseline knowledge of software engineering concepts and a working knowledge of the software standards/procedures in place within the Division. The use of training feedback in all training sessions has helped to identify improvements to be made in the training, and the kinds of courses which would be desirable in the future. The success of the overview training in stimulating a cultural change within the Division is largely a result of the management commitment demonstrated as a direct part of the training.

NATD Software Engineering Training Overview

- Opening remarks

- SETC video presentation

- NATD software standards and procedures

- Example

- Summary

- Future training

- Questions and discussion

D973 D29529.032

Figure 1
Training Agenda

Software Engineering Training /
Software QA Requirement
Quiz

Date: _____

What 5 significant things did you learn from this course:

1. _____
   _____
   _____
   _____
   _____

2. _____
   _____
   _____
   _____
   _____

3. _____
   _____
   _____
   _____
   _____

4. _____
   _____
   _____
   _____
   _____

5. _____
   _____
   _____
   _____
   _____

Figure 2
Course Quiz

Software Engineering Training / Software QA Requirement Course Evaluation

Date: _____

1. Name (optional): _____

2. Organization: _____

3. I perform the following tasks as part of my job responsibilities:
   - ☐ specify software   ☐ design software   ☐ code software
   - ☐ test software   ☐ verify software   ☐ control software
   - ☐ use software   ☐ manage software

4. I will be able to apply the course material to my job duties.
   - ☐ yes   ☐ no

5. Before I attended this course, I was familiar with software engineering concepts.
   - ☐ yes   ☐ no

6. Before I attended this course, I was familiar with:

   DP-3.7.1 (previously DP-3.2.9) Software Development   ☐ yes   ☐ no

   DP-3.7.2 (previously DP-3.2.4) Verification & Validation   ☐ yes   ☐ no

   DP-3.7.3 (previously DP-3.2.5) Configuration Control   ☐ yes   ☐ no

   DP-3.7.4 (previously part of DP-3.2.5) Error Reporting   ☐ yes   ☐ no

7. The length of the class was:
   - ☐ too long   ☐ too short   ☐ just about right

8. The material covered was:
   - ☐ too specific   ☐ too general   ☐ adequate for an overview

9. The video presentation was a valuable part of the course.
   - ☐ yes   ☐ no

10. The quality of the SETC video was:
    - ☐ excellent   ☐ good   ☐ fair   ☐ poor

11. The quality of the course slides was:
    - ☐ excellent   ☐ good   ☐ fair   ☐ poor

12. The example helped clarify the concepts.
    - ☐ yes   ☐ no

13. The course handouts were useful.
    - ☐ yes   ☐ no

14. In the future, I would prefer that the training be presented:
    - ☐ in the morning   ☐ during lunch   ☐ in the afternoon   ☐ after work

(Over)

**Figure 3
Course Evaluation - Part 1**

89

15. I would recommend attendance to my colleagues.
  ☐ yes   ☐ no
16. I have attended other software engineering training classes.
  ☐ yes   ☐ no
17. I would be interested in attending future software engineering training classes.
  ☐ yes   ☐ no
18. The type of software engineering training I would be most interested in is:

_____

_____

_____

19. I believe that NATD is committed to the implementation of good software engineering practices.
  ☐ yes   ☐ no
20. Other:

Thank you for your help.

Figure 4
Course Evaluation - Part 2

Familiarity with SE Concepts

Already familiar w/SE concepts (71.4%)

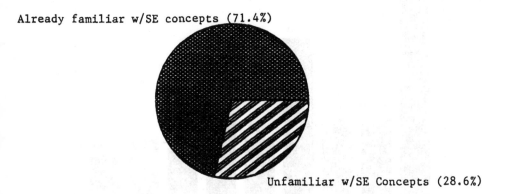

Unfamiliar w/SE Concepts (28.6%)

Ability To Apply Material To Job Duties

Able to apply material
(87.2%)

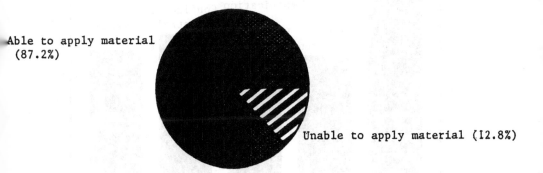

Unable to apply material (12.8%)

Figure 5
Evaluation Summary

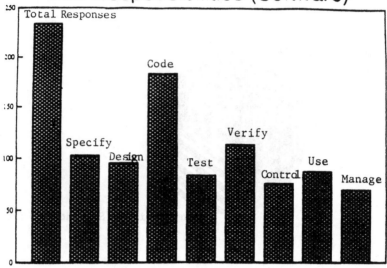

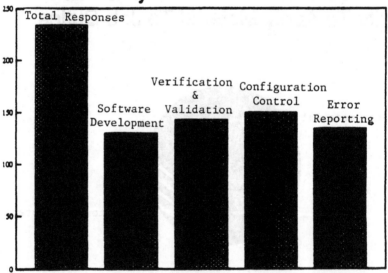

Figure 6
Evaluation Summary

Length of Class

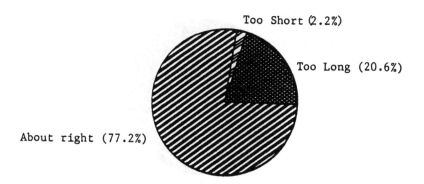

Too Short (2.2%)

Too Long (20.6%)

About right (77.2%)

Material Covered

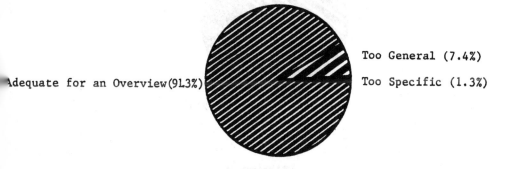

Too General (7.4%)

Too Specific (1.3%)

Adequate for an Overview (9L3%)

Figure 7
Evaluation Summary

Was Video Presentation Valuable

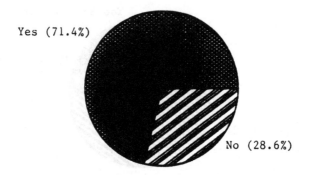

Yes (71.4%)

No (28.6%)

SETC video quality

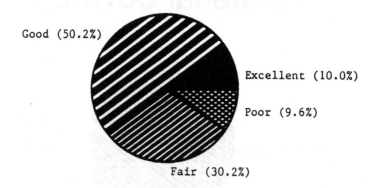

Good (50.2%)

Excellent (10.0%)

Poor (9.6%)

Fair (30.2%)

Figure 8
Evaluation Summary

Course Slide quality

Excellent (26.5%)

Poor (0.0%)

Good (66.5%)

Fair (7.0%)

Was the example helpful?

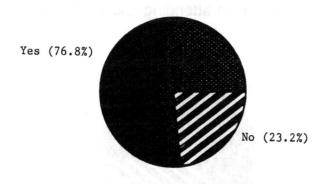

Yes (76.8%)

No (23.2%)

Figure 9
Evaluation Summary

Have you attended other SE Training ?

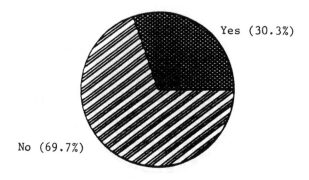

Yes (30.3%)

No (69.7%)

Are you interested in attending future SE Training?

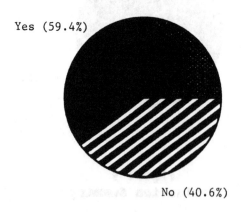

Yes (59.4%)

No (40.6%)

Figure 10
Evaluation Summary

Do you believe NATD is commited to good SE practices?

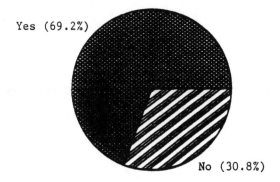

Yes (69.2%)

No (30.8%)

Would you recommend the course to your colleagues?

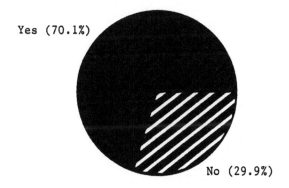

Yes (70.1%)

No (29.9%)

Figure 11
Evaluation Summary

REFERENCES

[1]   Pressman, Roger S., "Software Engineering Training Curriculum",
      R.S. Pressman & Associates, Inc., 1985.

BIBLIOGRAPHY

"American National Standard Guidelines for the Verification and Validation of Scientific and Engineering Computer Programs for the Nuclear Industry", ANS 10.4, American Nuclear Society, LaGrange Park, Illinois, May 1985.

"American National Standard IEEE Standard Glossary of Software Engineering Terminology", ANSI/IEEE Std. 729-1983, The Institute of Electrical and Electronics Engineers, Inc., New York City, New York, August 9, 1983.

"American National Standard IEEE Standard for Software Quality Assurance Plans", ANSI/IEEE Std. 730-1981, The Institute of Electrical and Electronics Engineers, Inc., New York City, New York, June 21, 1982.

"IEEE Guide to Software Requirements Specifications", IEEE Std. 830-1984, The Institute of Electrical and Electronics Engineers, Inc., New York City, New York, February 10, 1984.

"IEEE Standard for Software Configuration Management Plans", IEEE Std 828-1983, The Institute of Electrical and Electronics Engineers, Inc., New York City, New York, 1983.

"IEEE Standard for Software Test Documentation", IEEE Std. 829-1983, The Institute of Electrical and Electronics Engineers, Inc., New York City, New York, 1983.

"Controlling Software Projects", DeMarco, T., Yourdon Press, 1982.

"Making Software Engineering Happen", Pressman, R.S., Prentice-Hall, 1988

"Software Engineering Concepts", Fairley, R., McGraw-Hill, 1985.

"Software Engineering: A Practitioner's Approach", Pressman, R.S., 2nd Edition, McGraw-Hill, 1987.

INDUSTRIAL TRAINING FOR SOFTWARE ENGINEERS

P. Mann, A. Mason and M. T. Norris
British Telecom Research Laboratories
Martlesham Heath
IPSWICH IP5 7RE
England
Telephone - +44 473 642200

Abstract

Training software engineers to work in industry is a problem that has traditionally been tackled by the retraining of Computer Scientists, Electrical Engineers and Mathematicians. This initial skills conversion is not, however, a long term solution. The ever increasing rate of change of software technology can very quickly leave engineers out of date. While short term skills training is useful for meeting immediate needs, it does not provide sufficient breadth to keep staff up to date with a rapidly changing discipline. In order to remain competitive there is a need for a longer term mechanism to ensure that software engineers maintain an awareness and understanding of best practice.

This paper explains how a variety of training facilities have been combined to provide a coherent education package for software engineers in British Telecom.

1. Introduction

The skills shortage in the software industry is not a temporary phenomenon; it is the consequence of a process of rapid technological change which shows no sign of abating(1). The problem is exacerbated in the UK by the limited, and diminishing, supply of graduate engineers, mathematicians and computer scientists. High technology companies must, if they wish to continue competing in the market, ensure that their existing, experienced staff adapt to new technologies and techniques (2). Effective programmes of training are therefore an increasingly important element of running a large scale software business such as British Telecom.

Training in the software industry was, until quite recently, regarded as a short term remedy to immediate skill shortages, usually in fashionable but ephemeral products such as programming languages, design methods or management tools. The nature of training now required is, thanks to Moores law[1], more of a continuous learning process than the acquisition of a specific new skill.

In order to keep up with the phenomenal rate of change in software technology, the practicing engineer needs to be taken back over new foundations, not learnt at university or college (3). This implies a wide range of training courses covering new theory, its application and impact. Clearly, this cannot be done through the academic system alone - a coherent programme of continuing education, tailored to the needs of an individual company, is required.

This paper outlines a programme of continuing education for software engineers developed within British Telecom. The following two sections explain the background to the programme and the important influences that had to be taken into account in its creation. Subsequent sections describe the constituent resources that have been used to build the programme, the way in which it is organised and the results of its application. In order to illustrate the way in which training to meet new requirements is handled, the paper covers the PACE and METKIT programmes in some detail. The former provides material covering a broad range of general software topics, the latter specific techniques for software measurement.

---

[1]Moores law states that whenever there is an order of magnitude change in technology there is an accompanying qualitative change in the exploitation of that technlogy. (The law is attributed to Gordon Moore, founder of Intel)

2. Context of the programme

British Telecom (BT), the main telecommunications operator and supplier in the UK, currently employs in excess of 200,000 staff. In addition to network provision and maintenance, the company competes in many parts of the information technology market: from stored program control exchanges and large database products to small customer equipment.

Much of the advanced technology required by the network is provided by the company research laboratories at Martlesham. In their early days the laboratories specialised in telephone switching and transmission but with increasing use of digital techniques, the scope of activities has broadened. It is estimated that every year, several thousand staff years are being devoted towards software engineering.

In line with this broadening of technical focus, a specialist systems and software engineering unit was set up at the Laboratories in 1983. The role of this unit has been to transfer the most advanced software technology to the operational parts of BT. In the five years since its inception, the unit has been responsible for a number of major developments - the introduction of sophisticated software design tools (4,5), the provision of consultancy services to all the main operating units of BT and the initiation of a substantial long term research programme (6,7,8).

The rapid expansion of the software engineering unit (approximately 25% per annum) and its critical dependence on high calibre staff make it a very sensitive indicator of the effectiveness of training and education. Although the programme of ongoing education described here is available throughout the company, the remainder of the paper describes specific results from this unit.

3. Design of the programme

There are a number of important influences that have been taken into account in the development of the programme. These fall into two categories - first there are the external influences such as industry standards and practices, and second there are the internal requirements of the business.

3. 1 External Considerations

The main influences in this category are the Institute of Electrical Engineers (IEE), the National Computing Council (NCC) and the British Standards Institute (BSI).

The IEE and NCC published towards the end of 1988 a joint recommendation for the registration of software engineers (9). This effectively defines the level of knowledge and skill an individual requires to be recognised as a software engineer. Staff who are not in a position to comply with these requirements would probably find themselves limited in the range of projects they could work on.

The ISO9001[2] standard (10) defines the requirements which have to be met before a company in the UK can be registered as a quality approved supplier. With regard to software, the standard covers all aspects of design and implementation. A fundamental part of gaining BSI approval is the definition and maintenance of an appropriate training plan.

3.2. Internal Considerations

The first step in translating the broad requirement for effective training into a more concrete form has been the production of a published training strategy. This document serves a number of purposes:

- It sets a nominal budget for the programme.
- It defines the basic skills that are required.
- It makes the units policy on training and education visible to all staff.

The current strategy document is split into a number of sections which deal with training for new staff, training and education of existing staff and organisation and management. Within each of these sections the recommended level of spend and sources of information (see section 4 for more detail of these) are given.

The first part of the strategy, dealing with the training of new staff is designated the core as it covers the basic technical and managerial skills required to operate in unit. Most of the resources for core training (e.g. presentation skills, project management) are available in-house. This allows flexibility of provision as well as control over content.

---

[2] The BSI 5750 standard is usually quoted in this context. It is identical in content to the International Standards Organisation ISO 9001 document.

The portion dealing with ongoing education is less structured as it has to allow for a wide range of existing knowledge and expertise. Currently the main thrusts here are in design techniques (e.g. object oriented design, requirements specification methods), consultancy skills and emergent technologies (e.g. machine learning, formal methods). A range of sources are used for these; some short courses, some distance learning packages, etc. The requirements for this part of the programme are revised regularly so that suitable material can be found.

There are a number of operational issues that have to be addressed to ensure that the strategy is effectively implemented. First, local management must agree on a training plan with their staff (this is a prerequisite of ISO9001 registration). Coordination of training within the unit is managed through a nominated training officer. In addition to planning, monitoring and recording training within the unit, the training officer ensures that staff are kept aware of what is available. Finally the central systems training unit coordinates the overall programme by providing the required educational material.

4. Resources and Organisation

In order to meet the broad requirements of the unit, a number of different sources have been used within the programme. The main ones are outlined in this section. Particular attention is paid here to the PACE distance learning package and the METKIT project for the development of educational material in software measurement.

4.1. Euro-PACE

The European Programme for Advanced Continuing Education (Euro-PACE) (11) was originally conceived by five large European companies, as a means of supplying rapid and direct access to expertise in high technology subjects. These companies (British Telecom being one) became the founding sponsors of Euro-PACE. They were soon joined by a number of European universities and societies. To date there are 12 sponsoring companies.

The need for immediacy in high technology training is met by the use of satellite communication for information transfer. Lectures are transmitted from Paris and received at each location throughout Europe. These are complemented by supporting documentation and software packages (depending on course requirements) for each of the courses.

Students can immediately respond to course material by the use of PORTACOM. This is an Electronic Mail system based in Aarhus in Denmark. All of the course lecturers have their own account on this system, as do the Site Reception Managers. Students can use the PORTACOM facility so that questions can be asked on course topics and an answer, direct from the lecturer concerned, is usually returned the same day. For more urgent questions the students can use either Telephone or Facsimile services.

Over and above the pedagogic issues there is the opportunity to transmit a variety of European conferences. These can be received at each location as a 'Live Event' with the audience interfacing by PORTACOM.

Euro-PACE was launched in early 1988 with a limited pilot phase. The courses offered in this pilot were intended to cover 6 fields of special interest, from microelectronics to technology management, that were initially highlighted by the sponsors. In practice, however, the fields of Software Engineering and Artificial Intelligence proved by far the most popular. In August 1988 the full pilot phase was implemented. This phase offered 18 courses and 6 special events. The fields of Software Engineering and Artificial Intelligence were prominent with the following offerings:

> Real-Time software design
> Object oriented design and Programming
> Function Languages and Prototyping
> Software Engineering with ADA
> Natural Language Processing
> Prolog, logic programming (basic and advanced)
> Knowledge Engineering, Expert systems
> Live Event-Expert systems 88 Conference

More recent material in the 1989/90 and 1990/1991 programmes includes:

> Software quality, metrics and testing
> Database systems of the 1990's
> Self-organisation and neural nets
> AI in planning
> Constraint handling in Prolog (CHIP)
> International neural networks conference, 1990

Because the material is recorded on video, it is possible to use it to provide a scheduled lecture series on regular basis rather like a university course unit. Alternatively, the lectures can be viewed by individuals on a 'ad hoc' arrangement to suit particular requirements or constraints.

Over the two years since launch, British Telecom Research have had more than 250 students register with Euro-PACE, and have been actively involved with all of the Software and AI courses. The range of offerings under PACE has been extended since its inception and is now provides a comprehensive and integrated package for technical training in software engineering. The overriding consideration is that the transmissions present a very rapid means of disseminating leading-edge knowledge. This is undoubtedly achieved but, sometimes, at the expense of high quality: while the courses carry the expert authority, they are not all comfortable on camera. Likewise, support material and the use of animation and graphics is variable.

To illustrate the sort of material available in PACE, we can outline one particular course:

Subject - Object Oriented Design and Programming
Lecturer - Bertrand Meyer
Duration -18 hours(2 hours per week)
Support material - Book by Bertrand Meyer and copies of all transparencies used
Target audience-Software developers and system managers

This particular course has been taken by over 100 students (in 8 separate study groups). In each study group, the students could discuss the material amongst themselves and interact with Bertrand Meyer over the PORTACOM system. With this highly interactive capability Euro-PACE offers a cost effective answer to the problem of post graduate level continuing education. In some areas, for instance AI, some previously unobtainable material has been provided.

Overall, British Telecom has found sponsorship of EuroPACE to be a major asset: an extremely useful addition to other educational and training material on offer. It provides an immediate, state of the art knowledge base at an appropriate level.

4.2 Internal Courses

A number of internal courses have been developed by BT to provide the basic material which underpins the programme. Some of the current offerings, designed to ensure that staff with a range of different backgrounds can be brought to a known level of expertise, are listed below:-

Students can immediately respond to course material by the use of PORTACOM. This is an Electronic Mail system based in Aarhus in Denmark. All of the course lecturers have their own account on this system, as do the Site Reception Managers. Students can use the PORTACOM facility so that questions can be asked on course topics and an answer, direct from the lecturer concerned, is usually returned the same day. For more urgent questions the students can use either Telephone or Facsimile services.

Over and above the pedagogic issues there is the opportunity to transmit a variety of European conferences. These can be received at each location as a 'Live Event' with the audience interfacing by PORTACOM.

Euro-PACE was launched in early 1988 with a limited pilot phase. The courses offered in this pilot were intended to cover 6 fields of special interest, from microelectronics to technology management, that were initially highlighted by the sponsors. In practice, however, the fields of Software Engineering and Artificial Intelligence proved by far the most popular. In August 1988 the full pilot phase was implemented. This phase offered 18 courses and 6 special events. The fields of Software Engineering and Artificial Intelligence were prominent with the following offerings:

Real-Time software design
Object oriented design and Programming
Function Languages and Prototyping
Software Engineering with ADA
Natural Language Processing
Prolog, logic programming (basic and advanced)
Knowledge Engineering, Expert systems
Live Event-Expert systems 88 Conference

More recent material in the 1989/90 and 1990/1991 programmes includes:

Software quality, metrics and testing
Database systems of the 1990's
Self-organisation and neural nets
AI in planning
Constraint handling in Prolog (CHIP)
International neural networks conference, 1990

Because the material is recorded on video, it is possible to use it to provide a scheduled lecture series on regular basis rather like a university course unit. Alternatively, the lectures can be viewed by individuals on a 'ad hoc' arrangement to suit particular requirements or constraints.

Over the two years since launch, British Telecom Research have had more than 250 students register with Euro-PACE, and have been actively involved with all of the Software and AI courses. The range of offerings under PACE has been extended since its inception and is now provides a comprehensive and integrated package for technical training in software engineering. The overriding consideration is that the transmissions present a very rapid means of disseminating leading-edge knowledge. This is undoubtedly achieved but, sometimes, at the expense of high quality: while the courses carry the expert authority, they are not all comfortable on camera. Likewise, support material and the use of animation and graphics is variable.

To illustrate the sort of material available in PACE, we can outline one particular course:

Subject - Object Oriented Design and Programming
Lecturer - Bertrand Meyer
Duration -18 hours(2 hours per week)
Support material - Book by Bertrand Meyer and copies of all transparencies used
Target audience-Software developers and system managers

This particular course has been taken by over 100 students (in 8 separate study groups). In each study group, the students could discuss the material amongst themselves and interact with Bertrand Meyer over the PORTACOM system. With this highly interactive capability Euro-PACE offers a cost effective answer to the problem of post graduate level continuing education. In some areas, for instance AI, some previously unobtainable material has been provided.

Overall, British Telecom has found sponsorship of EuroPACE to be a major asset: an extremely useful addition to other educational and training material on offer. It provides an immediate, state of the art knowledge base at an appropriate level.

4.2 Internal Courses

A number of internal courses have been developed by BT to provide the basic material which underpins the programme. Some of the current offerings, designed to ensure that staff with a range of different backgrounds can be brought to a known level of expertise, are listed below:-

Pascal Programming
Aimed at graduate engineers, physicists, software technicians etc. Designed to teach the fundamentals of a structured programming language

Program development using dynamic data structures
Aimed at existing software developers. Designed to introduce the concept and use of complex structures to better represent real world data in a program. It is based on Pascal of C. Also deals with the problems of incorporating existing software into new systems, software maintenance and the need for good documentation standards in the production of software.

Introduction to Software Design
Aimed at anyone who is involved with the development of software. Uses the tried and tested software lifecycle model to highlight problem areas from requirements capture, through design and implementation to maintenance and enhancement. Also proposes methodologies which may assist at various stages in the development of large, medium or small software systems.

Discrete Mathematics for Formal Methods
Aimed at anyone who is likely to use formal methods such as VDM, Z, etc for the design and development of software. Covers the fundamentals of discrete mathematics necessary to be able to understand and use formal methods.

CCITT Specification and Description Language
Aimed at software developers who use the CCITT SDL standard as a design and development method. This standard is widely used in the specification and design of telecommunications systems.

The above courses are designed to complement one another and form a foundation level of basic training in software engineering. In addition to this technical foundation, a number of management skills courses have been developed to cover topics such as time management, consultancy skills & presentation techniques.

4.3. METKIT

In addition to providing education in established areas, BT is also anxious to start providing education in new and emerging areas, which are often ill-served by commercially available courses.
One area of high technology which has been perceived as of great importance in software metrics - the use of rigorous measurement applied to software (12). This is becoming increasingly important to aid processes such as cost estimation and the identification of modules likely to cause trouble in software systems.

With this aim in mind, BT has joined a consortium of software companies and educational establishments to work on the METKIT project. The METKIT project aims to provide an educational package for the teaching of software metrics.

METKIT is partly funded by the European Commission under the Esprit Programme (European Strategic Programme for Research and Development in Information Technology) - a ten year programme aimed at encouraging collaborative research in Information Technology.

The METKIT project came into being as a result of the realisation that - in Europe at least - vast sums of money are wasted on poor quality software. Measurement was seen as a way of helping to improve the quality of software. It was also seen as a way of helping to estimate the cost of producing and maintaining software and of evaluating and certifying systems.

Not only was there a lack of awareness of software metrics in the European software industry, there was also a lack of courses and few teaching materials. The METKIT Project aims to produce a set of teaching packages based on state of the art approaches to software metrication. Three main audiences for the material have been identified: managers, software engineers and academic students - the latter mainly undergraduates at university. The philosophy behind this was both to foster an awareness and to encourage the use of software metrics amongst people currently working in the industry. By providing material for students it is hoped that the use of metrics can be encouraged in the future.

In keeping with other training material, the courseware is modular in structure. The top level modules for each target audience give a birds' eye view of the field of software metrics. Lower modules then expand on the areas touched upon in the top module. Each of the METKIT modules is intended to be complete in its own right. There is no requirement for students to cover all the material and they need study only those modules which suit their interests and experience.

The topics covered in the top level modules include the following:

- A discussion of the present state of the software industry
- Measurement theory
- What can be measured in software engineering
- Software Engineering in practice

In the lower level modules, topics such as the following are addressed:

- Prediction models
- Products, processes and resources
- Goal definition
- Data collection and analysis
- How to set up a metrics programme

The major output of the project will be the teaching package modules consisting of teacher and student notes and sets of overhead projector slides. In addition some material will be produced as videos - probably the managers' modules. There will also be various ancillary materials. A metrics tools sampler and a survey of available tools are approaching completion. An interactive computer aided learning package which can be available at the software engineers terminal is also being developed.

METKIT is a three year project which started in February 1989. The work done in the first year consisted of research and planning - the current practice of industry and academia was surveyed and the needs for metrics were assessed. A certain amount of rationalisation and enhancement of existing metrics tool place.In the second year, the components of the teaching package were defined and prototype packages were developed. Some of these packages are now approaching completion.

In the third year it is expected that the packages will be tested in both industrial and academic environments. The feedback obtained will be used to refine and adjust the material as necessary.

At the end of the project, ownership of the materials will be vested in the partners who will be at liberty to use it for their own purposes or, indeed, to license it out to others.

In the case of BT considerable interest in the METKIT material has been shown to date. It is anticipated that the modules will find a ready use in software development units across the company.

4.4 Other Sources

The cost justification of producing, maintaining and providing the in-house courses is based upon three main criteria

• lack of suitable alternatives elsewhere (e.g. SDL).

- courses that have to be specialised for BT needs
- courses that attract a very high volume of students

This places great demands on the skilled resources required to develop and run courses, a difficulty that is partially overcome by buying-in existing commercial courses from training companies such as ICS and Yourdon, and also employing University staff to prepare and present bespoke courses on relevant subjects.This part of the programme is strengthened by BTs involvement with an Information Technology Associate Company Scheme (ITACS). This brings together sponsoring companies and the University of Strathclyde to design and develop state-of-the art software engineering and computer science courses on subjects such as Design using 4GLs, Evaluating and Selecting Information Systems Methodologies, etc.

5. Results

Despite the fact that it is very difficult to quantify the benefits of an effective programme, there are some facts and figures that do seem to have some relevance. This section discusses some of these indicators.

- Use of Training facilities

The training recommendations made in the strategy document, mentioned earlier, are closely adhered to. Time out to acquire new skill doesn't seem to have any detrimental effect on the software engineering unit's ability to compete - in fact its services are more in demand now than previously. Furthermore the pro-active development of special purpose training packages such as METKIT allows considerable control in establishing a common level of understanding and practice.

- Staff turnover[3]

The average staff loss from the software engineering research unit during 1990 was about 8%, mostly into other parts of British Telecom. The level of resignations from the unit is less than 1% . This is significantly lower than the norm for a high technology industry in the UK. It is true that this trend is not only due to a good training programme but it is an important factor.

- Cost of provision

The effort of organising and administrating the programme within the unit is

---

[3] BT regularly commissions independent surveys on its corporate image. These invariably reveal that the company is perceived as providing a good programme of training and that this is a strong motivator in joining and staying.

minimal - a total of less that a third of a staff year per annum. The cost of the training provided has been minimised by extensive use of the distance learning and in-house provisions. These are considerably cheaper than commercially available or bespoke training. To give some idea of the balance here, some 400 places are filled on in-house software engineering courses per year. Over the same period, 120 places are taken up on externally provided software engineering courses. The takeup of PACE training is detailed in the previous section.

6. Conclusions

There is no ready supply of appropriately trained people to staff the software industry: companies competing in this area of the market must be able to develop and maintain an adequate software technology capability.This can pose problems for large companies and there is a pressing requirement to capitalise on the skills of existing staff through a programme of continuing education. Such a programme has been developed within British Telecom Laboratories drawing on a number of different components. The nature of these components, their organisation and presentation as a coherent programme has been described here. We have also reported on some of the benefits derived.

Acknowledgements

The authors would like to acknowledge the Director of British Telecom Labs for permission to publish this paper. They would also like to thank the many friends and colleagues who contributed to this work.

References

1) "Software - A vital key to UK competitiveness" UK Cabinet Office report (HMSO books) ISBN 011 630829 X

2) 'The STARTS Guide' (- a guide to good software practice) prepared by UK Industry, the DTI and NCC, published by the Dept of Trade and Industry (1987)

3) Cohen B. "The education of the information systems engineer" Electronics and Power p203-5 (March 1987)

4) Tinker R. and Norris M., "Tools to support the design of systems", BT Tech Journal, Vol. 4, No. 3 (1986)

5) Norris M. T. and Jackson L. A., "An engineering approach to system design" Proceedings of Globecom 87, Tokyo (November 1987)

6) Stoddart A. G. and Tilley M. J., "Technology transfer within BT from research to the operating divisions" Proceedings of workshop on technology transfer, Pittsburgh (November 1987)

7) Jackson L. A., "Software system design methods and the engineering approach" BT Tech J Vol. 4 No. 3 (1986)

8) Norris M. T., "The role of formal methods in system design" BT Tech J Vol. 3 No. 4 (1985)

9) "Objectives for the software engineering certificate course" prepared by UK Industry, the IEE and NCC, published by the IEE and NCC

10) International Standards Organisation "Quality systems part 1: Specification for design, development, production, installation and servicing" Standard ISO9001

11) Euro-PACE secretariat, 7 place de la defence, Paris

12) Stockman S. G., Todd A. R. and Robinson G. "A framework for software quality measurement" IEEE Journal on selected areas of Communication, Vol. 3 No. 2 Feb '90

Software Engineering:
Graduate-Level Courses for AFIT
Professional Continuing Education

Dr. Nancy R. Mead, Software Engineering Institute
Lt. Col. Patricia K. Lawlis, Air Force Institute of Technology

Abstract: The Air Force has witnessed a shortage of qualified software engineering personnel, a dramatic increase in the use of software across all application areas, and an increasing complexity of systems subsequently requiring personnel to have higher software engineering skill levels. In addressing these issues, several Air Force commands worked with the Air Force Institute of Technology (AFIT) in developing a non-command-specific continuing education program in software engineering. The Software Engineering Institute (SEI) assisted Air Force personnel and AFIT faculty and staff in defining the curriculum and course content, and developing five graduate-level courses in AFIT's Professional Continuing Education program. The overall effort extended over a period of several years, from initial definition to the delivery of the first course(s). This paper describes the background and results of this unique collaborative effort, which included AFIT, the SEI, and SEI resident affiliates.

1. Introduction

Software is an area of increasing concern for government and private industry alike. The continuing increase in demand for software exceeds the increase in the productivity of software personnel across the board. The U. S. Department of Defense has a critical need to address this problem because of its increased reliance on "smart" software-driven weapons systems.

The Air Force has studied the problem, as have other organizations; and the Air Force Software Management Broad Area Review (1) highlights key issues. This review found that the Air Force is facing a shortage of qualified personnel and a dramatic increase in the use of software across all application areas. At the same time, the increasing complexity of systems is requiring higher skill levels.

To alleviate the problem, several Air Force commands agreed to work jointly with the Air Force Institute of Technology (AFIT) in developing a non-command-specific continuing education program in software engineering. The Software Engineering Institute (SEI) then became involved to assist Air Force personnel with their development effort.

This paper describes how the Air Force and the SEI worked together to select curriculum and subsequently develop courses that are now in use at the Air Force Institute of Technology. In Section 2, we briefly describe the two organizations chosen to develop the professional continuing education curriculum and discuss the reasons behind their effective collaboration. In the next section, we discuss the Course Development Workshop: how the curriculum was selected for development and how we conducted the workshop, which was the focal point for the initial development work. After presenting the outcome of the workshop, we consider lessons learned from the experience. Finally, we explore a possible future direction for this program, which is still in its initial stages.

2. Background of AFIT and the SEI

The Air Force Institute of Technology and the Software Engineering Institute share common goals—increasing the number of skilled software engineers and improving software engineering education. A brief look at the two institutes provides insight into the reasons behind their successful collaboration.

The Air Force Institute of Technology

The Air Force Institute of Technology is an unusual military organization. It is different from Air Training Command, which provides training (as opposed to education) for Air Force personnel in many areas, and from the Air Force Academy, which provides undergraduate education for budding Air Force officers. AFIT concentrates on graduate education and professional continuing education. Its mission statement includes the following (2):

- Provide in-residence graduate education (both master's and doctoral levels) in areas in which the Air Force will benefit from the unique military flavor that can be given to the programs.
- Provide professional continuing education programs for Air Force personnel, as needed.
- Conduct research relevant to Air Force needs.
- Provide coordination and administration for Air Force personnel receiving education (both undergraduate and graduate) at civilian institutions.

The Software Engineering Institute

The Software Engineering Institute is also an unusual organization. The only federally funded research and development center of its kind, the institute established an Education Program to address the shortage of qualified software engineering professionals resulting from (a) the increased demand for software throughout society and (b) the extended period required for an educational system to develop new academic programs and to graduate sufficient numbers of students from those programs. Rather than serving a particular type of student, the program works to increase the number of highly qualified software engineers by rapidly improving software engineering education throughout the academic, government, and industrial communities. It helps to change software engineering practice by building an educational foundation upon which further training for practitioners can be based.

The Education Program has two primary objectives: accelerating the development of software engineering programs in academia to increase the quality and quantity of the next generation of software engineers, and enhancing continuing education opportunities to improve the quality of the current generation of software engineers (3). The projects within the Education Program support the goal of establishing the SEI as the focal point for developing and disseminating software engineering education information and materials. The Continuing Education Project, in particular, works to effect organizational change by collaborating with industry and government to increase the ongoing availability of high-quality in-house educational opportunities for software practitioners. The project facilitates the initial offerings of courses and the development of educators by producing and delivering to educators courses on modern software engineering.

The Air Force and the SEI worked together on the course development for the AFIT program because each had objectives which could be met through this program. The initial Air Force objectives were to develop a series of five graduate-level courses in software engineering that would provide an adequate formal background to qualify a practicing computer professional as a software engineer, and to have a three-year pilot program in which a group of 320 of the best qualified Air Force software professionals take this entire set of courses. The initial SEI objectives were to provide leverage in software engineering education by helping to develop AFIT instructor skills, as well as course materials that could be delivered by AFIT, and to obtain course materials that could be used to expand the number of courses offered by the Continuing Education Project at the SEI.

Each organization had a number of key responsibilities in the overall effort. The Air Force was responsible for the following:

- Assign AFIT as the organization responsible for developing and teaching the courses.
- Select a curriculum as a framework for the courses.
- Provide six new instructor slots to AFIT to support course instruction. The slots came from the three sponsoring commands: Air Force Communications Command, Air Force Logistics Command, and Air Force Systems Command.
- Send the AFIT instructors who filled the new slots to the SEI for a Course Development Workshop to begin developing the courses.
- Develop a pilot program to offer the courses from October 1990 through September 1993 (FY91 through FY93), time enough for all 320 students to take all five courses.

At the same time, the SEI was responsible for these tasks:

- Work with AFIT in defining the curriculum.
- Establish a formal agreement with AFIT for the Course Development Workshop (4).
- Provide materials for courses in the SEI Master of Software Engineering program, along with other, additional course materials.
- Provide technical and administrative support to the AFIT instructors, as well as office space and equipment.
- Identify two resident affiliates to support the AFIT instructors.

3. Course Development Workshop

The goals of AFIT and the SEI and their mutual concern about continuing education point to a natural partnership between the two institutions. A six-month Course Development Workshop provided the means for implementing that partnership. The workshop focused the efforts of the SEI, enabling SEI staff to assist Air Force personnel and AFIT faculty and staff in defining course content and developing continuing education course materials. In the section below, we describe the curriculum decisions that were made in preparation for the workshop. The following section presents information about the workshop itself.

Selecting a Curriculum
When determining the courses that would comprise an appropriate software engineering curriculum for Air Force software professionals, AFIT used the graduate program developed by the SEI as a model (5). The SEI program leads to a Master of Software Engineering degree. AFIT uses the same model in its graduate program leading to a Master of Science degree with a Software Engineering specialty.

Based on the SEI model, AFIT identified the courses listed below, each of which was to be offered as a two-week course, with students dedicated to course work full-time for that entire time period. A two-week length was chosen for each course because it permits approximately 40 hours of lecture (the same number of hours that students get in AFIT graduate courses), along with approximately 30 additional hours which can be devoted to in-class project work. The first course is a prerequisite for the remaining four courses, which may be taken in any order. These course descriptions[1] formed the basis for Course Development Workshop activities (6):

WCSE 471 - Software Engineering Concepts - covers both an overview of software engineering life cycle activities and an overview of software engineering management.

---

[1]WCSE is the designator used for Professional Continuing Education courses by the Computer Science and Engineering Division of the AFIT Department of Electrical and Computer Engineering starting in October 1991 (FY92).

WCSE 472 - Specification of Software Systems - covers software requirements analysis and definition, system modeling techniques, and formal software specification languages and methods.

WCSE 473 - Principles and Applications of Software Design - covers the principles and concepts relevant to the design of large programs and systems.

WCSE 474 - Software Generation and Maintenance - covers the activities involved in the implementing and maintenance processes for software systems.

WCSE 475 - Software Verification and Validation - covers software verification and validation techniques and approaches.

Although the Professional Continuing Education program at AFIT does not contain all the courses required for a graduate degree, graduate-level courses were deemed appropriate to meet the program objectives. To ensure effective use of software engineering in Air Force systems, experienced Air Force professionals need to study the course materials at a level that enhances their ability to make the important decisions of an experienced middle manager. Lowering the level to that of undergraduate courses effectively makes the instruction appropriate for entry-level professionals rather than the experienced professionals targeted in this program.

Accomplishing graduate-level instruction in the Professional Continuing Education program has not been an easy task. PCE courses compress the amount of time available for instruction, making it difficult for the student to absorb the material. For that reason, typical instruction does not attempt to accomplish the higher comprehension levels required of graduate courses. In acknowledgement of this issue, the courses have been given upper undergraduate-level numbers in spite of the intended graduate-level instruction.

The difficulties experienced in developing graduate-level materials for continuing education courses are actually less significant than the difficulties in sustaining that level of instruction. Because of the common perception that professional continuing education instruction is at a lower level, there is continuous pressure to lower the entrance standards as well as to lower the level of instruction and the requirements for passing these software engineering courses. Given the objectives of this program, however, nothing less than graduate-level instruction is deemed appropriate. Hence, these standards must be maintained.

Conducting the Course Development Workshop

Staffing
Participants in the Course Development Workshop included AFIT personnel, SEI staff members, and SEI resident affiliates. The six AFIT instructors who participated in the workshop were: Dr. David R. Luginbuhl, James E. Cardow,

F. Michael Dedolph, Dawn A. Guido, John S. Robinson, and William Watson. All were Air Force captains; all had advanced degrees; and all had considerable experience in various aspects of software development.

The AFIT instructors were joined by Lyle Cocking from General Dynamics and Dr. J. Fernando Naveda from the University of Scranton, who provided the perspectives of industry and academia. SEI employees participated as advisors, reviewers, and subject matter experts. The SEI also provided library, computing, and video studio facilities, and gave graphic and administrative support.

Before the Course Development Workshop began, the AFIT participants completed a knowledge/skill questionnaire to help determine the scope of expertise of the group. The results were used to assign technical areas to the AFIT participants and to identify gaps to be filled by SEI or external experts.

Scheduling

An ambitious schedule was set for course development. Significant milestones for each organization are listed below.

Significant AFIT milestones were:

- Period of residence for AFIT instructors at the SEI - 1/90-7/90
- Dry run of Software Engineering Concepts, the foundations course - 9/90
- First course offering:
    - Software Engineering Concepts - 10/90
    - Specification of Software Systems - 2/91
    - Principles and Applications of Software Design - 3/91 (later moved to 10/91)
    - Software Generation and Maintenance - 3/91
    - Software Verification and Validation - 4/91 (later moved to 12/91)

The significant SEI milestones were:

- Contract award; formal agreement with the Air Force commands - 12/89
- Period of AFIT participants' residence at the SEI - 1/90-7/90
- Interim report by the SEI delivered to the Air Force - 9/90
- Dry run of Software Engineering Concepts course - 9/90
- Final report delivered to the Air Force - 3/92
- Contract end - 3/92

The Air Force Institute of Technology also developed a complete plan for delivery, with instructor teams assigned. This was for their internal use in scheduling course offerings.

Reviews

The course development process included three reviews. A preliminary review focused on the outline and goals for the module. An optional interim review addressed the outline and some of the course material (slides and instructor notes). The final review included complete course materials: slides, instructor notes, annotated outline, exam questions and answers, and exercises. Once a module passed final review, it went into configuration management, along with copies of readings that would be used with the module.

Level of Instruction

At the workshop, all participants were sensitive to the concerns about level of instruction and comprehension that we discussed earlier. Course developers were aware of the need to ensure student participation, which translates into a higher comprehension level. Thus, a large portion of each of the five courses is devoted to laboratory work. Some of the courses emphasize one large group project. This brings a sense of realism to the classroom because software engineering is typically used on systems that cannot be completed by an individual. Software engineers must learn to work effectively within groups, and this learning begins in the classroom. In some of the courses, students also receive numerous smaller problems that require them to apply the course material. This activity provides important reinforcement for materials presented in classroom lectures.

Built into the Professional Continuing Education program is motivation for students to participate in the course learning experiences—instructors assign grades. Students who fail to successfully complete the first course in the series (WCSE 471 - Software Engineering Concepts) cannot take any of the other courses. And students who fail to complete all five courses do not receive the recognition of having completed the requirements for becoming an Air Force software engineer. Although the ramifications of this have not yet been made clear by Air Force policy, the intent is to make the completion of all five courses as significant to an Air Force software professional as the completion of a software-related graduate degree, and possibly even more significant than the completion of any other type of advanced degree.

4. Outcome of the Workshop

During the six-month period of residence at the SEI, participants in the workshop, largely under the direction of Dr. Nancy Mead, completed roughly 40% to 50% of the course materials. The completion level per course was as follows:

- Software Engineering Concepts - 52%
- Specification of Software Systems - 40%
- Principles & Applications of Software Design - 50%
- Software Generation and Maintenance - 38%
- Software Verification and Validation - 42%

Under the supervision of Dr. (Lt. Col.) Pat Lawlis, the development effort continued after the instructors returned to AFIT. A briefing and status report on the overall effort was given at the 1990 SEI Affiliates Symposium (7). All six instructors worked on completing the Software Engineering Concepts course. After a dry run, this course was delivered as scheduled starting in October 1990. For development of the other four courses, the team split into two smaller teams of three people each. All course development is now a team effort. The Specification of Software Systems and Software Generation and Maintenance courses have been offered starting in the first half of 1991. The remaining courses will be offered starting in the fall of 1991, so that all five courses will have been offered by the end of an 18-month period.

After the workshop, SEI participation continued at a lower level, with attendance at the first dry run and subsequent meetings and conversations. In addition, AFIT faculty and Air Force Academy faculty reviewed materials and participated in the dry run. AFIT constructed new classrooms, and provided furniture, equipment, and administrative support to the program.

Demand for the classes has been very high. Classes are full (20 students each) and additional students are on waiting lists. Screening for all class slots is currently done through the sponsoring Air Force commands.

Feedback from the initial offerings has been excellent. For the early offerings, students were asked to critique individual lectures as well as the overall course. For the overall course, *Job applicability* rated a mean of 3.8 out of 5.0. *Quality* of the course rated 4.2 out of 5.0. *Overall satisfaction* with the course rated 4.0 out of 5.0.

One difficulty that has not yet been properly addressed is how to give appropriate credit to the students completing all of these courses. Although the material is presented at a graduate level, a direct correlation cannot be made between taking a PCE course with 40 lecture hours over a 2-week period and taking a graduate course with 40 lecture hours over a 10-week period. In spite of the care taken to maximize student comprehension, the student who learns the material in 2 weeks will still not retain as much as the student who takes the course in a regular 10-week school term.

This does not mean that credit should not be given, but it does mean that there are no current standards for either how much or what type of credit should be given. Some favor granting a number of graduate credits for the completion of all five courses (rather than for each course), while others argue that awarding continuing education units (CEUs) would be more appropriate. AFIT is currently wrestling with this problem. Overall, the most important matter is for students to receive some type of credit.

5. Lessons Learned

The Course Development Workshop was the first of its kind at the SEI, and perhaps anywhere. It included a mix of people from industry, government, and academia who had never worked with one another. The schedule was very ambitious. The number of people assigned was roughly half of what would have been needed under ideal circumstances to do the job. Therefore, it is natural that some things did not go as smoothly as desired. On the other hand, there were some aspects that worked very well. This section is an attempt to document lessons learned, both good and bad, so that other efforts can benefit in the future.

One of the unstated objectives of the effort was instructor development. In that regard we believe the program was highly successful. By the end of the SEI residence period, all the participants had acquired the needed knowledge base, arrived at a standardized way of documenting the course material, and produced a number of course modules. For those who were already well versed in these areas, technical contacts were established for future use.

In addition, the following had a positive effect on the effort:

- The Macintosh environment that was used for the course materials was a good environment for course development. It was not overly difficult to learn, and the electronic medium made updates and configuration management easy to accomplish.
- The SEI library facility provided a considerable amount of support; it is a unique resource for software engineering materials.
- The brief weekly status meeting helped in tracking status without requiring significant overhead in terms of time.
- The review process helped to ensure consistent course material and quality across the courses.

There were other factors that resulted in lower productivity for the group, and these should be kept in mind for future efforts of this type:

- The Statement of Work contained some vague language, which caused misunderstandings that had to be resolved during the project. Although it does not need to be lengthy, the statement should be precise.
- The SEI focal point changed during the project. The first person was heavily involved. After he left, no one was dedicated to the AFIT effort full time for several months. For optimum success, there should be a full-time focal point with no midstream changes.
- The AFIT focal point also changed during the development period. Neither was resident at the SEI, which limited their ability to provide leadership. For optimum success, on-site leadership is needed (see next bullet), and such an effort requires a single focal point throughout.
- Since all the on-site participants from AFIT were of equal rank, there

was no clear leadership within the group. Management by consensus did not work well.

- None of the AFIT participants had worked together before. Many of them had not been part of an education team effort, and many of them needed to do research prior to starting course development. It would have been more productive for them to spend three months (or so) working through the group dynamics and research prior to coming to the SEI. In that way, the time at SEI could have been dedicated entirely to course development.

Overall, the objectives for course completion were extremely ambitious. Only a set of subject matter experts who had worked together as a team could have accomplished the objectives, given strong continuous leadership on the part of AFIT and strong continuous support on the part of SEI.

The AFIT team was a strong technical team; but not all of them were subject matter experts, none had worked together before, and none were experienced in team teaching. On the other hand, if they would have had all those attributes up front, the instructor development noted above would not have taken place. Overall, the staffing was appropriate, but more time should have been allowed to make this effort a total success. As it stands, we view the effort as a qualified success.

The recommendations for undertaking a similar effort in the future can be deduced from the lessons learned. The team should be assembled prior to the period of residence. If they have not been involved in team teaching before, more time is needed for course development. If they are not experts in their subject matter areas, again, more time is needed for course development. Strong leadership and support are essential.

All the positive aspects of the Course Development Workshop are also needed for success. These include instructors with good leadership skills, extensive software experience, advanced degrees, teaching experience, enthusiasm, and the desire to make a difference in the way software is developed by the Department of Defense.

6. Future Plans

Although the pilot of this program has not yet completed its first year, the Air Force has already approved the program to continue beyond the pilot. Current plans do not include any additional courses; rather, the focus is on different modes of presentation for the existing courses. There are two primary motivations for examining alternative modes of presentation: reducing expenses and reaching more students.

Methods are already being considered for presenting the Software Engineering

Concepts course to students in their own workplaces rather than requiring them to attend AFIT in residence. Significant savings may be possible if two AFIT instructors can travel to the location of 20 students instead of the Air Force paying the expenses of 20 students to travel to AFIT. Of course, this presumes that all project work can be accomplished at a location remote from AFIT. For the Software Engineering Concepts course, this is a good possibility; but it is more doubtful for the other courses.

It is also clear that many more than 320 Air Force software professionals need to be upgraded to software engineers every three years. Yet with the initial pilot program schedule, it is not possible to reach more students. Six instructors must work full-time to provide all the offerings required for 320 students to complete the program in three years, assuming 20 students per offering. Replacing in-residence offerings with remote offerings does not increase the total number of students who can take the courses in any given time period. To reach more students, it is necessary to increase the number of instructors or change the methods of presentation so the instructors can reach more students at one time. It is unlikely that AFIT would increase the number of instructors involved in this program. This brings us to changing methods, moving into an area often referred to as distance learning, where students and instructors are not at the same location. Distance learning could be accomplished by videotape, teleconference, computer-based instruction, or (more likely) some combination of these and other techniques for increasing the number of students per instructor hour.

It is very possible that all five courses will eventually be put in the distance learning mode. In fact, the program cannot be completely effective for the Air Force unless all the courses are more readily accessible than the current offerings. However, because distance learning has not previously been used for this type of graduate-level professional continuing education, many questions must be answered before plans can be made. These questions include, but are not limited to:

- What are the effective combinations of distance learning modes for these courses?
- Can the distance learning version of a course accomplish the same objectives as the in-house version? Should it?
- What are the resources required to develop a distance learning version of one of these courses?
- Can SEI resources contribute to this effort effectively?
- How many students would typically be enrolled in a distance learning version of this type of course in a year?
- What are the resources required to offer a distance learning course of this type to the required number of students, maintaining enough graded exercises to ensure an appropriate level of student learning?
- Is the Air Force willing to commit the necessary resources to complete this program in a distance learning mode?

We will begin to find answers to these questions only if AFIT gains experience with the distance learning mode. AFIT is currently working toward a capability to develop distance learning courses, and the Software Engineering Concepts course is expected to be one of the first to be developed using this capability. However, a new distance learning version of the course will not be available for at least another year, even if full funding is realized. After this course has been developed and offered to a significant number of students as a distance learning course, informed decisions can be made as to what the next step in software engineering instruction should be.

Perhaps it is even premature to consider all the above questions now. The in-residence program has not been in place long enough to answer questions such as:

- What is the actual level of instruction of each of these courses?
- Do the courses make a consistent, effective set?
- Does the series of courses meet the Air Force objectives?
- Will full funding be continued for the in-residence courses?

It is promising that the AFIT continuing education courses in software engineering are experiencing early success; the Air Force maintains high expectations for the effect this program will have on its software professionals. It is safe to say that the program will have a profound effect on the way the Air Force does its future software business.

7. References

1. U.S. Air Force, *Air Force Broad Area Review on Software Management: Findings and Recommendations,* Dec. 19, 1989.

2. Air Force Institute of Technology, *AFIT Catalog, 1989-91.*

3. Software Engineering Institute, *Quarterly Update 3Q90,* Carnegie Mellon University, Pittsburgh, Pa., July-September 1990.

4. Software Engineering Institute, *Technical Objectives and Plan (TO&P) for Collaborative AFIT Course Development #1-002.*

5. Ardis, Mark and Ford, Gary, *1989 SEI Report on Graduate Software Engineering Education,* CMU/SEI-89-TR-21, DTIC: ADA 219018. An updated report by Gary Ford is forthcoming: *1991 SEI Report on Graduate Software Engineering Education,* CMU/SEI-91-TR-2 (DTIC number has not yet been assigned).

6. AFIT School of Engineering, *Professional Continuing Education,* Class Schedule for FY91.

7. Dedolph, F. Michael, "Course Development Workshop." Presentation given at the SEI Affiliates Symposium, Sept. 12, 1990, Pittsburgh, Pa.

This work is sponsored by the U.S. Department of Defense.

"Panel on Curriculum Issues"

Moderator: *Gary Ford*
Software Engineering Institute

Computing Curricula 1991 -
Its Implications for Software Engineering Education

Bruce H. Barnes, National Science Foundation
Jean B. Rogers, Hewlett Packard CBU

Computer Based Systems Engineering
Workshop

Jonah Z. Lavi, Ashok, Israel Aircraft Industries
Ashok Agrawala, University of Maryland
Raymond Buhr, Carleton University
Ken Jackson, SD-SCION UK Ltd.
Michael Jackson, Bernard Lang, Inria

COMPUTING CURRICULA 1991
ITS IMPLICATIONS FOR SOFTWARE ENGINEERING EDUCATION

Bruce H. Barnes
Computer and Computation Research
National Science Foundation
1800 G Street, NW
Washington, DC 20550
(202) 357-9747

Jean B. Rogers
Hewlett Packard CBU
1700 South Baker St.
McMinnville, OR 97128
(503) 472-5101

Abstract

The report Computing Curricula 1991 contains curricula recommendations for baccalaureate programs in the area of computing, which includes programs with the titles "computer science," "computer engineering," "computer science and engineering," and other similar titles. Its recommendations provide a uniform basis for curriculum design across all segments of the educational community -- schools and colleges of engineering, arts and science, and liberal arts. That report is also the first comprehensive undergraduate curriculum report to be jointly prepared and endorsed by the Association for Computing Machinery and the Computer Society of the IEEE.

The guidelines provide coverage of new and updated subject matter, including a detailed breakdown of individual lecture and laboratory topics. Fundamental areas of concern in curriculum planning are also addressed: program goals; course design and sequencing; integration of laboratory work; the role of programming and other related educational experiences.

Because the computing field is changing and because guidelines must be applicable to a variety of programs, the report focuses on the process of curriculum design in the discipline of computing. Instead of providing a detailed design for a curriculum in computing, the report provides a set of requirements for programs of study in this area. These include a collection of computing subject matter topics to be included in every student's program and a set of advanced elective subject matter topics. Also included are course requirements in mathematics and science.

This paper considers the implications of the report for programs specializing in software engineering. The basic recommendations of the report are presented and discussed. A comparison of the implementation with the SEI Undergraduate Curriculum in Software Engineering will be given.

A joint Task Force of the Association for Computing Machinery and the IEEE-Computer Society has recently produced a set of recommendations for baccalaureate programs in computing. These have been prepared and endorsed by the two societies and have been published as Computing Curricula 1991 [1]. The primary objective of the Task Force report is to provide curricular guidance for implementing undergraduate programs in the discipline of computing. This includes programs in computer science and/or engineering with an emphasis on software engineering. In this discussion we will briefly outline the main features of the report and discuss their relationship to software engineering education. This also includes the report's sample curriculum for preparing students for entering the field as computing professionals with a strong background in software engineering. It will conclude with a comparison of these recommendations with the SEI Undergraduate Curriculum in Software Engineering [3].

REPORT FROM THE TASK FORCE

The report is divided into three parts. The first section entitled "Designing Undergraduate Curricula in Computing", provides background and a set of requirements for all students majoring in computing. The second, "Details of the Subject Matter" gives a detailed set of subject matter material that should be a required part of every student's education along with a set of recommended elective subjects. Finally a set of "Sample Curricula" are presented, one of which has a strong emphasis on software engineering.

The report lists a number of general goals for undergraduate programs in computing. These include preparing students to understand the field of computing, both as an academic discipline and as a profession. Thus, any program must provide a coherent and broad based coverage of the discipline of computing. Also the program must fit within the institutional framework in which it is housed. While each program and institution will emphasize different objectives, each program will help prepare student for graduate study in the discipline of computing, entry into the computing profession and preparation for the general challenges of professional and personal life. Another goal is to expose the student to the social and ethical issues associated with the computing field. The graduate of programs in computing should be able to apply the knowledge to solve constrained problems in the field at an appropriate level. Finally the student should have a sufficient understanding of the rich body of theory underlining the field of computing to appreciate the intellectual depth of the field and to be able to grow in his or her understanding of it.

All of these are, of course, appropriate goals for a software engineering oriented program. For software engineering one would also want to add one or more goals that relate more directly to software engineering. One would like such a program to thoroughly ground the student in the fundamentals of software engineering. The program should also prepare the student to function effectively in the field at an entry level position.

SUBJECT MATTER AREAS

The report uses the definition of the field as specified in the ACM/IEEE-CS report "Computing as a Discipline [2]." That report divides computing into nine subject matter areas. These are:

Algorithms and Data Structures,
Architecture,
Artificial Intelligence,
Data Base and Information Retrieval,
Human-Computer Communication,
Numerical and Symbolic Computation,
Operating Systems,
Programming Languages,
Software Methodology and Engineering.

While this subdivision is somewhat arbitrary, it provides a reasonable way of organizing the field. It is important to note that software engineering is one of the nine subareas. It is currently the only one where special undergraduate programs are being implemented. Traditional computer engineering programs emphasize a blend of these nine subareas with some specialization in architecture, but that is not usually a special program. Some programs that emphasize preparation for graduate education will include a considerable amount of theory in their program, but again these would not be considered special programs. Only software engineering has both the depth and breadth of subject matter material and a sufficiently large employment base to make a special program viable, and a specialized program in software engineering will easily fit within the structure of the Curricula 1991 report.

The "Discipline of Computing" report also discusses three processes: theory, abstraction and design. Like all other programs, a program specializing in software engineering should have a balance of all three processes deeply embedded in the program. Since design is one of the distinguishing feature of engineering, this process will play a bigger role in a software engineering program than in the traditional computer science program. Thus, some elements of design should appear in most computing courses and at least one course should have design as a major theme.

Along with the definition of the discipline and the three processes, social and professional issue provide the context in which programs in computing are offered. Since computing plays such a major role in human activity, the Computing Curriculum 1991 report added a tenth subject matter section to the definition of computing called Social, Ethical, and Professional Issues, which was not included in "Computing as a Discipline." Since software engineers are likely to be involved in projects that affect society and the people in it, they must be able to understand the consequences of their efforts.

RECURRING CONCEPTS

The report also identified a set of basic ideas, called Recurring Concepts. These recurring concepts are significant ideas, concerns, principles and processes that help to unify the discipline. An appreciation for the pervasiveness of these concepts and the ability to apply them in appropriate contexts is one indicator of a graduate's maturity as a computer professional. These recurring concepts can be used as underlying themes that help tie together curricular materials into cohesive courses.

Each recurring concept listed in the report:

o   Occurs throughout the discipline
o   Has a variety of instantiations
o   Has a high degree of technological independence

Thus, a recurring concept is one that pervades the discipline and is independent of any particular technology. A recurring concept is more fundamental than any of its instantiations. A recurring concept has established itself as fundamental and persistent over the history of computing and is likely to remain so for the foreseeable future. Not only do they recur throughout the discipline, they do so across the nine subject areas and across the levels of theory, abstraction and design. Furthermore, most are instances of even more general concepts that pervade mathematics, science and engineering.

Below is a list of the 12 recurring concepts that were identified as fundamental to computing:

Binding,
Complexity of large problems,
Conceptual and formal models,
Consistency and completeness,
Efficiency,
Evolution,
Levels of abstraction,
Ordering in space,

```
Ordering in time,
Reuse,
Security,
Tradeoffs and consequences.
```

Since these concepts are also principle design criteria, they play a special role in software engineering education. Tradeoffs and consequences is what design is all about. Students must learn to make these evaluations. Levels of abstraction is the fundamental tenant of the software life cycle. The complexity of large problems is always one of the big challenges in software design. Deciding when to finalize or bind a decision is the key point in software development. Thus, the recurring concepts could play a special role in teaching software design and development.

PROGRAM REQUIREMENTS

Now that the context for the curriculum has been established we can define the requirements for a program. Subject matter is, of course, the main ingredient in any program. Since the report is designed to be applicable to a large variety of programs set in a diverse group of institutions, the report does not specify particular courses. Instead it provides a broad selection of topics taken from all ten subject areas of computing. These topics are identified as "Common Requirements." The common requirements are presented as a collection of "Knowledge Units". These can be combined in various ways to form different sets of courses, or implementations, in different academic settings. These will be discussed further in the section on subject matter. The common requirements ensure breadth in each program. Depth is realized through additional elective subject matter material depending on the goals of the particular program and faculty expertise. Some suggested additional material is given in the section on subject matter.

In addition to courses in computing, the curriculum includes courses in other areas and other experiences. One of these, programming experience, is an essential part of every student's program. This is especially true for student specializing in software engineering. The roles that computer programming plays in an undergraduate program in software engineering education are many and varied. These roles can be grouped in five areas; intellectual, professional, pedagogical, motivational, and cultural.

Developing the intellectual capabilities of each student is the primary goal of every undergraduate program. In software engineering programming is essential to that development. Each of the three processes, theory, abstraction and design are fundamental to the intellectual development of each student. Computer programming and abstraction are intimately intertwined, since a program is an abstraction. In developing a computer program one must make an abstraction of what the program is to model and then encode that abstraction in a programming language. Programming can also help develop the student ability to think logically, carefully and completely. These are the fundamental ingredients in theory and must be mastered, if the theoretical aspects of computing are to be understood. If both programming and software design are interpreted in the broadest sense, the words are synonymous. They both involve understanding the problem, devising a solution to the problem, and organizing and encoding the solution.

In the professional role, programming is a major part of many computer specialists daily activities, especially young professionals. Software engineers must be able to perform at a reasonably proficient level early in their careers. Thus, students in a computing program with a strong emphasis on software engineering must have completed a considerable number of different programming projects, at least one of which is a major project involving most of the activities in the software life cycle.

Computer programming has turned out to be one of the best pedagogical tools of the twentieth century. One soon learns the depth of their understanding in an area when one begins to program in it. A good device for learning about a theoretical area such as Turing machines is to program in a simulator of one. Programming an algorithm and experimenting with it is a good way to learn about an algorithm and its performance.

Programming is a great motivator because it is both challenging and fun. Students enjoy it and get a great sense of accomplishment upon completing a difficult assignment. Programming is part of the culture of software engineering. One has not passed through the rites of initiation until one has been up several late nights finishing a project. If students understand that programming will help in their intellectual development, professional growth, and subject matter mastery, they will put extra effort into it and be rewarded accordingly. It is also true that much of the insight in computing is transmitted through software products. Thus, students must be able to read and understand the various software work products.

LABORATORY EXPERIENCES

The report stresses the role of laboratories in the undergraduate curriculum and details how these very important activities can be integrated into an undergraduate program. The learning process occurs as a result of interactions among student, instructor, and the subject matter.

Laboratories demonstrate the application of principles to the design, implementation, and testing of hardware and software systems. Laboratories also emphasize techniques that utilize contemporary tools and lead to good experimental methods, including the use of measuring instruments, diagnostic aids, software and hardware monitors, statistical analysis of results, and oral and written presentation of findings. The laboratories should augment the instruction that takes place in the lectures by having clearly stated objectives that complement the lectures.

The laboratory exercises are included in the Suggested Laboratories part of each knowledge unit and provide a diverse set of learning experiences. Some involve the execution of hardware, software, or simulators to observe some phenomenon, either by data collection or by visualization. Others are designed to increase student expertise in software methodology through the development of alternative design and implementation techniques. Still other laboratories are similar to science experiments because they involve hypothesis formation and testing. These types of laboratory experiences combine to increase student problem solving ability, analytical skill, and professional judgement.

Beyond programming and laboratories, undergraduates in computing should have additional educational experience that help them develop the capacity for critical thinking, problem solving, research methods, and professional development. These experiences can be incorporated into the classroom activities, laboratories, and extracurricular activities of the undergraduate program. The report divides these experiences into three areas: working as part of a team, communication, and familiarization with the profession. These are also very important aspects in the education of software engineers.

KNOWLEDGE UNITS

As mentioned earlier the report specifies a collection of subject matter material that is to be included in each program of study. This material is arranged by the nine subject areas given in the "Discipline of Computing" report and the tenth area of Social, Ethical, and Professional Issues. This material is further organized into "knowledge units". A knowledge unit is understood to designate a coherent collection of subject matter that is so fundamental that it should occur in every undergraduate curriculum. They can, however, be introduced within any of several alternative course structures.

It is interesting to note that approximately 16% of the time allotted for the knowledge units are associated with Software Methodology and Engineering. A summary of the knowledge units is given below with the approximate number of hours in each area.

Algorithms and Data Structures (47 lecture hours)
Architecture (59 lecture hours)
Artificial Intelligence & Robotics (9 lecture hours)
Database and Information Retrieval (9 lecture hours)
Human-Computer Communication (8 lecture hours)
Numerical and Symbolic Computation (7 lecture hours)

Operating Systems (31 lecture hours)
Programming Languages (46 lecture hours)
Software Methodology & Engineering (44 lecture hours)
Social, Ethical, and Professional Issues (11 lecture hours)

A complete curriculum will include not only the common requirements but also certain additional material. This advanced and supplemental material gives each individual student an opportunity to study the subject areas of the discipline in depth. The curriculum should provide depth of study in several of the nine subject areas beyond that provided by the common requirements. Students normally achieve that depth by completing several additional courses in this part of the curriculum. The number of such courses will vary in accordance with institutional norms.

The topics in the following list should be considered as areas where courses may be developed to provide in-depth study in advanced undergraduate and graduate courses. Other topics beyond these as important as well, but will vary with the particular interests and expertise of the faculty in individual programs.

Advanced Operating Systems
Advanced Software Engineering
Analysis of Algorithms
Artificial Intelligence
Combinatorial and Graph Algorithms
Computational Complexity
Computer Communication Networks
Computer Graphics
Computer-Human Interface
Computer Security
Database and Information Retrieval
Digital Design Automation
Fault-Tolerant Computing
Information Theory
Modeling and Simulation
Numerical Computation
Parallel and Distributed Computing
Performance Prediction and Analysis
Principles of Computer Architecture
Principles of Programming Languages
Programming Language Translation
Real-Time Systems
Robotics and Machine Intelligence
Semantics and Verification
Societal Impact of Computing
Symbolic Computation
Theory of Computing
VLSI System Design

OTHER CURRICULAR CONCERNS

Mathematics is an essential part of every undergraduate program in computing. The report recommends a minimum of half year, 15 credits, of Mathematics. This would include Discrete Mathematics, Calculus and a choice of Probability, Linear Algebra, Advance Discrete Mathematics or Mathematical Logic. Software Engineering programs may require more than this. Parnas [5] has recommended a substantial amount of mathematics for practitioners in this area.

Science is important in computing curricula for three reasons. First, as well-educated scientists and engineers, graduates of computing programs should be able to appreciate advances in science because they have an impact on society and on the field of computing. Second, exposure to science encourages students to develop an ability to apply the scientific method in problem solving. Third, many of the applications students will encounter after graduation are found in the sciences. For these reasons, all computing curricula should include a component that incorporates material from the physical and life sciences. Ideally, courses in this component are those designed for science majors. Programs intended to prepare students for entry into the profession should require a minimum of one-half year of science. This normally includes a year-long course in a laboratory science and additional work in the natural sciences.

Part one of the report concludes with a discussion of curriculum design and implementation and some related concerns, such as faculty, libraries, and service courses. These are generic in nature and no more relevant to software engineering than other areas of computing. The one exception would be this issue of accreditation. This is a complicated issue beyond the scope of this report. Ford has an interesting discussion of accreditation in his report [3].

SOFTWARE METHODOLOGY AND ENGINEERING KNOWLEDGE UNITS

Part two of the report gives the details of the subject matter. The knowledge units are specified in considerable depth, while the advance/supplemental material is specified on much less detail. In some cases only titles are given. Software Methodology and Engineering is specified at about the level of an advanced course for general computing majors, but not enough for student with a heavy concentration in this area. Much of the effort of the task force went into the definition of the common requirements and knowledge units and they form an essential part of the report.

The details of the knowledge units in the area of Software Methodology and Engineering are included here to illustrate the structure of the knowledge units and to give some flavor the kind and amount of material in this area that should be included in every student program of study.

SOFTWARE METHODOLOGY AND ENGINEERING

The knowledge units in the common requirements for the subject area of Software Methodology and Engineering emphasize the following topics: fundamental problem solving concepts, the software development process, software specifications, software design and implementation, verification, and validation.

SE1: FUNDAMENTAL PROBLEM-SOLVING CONCEPTS

Introduction to the basic ideas of algorithmic problem solving and programming, using principles of top-down design, stepwise refinement, and procedural abstraction. Basic control structures, data types, and input/output conventions.

Recurring Concepts:
conceptual and formal models, consistency and completeness, levels of abstraction.

Lecture Topics: (16 hours minimum)
1. Procedural abstraction; parameters
2. Control structures; selection, iteration, recursion
3. Data types (e.g., numbers, strings, booleans) and their uses in problem solving
4. The software design process; from specification to implementation; stepwise refinement; graphical representation

SE2: THE SOFTWARE DEVELOPMENT PROCESS

Introduction to models and issues concerned with the development of high quality software. Use of tools and environments that facilitate the design and implementation of large software systems. The role and use of standards.

Recurring Concepts:
complexity of large problems, conceptual and formal models, consistency and completeness, levels of abstraction.

Lecture Topics: (eight hours minimum)
1. Software life-cycle models (e.g. waterfalls, prototyping, iterative development)
2. Software design objectives
3. Documentation
4. Configuration management and control
5. Software reliability issues; safety, responsibility, risk assessment
6. Maintenance
7. Specification and design tools, implementation tools

SE3: SOFTWARE REQUIREMENTS AND SPECIFICATIONS

Introduction to the development of formal and informal specifications for defining software system requirements.

Recurring Concepts:
Complexity of large problems, conceptual and formal models, levels of abstraction, reuse.

Lecture Topics: (four hours minimum)
1. Informal specifications
2. Formal specifications; preconditions and postconditions, algebraic specifications for ADT's.

SE4: SOFTWARE DESIGN AND IMPLEMENTATION

Introduction to the principal paradigms that govern the design and implementation of large software systems.

Recurring Concepts:
complexity of large problems, conceptual and formal models, consistency and completeness, reuse

Lecture Topics: (eight hours minimum)
1. Functional/process-oriented design
2. Bottom-up design; support for reuse
3. Implementation strategies (e.g., top-down, bottom-up, teams)
4. Implementation issues; performance improvement, debugging, antibugging

SE5: VERIFICATION AND VALIDATION

Introduction to methods and techniques for verification and validation of software systems.

Recurring Concepts:
consistency and completeness, efficiency, trade-offs and consequences.

Lecture Topics:
1. Using pre- and post-conditions, invariants, elementary proofs of correctness.
2. Code and design reading, structured walk-throughs
3. Testing (e.g., test plan generation, acceptance testing, unit testing, integration testing, regression testing)

EXAMPLE CURRICULUM

The report concludes with a large appendix containing twelve sample curricula. Nine of the samples have the common goal of the preparation the graduates for entry into the computing profession. Each of these was designed to be consistent with curricular requirements of the relevant professional accreditation body (EAC/ABET or CSAB/CSAC). One of these has a strong software engineering emphasis. It was designed to meet or exceed the current CSAB/CSAC minimum requirements in science and mathematics, computing (i.e. "computer science"), and humanities and social science. It is in included here to illustrate how the Curriculum 1991 report can be used to shape curricula in software engineering.

A PROGRAM IN COMPUTER SCIENCE (SOFTWARE ENGINEERING EMPHASIS)

Goals and Features of this Program: This program leads to the B.S. in computer science in such a way that students concentrate their studies on the principles and applications of software engineering. The foundation of this curriculum is a sequence of fundamental courses in software engineering. The curriculum emphasizes software development, large software systems design, programming paradigms, operating systems, and a capstone software project.

This program prepares students for a career in computing, providing a foundation for lifelong learning through professional development and/or graduate study.

Summary of Requirements: This program of study requires 40 semester courses, with credit-hours distributed as follows:

12	hours of science electives
18	hours of mathematics
36	hours of humanities and social sciences (including 12 hours of English)
34	hours of required computer science
9	hours of computer science electives
_21_	hours of free electives
130	TOTAL

Course Descriptions

The introductory sequence of two courses, Introduction to Software Engineering and Software Methodology, act as the cornerstone for this curriculum. Within these courses, students will be introduced to programming in the context of solid software engineering practices. No assumptions about prior programming experience are made, although prior experience with editors and program execution is helpful.

Historically, the introductory course sequence has introduced a procedural programming language, although functional languages have also been popular. For this program, however, departments might choose to use an object-

oriented analysis style, introduce the message-passing model
of computation, and use internal implementation of objects to
show data and procedures. This would leave inheritance until
the second course, where students can begin using system-
defined objects such as lists and arrays as the basis for
developing their own ADT's.

C101 - INTRODUCTION TO SOFTWARE ENGINEERING

Topic Summary: This course introduces programming and
software engineering. The methodology may be based on
functional analysis or object-oriented analysis as described
above. Discussion of fundamental algorithms and data
structures is included, focusing on ADT's throughout. User
interfaces should be covered in the specification of
programming tasks. The historical and social context of
computing will be discussed, integrated with other course
material.

This four credit-hour course contains 35 KU lecture hours
selected from Algorithms and Data Structures, Human-Computer
Communications, Software Methodology and Engineering, and
Social, Ethical, and Professional Issues.

Prerequisites: None

C102 - SOFTWARE METHODOLOGY

Topic Summary: Continuing in software engineering methodology
with focus on life-cycles, analysis, specification
documentation of the process as well as documentation of the
product, this course again will include ADT's and the
beginning of careful analysis of some algorithms. The design
of human/program interfaces continues in this course and
performance concerns are introduced. An important
social/professional topic is the discussion of intellectual
property rights.

This course is a four credit-hour course with 37 KU
lecture hours selected from Software Methodology and
Engineering, Architecture, Human-Computer Communication, and
Social, Ethical, and Professional Issues.

Prerequisites: C101

C203 - SOFTWARE DEVELOPMENT

Topic Summary: This course expands the software engineering
instruction to larger projects, particularly addressing the
problems of scaling up process and product. Software
evolution and maintenance concerns are also emphasized. In
this context, students should study the impact of calculation

intensive computation, using and discussion particularly numerical analysis packages. Search strategies and other artificial intelligence techniques are introduced as large-problem approaches, along with other discussion, the problem solving strategies from an algorithm analysis point of view.

This is a four credit-hour course with 40 KU lecture hours selected from Algorithms and Data Structures, Artificial Intelligence, Numerical and Symbolic Computation, and Software Methodology and Engineering. '

Prerequisites: C102

C204 - PROGRAMMING PARADIGMS

Topic Summary: Various programming languages are studied from three points of view:

1. the paradigms and models they express (e.g., the von Neumann machine)
2. the levels of abstraction they represent (e.g., assembly language, fourth generation)
3. the way they are defined and implemented (e.g., translators)

This course contains 39 KU lecture hours selected from Architecture, and Programming Languages.

Prerequisites: C102

C305 - SOFTWARE SYSTEMS

Topic Summary: This course looks at large scale applications problems, such as database problems, large expert systems, real-time, distributed and concurrent system problems. As much of the material on distributed and concurrent systems will be presented in survey form and as a result, not include lab assignments, instructors can use this course for other lab experiences, such as practice in porting between systems or configurations.

This course contains 32 KU lecture hours selected from Algorithms and Data Structures, Architecture, Data Base and Information Retrieval, Operating Systems, and Programming Languages.

Prerequisites: C203

C306 - FORMALISMS AND COMPUTATION

Topic Summary: The use of representation and manipulation and the application of formal systems in computation are the focus of this course. Logic, sets, algebra, complexity and computability will be discussed and exemplified. An introduction to digital logic and elementary digital systems is integrated with the theoretical treatment of these issues.

This course contains 40 KU lecture hours selected from Algorithms and Data Structures, Architecture, and Programming Languages.

Prerequisites: C204, Discrete Mathematics

C307 - OPERATING SYSTEMS

Topic Summary: Organization and implementation of operating systems, including time and space management, control and robustness of a variety of systems are studied. While the assembly language used in C204 may have been simulated, in this course students should use a real assembly language and program real machine interaction.

This course contains 42 KU lecture hours selected from Architecture and Operating Systems.

Prerequisites: C204

C407, 408 - CAPSTONE PROJECT SEQUENCE

Topic Summary: This two-semester course presents the student with a strong experience in software engineering. Students, working in teams, investigate, design, implement and present to their classmates a significant software project. The project should solve a significant, complex and hopefully generalizable problem, dealing with constraints and trade-offs in the solution. The course includes study of a certain amount of project management concerns (planning, scheduling, assessing progress, recognizing hard parts of a problem, but not personnel management or specific leadership training). While students are working on their project, instructors will want to use lecture time to cover issues of professional responsibility, risks, and liabilities. They also may want to use lecture time to cover such technical topics as international concerns, metrics and measurements methods, quality assurance processes and time-to-market economics.

This is six credit-hour course, containing 6 KU lecture hours for Social, Ethical, and Professional Issues

Prerequisites: C306

TYPICAL STUDENT SCHEDULE

Freshman Year

First Semester			Second Semester		
Engl 101	3	English I	Engl 102	3	English II
Math 101	4	Disc. Math I	Math 102	4	Disc. Math II
C101	4	Intro to Soft. Eng.	C102	4	Software Methodology
Sci Ele.	3	Sci. Ele.	Sci. El.	3	Science Ele.
HU/SS	3	HU/SS Ele.	HU/SS	3	HU/SS Ele.
	17			17	

Sophomore Year

First Semester			Second Semester		
Sci. El.	3	Sci. Ele.	Sci. El.	3	Sci. Ele.
Math 201	3	Math Topics for Comp. Sci.	Math 203	4	Calculus
C203	4	Software Dev.	C204	4	Programming Paradigms
Engl. El.	3	Engl. Ele.	Engl. El.	3	Engl. Ele.
HU/SS	3	HU/SS Ele.	HU/SS	3	HU/SS Ele.
	16			17	

Junior Year

First Semester			Second Semester		
C305	4	Soft. Sys.	C307	4	Operating Sys.
C306	4	Formalisms & Computation	CS El.	3	Comp. Science Elective
Math El.	3	Math Ele.	HU/SS	3	HU/SS Elective
HU/SS	3	HU/SS Ele.	Elect.	3	Elective
Elect.	3	Elective	Elect.	3	Elective
	17			16	

Senior Year

First Semester			Second Semester		
C407	3	Soft. Eng. Project I	C408	3	Software Eng. Project II
CS El.	3	CS Ele.	CS El.	3	CS Elective
HU/SS	3	HU/SS Ele.	HU/SS	3	HU/SS Elective
Elect.	3	Elective	Elect.	3	Elective
Elect.	3	Elective	Elect.	3	Elective
	15			15	

ADVANCED COURSES - Any of the following courses can be offered as advanced electives to complete the major.

- o   Artificial Intelligence
- o   Database Principles
- o   Semantics and Verification
- o   Compiler Design
- o   Networks and Distributed Computing
- o   Computer Graphics
- o   Parallelism and Concurrency
- o   Simulation
- o   Numerical and Symbolic Computation

COMPARISON WITH THE SEI UNDERGRADUATE CURRICULUM IN SOFTWARE ENGINEERING

The Software Engineering Institute at Carnegie Mellon University has developed a recommended curriculum in Software Engineering [3] [4]. This section of the report will present a comparison between the SEI curriculum and the sample curriculum given in the task force report [1]. As will be seen, the report has more similarities than differences. Since the two were independent, this indicates some convergence in what should constitute an undergraduate curriculum in Software Engineering.

Ford lists five design constraints for the SEI effort. Our curriculum also was guided by five similar constraints. This curriculum is for a B.S. degree in computer science with an emphasis on Software Engineering. The SEI curriculum is for a degree in Software Engineering. While one is a science curriculum and one is an engineering curriculum, they have remarkably similar structure. This curriculum was designed to meet the subject matter requirements for CSAC accreditation, while the SEI report meets the requirements of both ABET and CSAC.

The SEI report contains a very careful and thorough development of the subject matter of Software Engineering. This material is then organized into undergraduate courses. The sample curriculum did not attempt to include the material listed in the SEI report. However, much of it is included in the sample curriculum and with an appropriate selection of computer science electives, most of the material could be included in the sample implementation. Both incorporate the knowledge unit specified for all curriculum as given the task force report. Since the SEI report was prepared from a draft before the final report was presented, there are minor variations from the final set of recommended knowledge units. These are not many nor serious and could be easily adjusted to accommodate the final recommendations. Both curricula attempt to be pedagogically sound. There are some differences in approach which will be discussed later.

The SEI Curriculum includes 120 semester hours which is typical of science programs, while the sample curriculum includes 130 semester hours which is more usual in engineering. If we modify the sample curriculum to reduce the hours to 120 by removing one science elective, two humanities and social science electives and one free elective and add two credits to computer science then both programs have the same number of hours in each category. This is not surprising because both attempted to conform to CSAC guidelines.

While the sample curriculum does not attempt as complete a coverage of the field of Software Engineering as does the SEI Curriculum, never-the-less, it includes much of the same material. Explicit listing of topics beyond the knowledge units is not given in the sample curriculum as they are in the SEI curriculum, so one has to extrapolate from this course title, description and the selection of knowledge units to see what topics would be included. We expect that all of the material in Software Analysis #1 and #2, but only a small portion of Software Analysis #3 would be included. Likewise, all of Software Architecture #1 and a large portion of Software Architectures #2 and #3 are included in the sample curriculum. However, only about 1/2 of Software Architecture #4 would be represented. In the Computer Systems area, very little of Computer Systems #3 would be in the non-elective material in the sample curriculum would be included, but most of the material in Computer Systems #1 and #2 would be.

The software process area is where the two programs differ the most, reflecting the different titles of the two programs. The SEI Curriculum is for an undergraduate degree in Software Engineering while the task force sample curriculum is for a Computer Science degree with an emphasis in Software Engineering.

The SEI program has four courses in the area with substantial projects in three of these courses. Generally, this portion of the curriculum is designed to educate students to participate effectively in large software system projects which are built by teams of developers. It provides a very thorough coverage of software processes. There is an emphasis on formalism and the use of tools.

The Task Force Curriculum on the other hand, leads to a B.S. in Computer Science in such a way that students concentrate their studies on the principles and applications of software engineering. The software process component is spread over a small number of courses including other material and is completed with a capstone project sequence of two courses. While sound software engineering procedures are taught and adhered to, is does not provide a complete coverage of all of the subareas of software engineering. These are left for the electives, graduate training or on the job training, if the student decides to make software engineering his/her professional goal. While it does not give the student the depth of coverage in software engineering, it provides opportunities for further educations and/or employment.

Pedologically, there is also a difference in approach; the SEI program divides software engineering knowledge and process into its four most logical subcomponents and organizes the curriculum around the four areas with courses defined in each area. The Task Force takes a different approach and integrates the material in such a way that topics from more than one subarea are included in most courses. Both approaches are valid and can provide the student with an excellent education.

ACKNOWLEDGEMENTS

The authors would like to thank Terry Bollinger and John Cherniavsky for their critical review.

REFERENCES

[1] ACM/IEEE-CS Joint Curriculum Task Force. Computing Curricula 1991. Technical report, ACM Press and IEEE-CS Press January 1991.

[2] Peter J. Denning, Douglas E. Comer, David Gries, Michael C. Mulder, Allen B. Tucker, A. Joe Turner, and Paul Young. Computing as a Discipline. Communications of the ACM, 32(1): 9-23, January 1989.

[3] Gary Ford. 1990 SEI Report on Undergraduate Software Engineering Education. Technical report CMU/SEI-90-TR-3, Software Engineering Institute, Carnegie Mellon University, Pittsburg, PA, March 1990.

[4] Gary Ford. The SEI Undergraduate Curriculum in Software Engineering, SIGCSE Bulletin, (23)1:375-385, March 1991

[5] David L. Parnas. Education for Computing Professionals. Computer, 23(1):17-23, January 1990.

COMPUTER BASED SYSTEMS ENGINEERING WORKSHOP

Jonah Z. Lavi, Israel Aircraft Industries, Workshop Chair
Ashok Agrawala, University of Maryland
Raymond Buhr, Carleton University
Ken Jackson, SD-SCION UK Ltd.   Michael Jackson
Bernard Lang, Inria

Abstract

Modern computer based systems are complex multi-systems consisting of many connected individual subsystems; each one of them is typically also a multicomputer system. The subsystems in a multi-system can be either geographically distributed or locally connected systems. Typical examples of computer based systems are medical systems, process control systems, communications systems, weapon systems and large information systems.

The development of these complex systems requires the establishment of a new engineering discipline in its own right, Computer Based Systems Engineering - CBSE. The definition of the discipline, its current and future practice and the ways to establish and promote it were discussed in an international IEEE workshop held in Neve-Ilan, Israel in May 1990.

The major conclusion of the workshop was that CBSE should be established as a new field in its own right. To achieve this goal, the workshop participants recommended that the IEEE Computer Society shall set up a task force for the promotion of the field, the establishment of CBSE Institutes and the development of the educational framework of CBSE. The paper describes the major findings of the workshop that led to these conclusions and recommendations.

1 BACKGROUND

Modern computer based systems are complex multi-systems consisting of many connected individual subsystems; each one of them is typically also a multicomputer system. The subsystems in a multi-system can be geographically distributed (e.g. in information systems), or locally connected systems (e.g. in aircraft avionics systems). Typical examples of computer based systems are medical systems, process control systems, communications systems, weapon systems and large information systems.

The development of these complex systems requires the establishment of a new engineering discipline to be named *Computer Based Systems Engineering - CBSE*. This should be a discipline in its own right. CBSE is not just a grouping of application specific disciplines such as process control, software engineering, or avionic systems engineering, although these are obviously important. CBSE is a new discipline that is concerned particularly with techniques, methods, and processes for handling the new kind of complexity created by joining multiple components and diverse areas of expertise in a single computer based system project. The discipline has been slow to emerge because it has taken a while for the fact to become apparent that explosions in both technology and requirements have created a new kind of complexity that demands such a discipline. CBSE requires the knowledge of interdisciplinary techniques, methods and skills considering multiple aspects together with application specific knowledge. These have to be taught and practiced as a holistic discipline and approach.

The need to address CBSE is currently gaining increasing recognition. For example, the "Call for Papers" of the coming International Software Engineering Conference states "the engineering of software is becoming the engineering of computerized applications." Therefore the selected theme of ICSE13 is "System Design: Research and Practice."

In spite of the rapidly increasing demand for computer based systems, the supply of engineers experienced in this new field is very limited. This is due to a lack of institutions which educate such engineers, the limited number of groups in academia and industry devoted to the research and development of necessary engineering methods and tools and a lack of conferences and journals. Also, the industry lacks experienced engineers who can train the needed computer based systems engineers. Furthermore, management in most companies has not yet realized the need for comprehensive computer based systems engineering and does not impose it on their project managers. As a result many systems are developed without considering overall systems issues. This causes excessive development costs, delayed schedules, unnecessary development cycles, and undesired and poor performance. Many of these systems are also unsafe and unreliable.

Engineers and experts actively working in this rapidly emerging discipline were trained either in computer science departments or electrical engineering departments. Almost none of these departments is training computer based systems engineers capable of handling the holistic problems and issues that have to be addressed during Computer Based Systems (CBS) development. Software Engineering curricula attempts to cope partially with the area. Unfortunately, software engineering is taught mainly in individual courses and has not emerged into full university curricula. One of the reasons is that software engineering handles only a very limited part of the issues involved in CBSE. Therefore, it is very hard to "sell" software engineering as a useful discipline, both in academia and in the industry. Some universities have already realized this need and have started or proposed both undergraduate and graduate programs in CBSE. (BOUN89, CAUN90, PARN90).

2   THE NEVE-ILAN WORKSHOP

The organization of an international workshop was recommended by the CompEuro 90 conference program committee which selected as the main theme of the conference "Systems Engineering Aspects of Complex Computer Based Systems". The committee realized the necessity to support the development of such systems by a new, previously undefined discipline of CBSE. The workshop was devoted to the promotion of this new discipline.

The Neve-Ilan CBSE workshop was sponsored by the Israel Section of the IEEE and the Israel Chapter of the Computer Society. It took place in Neve-Ilan, Israel in May 1990 prior to CompEuro 90.

The major objectives of the workshop were

1. To define the computer based systems engineering discipline, its contents and problematics, discuss the state of the art and investigate the reasons why it is not widely recognized as an active field of teaching and practice.

2. To discuss the promotion of computer based systems engineering as an acknowledged engineering discipline in industry and the academia.

The 28 participants of the workshop came from nine countries and from a wide spectrum of academic and industrial backgrounds. The discussions of the workshop and the conclusions reached by its participants are summarized in the following sections. It is worth noting that in spite of the fact that a significant portion of the workshop discussions took place in isolated working groups, the participants easily reached a consensus in their conclusions.

3   DEFINITION OF THE DISCIPLINE

Computer Based Systems Engineering - CBSE, means the engineering of Computer Based Systems, which are a specific class of systems. It is an inter-disciplinary branch of engineering, merging systems, computing, software, electronics, management and application disciplines and techniques. It is very much concerned with the decomposition of systems, the allocation of development responsibility for specific system components (to specialist developers or manufacturers) and with the subsequent composition of these system components to produce the final system. Its approach is holistic, involving trade-offs between the various specialized disciplines and the technical co-ordination of development efforts across the complete project.

It is difficult to define the class of computer based systems explicitly. Therefore we chose instead to describe it by listing their typical attributes enumerating some of the important engineering technologies and some of the existing scientific foundations of those technologies.

3.1 Attributes of Computer Based Systems

We are concerned with computer-based systems engineering, rather than with systems engineering in general. We therefore require as a primary attribute, that every relevant CBS should include major software and digital computer components.

We divided the other attributes into structural and behavioral attributes. In both cases, these attributes are typical of such systems; not all of them are required to coexist simultaneously.

The structural attributes of CBS we identified were

Distributed the computations performed by the system are distributed among several computing nodes.

Internally Communicating the system contains one or more internal communication systems.

Heterogeneous the system contains components of several different types - for example computers of different architectures, software written in different languages, buses using different communication protocols.

Embedded the system is embedded within and controls a larger system.

Complex the design and implementation of the system involves the mastering of substantial complexities.

Multifaceted because of its complexity, the system can not be adequately described from a single point of view, but demands description from many points of view.

The behavioral attributes we identified were

Safety-critical failure or malfunction of the system is dangerous to human life or health, or property.

Tightly time-constrained given the other constraints on the system resources, there is a significant engineering problem in meeting the response-time requirements.

Control-interactive the system interacts with human operators and is controlled, at least in part, by this interaction.

Event-driven the system is required to respond to events occuring in its environment.

Externally Communicating the system is coupled to other systems by external communications.

Dynamically Reconfiguring the system is subject to dynamic changes in its configuration, and these changes must be accommodated without significant interruption of the system function.

3.2   Important Engineering Technologies

As the systems we are concerned with have major software and hardware components, all the technologies of software and hardware engineering are clearly important. However, some seemed to stand out as particularly important for the engineering of CBS rather than of its components. Among these we included

Synthesis technologies such as discretisation of continuous domains, formalization and abstraction, fault-tolerant design, interface design, design of Human-Computer Interfaces, circuit design and rapid prototyping.

Analysis technologies such as hazard analysis, testing and verification, interface analysis, circuit analysis, reliability analysis, performance analysis, risk analysis and dataflow analysis.

Supporting technologies such as technical documentation, configuration management, quality engineering and management of interdisciplinary communication. The supporting technologies especially emphasize the fact that Computer Based Systems Engineering cannot be a solitary activity of a single engineer, but necessarily involves many people and hence the management of their interactions.

Application domain technologies pertinent to each application.

3.3   Scientific Foundations

Many of the scientific foundations of CBSE technologies are simply the foundations of software or electrical engineering. Among these we included circuit theory, graph theory, set theory, Boolean algebra, logic, formal language and automata theory and analysis of algorithms.

Others are more directly concerned with systems engineering rather than with the understanding and design of complex assemblies and structures. Among these we included systems theory, control theory, probability and statistics, measurement theory, and models of concurrency.

We felt that not all the necessary scientific foundations for the discipline are currently available. The missing ones will emerge with the development of the field.

4   CBSE PRACTICE

4.1   Current Practices and Methods

It was felt that current practice and methods rely far too much on ingenuity of the designers. The following specific criticisms were identified:

Lack of Engineering Technologies There is a great lack of methods necessary for the analysis and the design of complex CBS. Especially missing are the interdisciplinary "Glueing Techniques" discussed in the next paragraph.

Missing "Glueing" Techniques A fundamental vital requirement within systems engineering in general and in CBSE in particular is to analyze how the systems' components work together as a complete purposeful system. The interdisciplinary nature of CBSE interfaces and inter-dependencies between the components cross various disciplines. Currently there is little or no generally accepted understanding of how to express and analyze these inter-disciplinary interfaces, dependencies and trade-offs.

Unrealistic Expectations and Methods A significant number of the CBS projects are document driven (BOEH88). This approach is wrong because essentially it means that the documentation standard is being used as a basis for a development methodology and process.

There is a widely accepted myth that top-down development is possible. It is known to be a fallacy in systems engineering. In practice, most systems are analyzed by the team through discussions and false starts in an iterative process looking at many different views. Based only on these elaborations, a structure is devised with which the design team is content. This design is then normally presented in a top-down manner reducing the complexity of the presentation.

Much effort is expended in many projects attempting to keep anything to do with implementation out of requirements documents. This approach was proven wrong many years ago (SWAR82).

Logical designs used by the ADP community neglect all physical constraints which might be introduced during the implementation phase. Such a design is of little, if any, practical value because a design which does not address the imposed constraints is not a practical one.

Another myth, which pervades the industry especially in the software aspects of CBSE, is the concept of the perfect and complete CBS specification. Such a thing never exists. Systems have to be designed for change (PARN79).

4.2 Future Practice

The discussion on how future practice should develop was very wide ranging. Naturally the issues which have been addressed in the previous section should be remedied in the future. Some of the following issues regarding the future practice of CBSE were identified:

4.2.1 Methods and Techniques

The development of modern CBS will require new methods and methodologies supporting the engineering of these complex systems. Methodologies were defined at the workshop as the "collections" of techniques, processes and heuristics. Any particular methodology consists of

Techniques used to capture information in a particular format such as electronic and mechanical diagrams, Entity Relationship Diagrams, Data Flow Diagrams and State Transition Diagrams.

Processes which are applied to organize the derivation and the capture of the information using one or more of the techniques.

Heuristics which guide the engineers how to proceed in specific circumstances.

It is important to recognize that existing techniques are not capable of capturing the complete information necessary for the requirement specification or the design and their analysis. Thus there is currently a need to supplement the information captured by the more formal techniques with text in a natural language. This type of information is notoriously vague and ambiguous.

It follows, therefore, that we should concentrate on the development of specific new techniques which fill the gaps left in existing methodologies and consequently reduce the use of natural languages.

It was also noted that the number of techniques is much smaller than the number of methodologies. This is analogous to the restaurant industry in which the number of basic ingredients is much less than the number of possible menus. There is an increasing trend towards a "mix and match" approach in which each project selects the set of techniques appropriate to the project.

The criteria used in the selection include

- application type
- customer/user environment (e.g. special constraints such as safety security, availability)
- understanding of the problem
- previous experience in the use of the methods.

This approach was welcomed by the group as it represented new awareness in the industry that there is no universal panacea for CBSE development.

Tools to support these techniques should ideally

- deliver the information in a machine readable format
- record the information onto a coherent data model covering the complete development, allowing the information to be viewed from different viewpoints.
- provide the possibility of prototyping different aspects of the system based on the recorded information, for example, software, hardware, hydraulics.

4.2.2   The Development Process

It was recognized that the CBS development process must involve rapid iteration early in the life-cycle in order to arrive at a system architecture embodying the required constraints, functionality and testability which can form the basis for estimation and planning with an acceptable level of risk. Thus we envisioned the development process as being a multi-pass process driven by the need to reduce risk.

The diagram in figure 1 encapsulates our view of the future development process. The process starts with the initial concept which is assumed to be quite vague. This

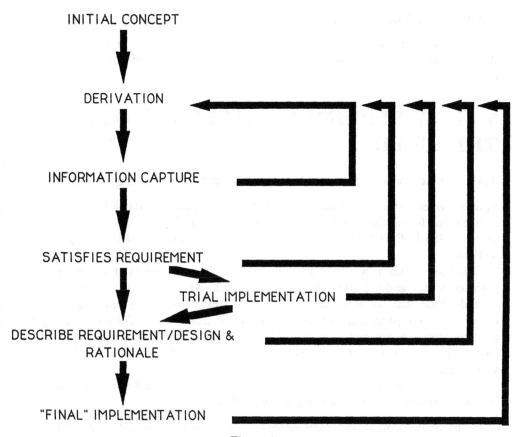

Figure 1:

is followed by an iterative derivation process which is initially concerned with gathering/creating information and then capturing the information in a form which is adequate for communication within the team responsible for the derivation. The same process is applied to the creation of the requirement and the design. In this way a large number of ideas are rejected, and the embryo design is modified until an adequate result is achieved agreed upon by the developers and the customers.

It is imperative that this iterative process should be performed as rapidly as possible. This process should include rapid prototyping techniques useful in the validation of the concepts and the design. Once the wider consensus is reached it is possible to begin the process of formally describing the design. This is a slower, time consuming activity.

Figure 1 also shows an additional branch labelled trial implementation. This option exists because for some systems, the only way to reduce risk to an acceptable level is to partially implement it!

4.2.3 Risk Management

Risk management is a vital technique for successful development of CBSE projects. However, current understanding of it leaves much to be desired and needs further research.

5 ESTABLISHMENT AND PROMOTION OF THE FIELD

5.1 The Need for a New field and its Recognition

In the previous section CBSE has been described both in terms of its basic scientific and technological foundations, and in terms of the current and future industrial engineering practice. Should CBSE then be promoted as a field of its own, and if so, why, where, and how?

The need for the new CBSE discipline has emerged as a result of an explosion in both technology and requirements that has created new complexities. Hence, it must be understood that the essential motivation for establishing and promoting CBSE is not to promote a particular technical lobby, but to create the conditions necessary to properly meet the pressing current and future needs of this critical field for modern technology, both in terms of technical know-how and in terms of an adequate supply of competent resources.

The need for the recognition of CBSE as a distinct engineering discipline may have several motivations, either technical, sociological or political:

- The existence of specific problems requires research, teaching and the development of new technologies.

- More qualified professionals are needed to meet the growing demand for the development of large and complex CBSs. This need can only be met if the discipline is recognized, so that competent professionals are attracted and educated.

- People working in CBSE should be recognized as specialists in their own field.

- Special CBSE technologies should be recognized by all concerned, especially industry, academia and government.

5.2 How to Establish CBSE

Establishing a new field, even when it already has a virtual de facto existence as is the case with CBSE, requires efforts in several directions to give it coherence, boundaries and dynamics. These efforts include

- Defining an internal identity, in other words the scientific and technical contents of the field.

- Creating or clearly identifying the academic and industrial communities.

- Building an educational structure.

- Establishing an external identity to be recognized by other technical communities.

5.2.1 Defining The Identity of CBSE

In order to establish the field, it is essential to first give it a distinct identity. This starts with the identification of the relevant areas of science and technology and their relative importance, as we have done above, and the understanding of how they interact and complement each other. This must lead to a recognized definition of the field, and to the establishment of a common language and frame of reference accepted by the people active in the field.

The unique aspects of CBSE must be clearly emphasized, since many of the concerned areas are shared with other disciplines. In particular, though the formal mathematical or technical context may be the same for some problems, the emphasis of CBSE can be qualitatively or quantitatively different.

Finally, we must identify clearly all those problems that are more specifically relevant to CBSE, whether of a practical, research or managerial value.

5.2.2 Establishing a Common Terminology

The problem of establishing a common terminology appears a major and crucial objective. It is unfortunately true that in emerging fields, such as those related to computing, the lack of a standard terminology is too often an obstacle to technical communication and cooperation. The problem is compounded when interdisciplinary work brings together a wide variety of concepts, approaches and thought habits. Also CBSE has inherited from computer science the regrettable practice of using overloaded (or "underloaded") buzz-words as reference concepts.

Indeed, several such words were identified during the Neve-Ilan CBSE Workshop. For example:

Analysis and synthesis is for some of us more or less synonymous with top-down vs bottom-up development in mathematical proofs. However a more common meaning in CBSE is that synthesis corresponds to the decomposition of a system into components while analysis is the examination of the structure thus obtained to determine whether it fits the original problem requirements.

Object Orientedness is probably the most overloaded and least defined of all buzz-words. It can cover a variety of concepts and techniques, many of them essential to CBSE.

Holistic properties that characterize a system as a whole are not understood by everyone as covering the same scope.

5.2.3 Creating the academic and industrial communities

The existence of any technical field or discipline depends entirely on its promoters and practicioners. Though this document and the workshop that produced it are a clear sign of an existing community that recognizes itself as dealing with CBSE, it has to better assert its role, actions and concerns. In particular, it must reinforce its ties and attract concerned professionals using conventional means such as specialized forums (journals, conferences, workshops) and recognized professional organizations.

5.2.4 Building an Educational Structure

Practicing CBS professionals learned their skills on the job, much as computer professionals did 25 years ago. However, this incurs high costs and cannot supply industry with the increasing number of adequately educated professionals required by the growing number of computer based systems and their complexity. Hence an educational structure has to be developed that will produce a sufficient supply of CBS Engineers, both by attracting people to this field and by making adequate curricula available.

This necessary CBSE educational framework is described later in the paper.

5.2.5 Establishing an External Identity

The last requirement is to have the field recognized by other communities. Such recognition will reinforce the internal identity of the CBSE community itself. More importantly, it is an essential step for the achievement of its goals through sensitization of the following communities:

Academia which has to offer new curricula and to support research in this new field.

Industry which should urgently be made more aware of the rapidly developing CBSE technology and the needs of its professionals and the need for them.

Government bodies who are CBS customers and funders of large research projects and long term educational efforts.

The general public who should be made aware of the new technology helping to attract new people to become CBSE professionals.

Establishment of this external identity requires lobbying and much public relations to make CBSE better known. In this respect, it is of particular importance to carefully analyze CBSE's relationship to other fields of Engineering and Computer Science, with respect to both its intersections and its differences.

5.3 Promotion of CBSE

CBSE should be promoted on many fronts. Some of them were suggested at the workshop.

5.3.1 Creating an IEEE Computer Society Task Force

The first and most important recommendation is to form a task force within the IEEE Computer Society to establish the identity of the field according to suggestions made in the previous paragraph. This should be done by organizing additional workshops and conferences and promoting the need to establish research institutes and the necessary educational programs.

5.3.2   Establishing CBSE Institutes

It was recommended that a major step to achieve the previously outlined objectives is the creation of an institute or several institutes for CBSE. Such institutes will be the flagship that will embody the existence of the field and give it visibility. More concretely their objectives will be as follows:

Research in CBSE and CBSE related fields. This research should include experimental work on large scale CBS. Such systems that better exhibit the full problems, are often too large to be developed within an academic environment. During the workshop an initial list of research topics was identified as necessary for the development of theories, methods, techniques, representations and tools in the following areas:

- De/Re-composition
- Continuity within and between the life cycle phases
- Trade-off and evaluation studies
- Holistic properties of CBS
- Testing of CBS and the analysis of test results
- Performance prediction
- Distributed control issues
- Risk management techniques.

Education in cooperation with universities and industry. This activity should stress advanced teaching especially of already experienced professionals. It will also include the creation of new curricula and the analysis of the effectiveness of existing curricula according to the evolution of the state of the art and present industrial needs.

Technology transfer to industry, particularly through training of professionals on the Institute projects, or simply by demonstrations based on the Institute projects.

Another major requirement will be the creation of a center of expertise as a focal point for a number of activities related to the promotion of CBSE.

To be successful, such institutes must have a critical mass of resources, man-power and expertise. Considering the cost and complexity of the objects being studied, this implies large institutions with a national or international scope sponsored by all the concerned parties namely, governments, industry and academia.

The institutes will hopefully develop competence in all the technical areas of concern to CBSE, keeping CBSE as a guideline but seeking technical excellence in each of these areas.

Though such a creation is always the source of much controversy, which is by itself a way of attracting attention to the existing problems and needs - there are many success stories. In neighboring fields France has successfully created INRIA (Institut National de Recherche en Informatique et en Automatique) for computer science and control, and LAAS (Laboratoire d'Automatique et d'Analyse des Systemes) for control, and systems analysis. Great Britian has created SIRA an institute devoted to industrial automation and measurement. In the USA the Software Engineering Institute and MCC are contributing significantly to the advancement of the field.

5.3.3 Establishing the Educational Framework of CBSE

CBSE education raises problems that require a somewhat original approach:

The basic scientific knowledge required covers many different scientific domains, which a single individual cannot grasp in depth. Hence, a proper balance has to be found in curricula to provide adequate knowledge in each. In some cases, finding unifying concepts could possibly reduce the learning load, and this is certainly an object for CBSE research.

Much of the difficulty of CBSE is due to the size and complexity of the systems considered. This cannot usually be taught within an academic environment and requires cooperation with industry or the proposed CBSE Institutes, either through participation in a real CBSE project, or through the teaching of professionals involved in such projects.

The teaching of the problems related to the development and management of complete systems should be limited to people who have already some professional experience and sufficient command of the supporting disciplines.

Hence, it has been the consensus of the workshop participants that academic teaching of CBSE students should clearly distinguish between undergraduate and graduate education. While undergraduate education must of necessity concentrate on the supporting disciplines, it can also serve to sensitize students to the specific problems and complexities of CBSE. However, deep treatment of the overall systems view should be reserved for the graduate level education, addressing students who are mature and hopefully have some basic professional experience as support and motivation for their study of the field.

Educational curricula at various levels should also be developed for practitioners already active in the field who don't have adequate education.

Another consequence of the uniqueness of the field is that people with industrial experience should play a substantial role in the teaching of CBSE, especially at the graduate level.

The development of CBSE curriculae should be based on

- the recommendation of experts (e.g. [Parnas-90]),
- industrial experience and industrial needs,
- practical experience in existing programs (e.g. [CAUN90]).

The success of programs that have already been in existence for several years in some universities is in this regard extremely encouraging.

Finally, although we do recommend the creation of CBSE institutes as focal points for the field, we believe that CBSE programs can be created in academic environments by introducing new curricula, and do not necessarily require the creation of new structures (e.g. new departments) though of course, such a creation can give more strength, depth and commitment to a program.

References

[BOEH88] Boehmm B. W.,"A Spiral Model of Software Development and Enhancement", IEEE Computer, May 1988, pp. 61-72.

[BOUN89] (-), "Boston University, College of Engineering, Graduate Program, Masters Program in Computer and Systems Engineering", Boston Massachusetts, 1989. (An initial attempt made by Prof.J. Brackett to develop a program close to CBSE).

[CAUN90] (-), "Carleton University, College of Engineering, Under Graduate and Graduate Program of the Department of System and Computer Engineering", Ottawa, Canada 1990. (An existing program in CBSE taught for the last five years).

[PARN79] Parnas, D. L., "Designing Software for Ease of Extension and Contraction", IEEE Transactions on Software Engineering, Vol.SE-5, No. 2, pp.128-137.

[PARN90] Parnas, D. L., "Education for Computing Professionals", IEEE Computer, January 1990, pp. 17-22.

[SWAR82] Swartout, W., Balzer, R., "On the Inevitable Intertwining of Specifications and Implementation", Communications of the ACM, Vol. 25, No. 7, July 1988, pp. 438-440.

6 Acknowledgements

We would like to thank all workshop participants for their valuable contribution to the success of the workshop. Members of the program committee were J.Z. Lavi, Israel; A.K. Agrawala, USA; M. Jackson, GB; B. Lang, France; H.U.Steusloff, Germany and A. Yehudai, Israel.

The participants in the first working group, defining the discipline, were M.Jackson, England, Chairperson; N.Fenton, London City University; A.Melton, Kansas State University; H.Rischel, Technical University of Denmark; F. Rosenberg, Israel Aircraft Industries; A.Schill, University of Karlsruhe; A.Yehudai, Tel-Aviv University; M.Winokur, Israel Aircraft Industries.

The participants in the second working group, studying the CBSE practice were K.Jackson, SD-SCICON England, Chairperson; M.Arreguy, Ministry of Public Administration, Cordova, Argentina; D.Blank, ibid; M.Boason, Hollandse Signaalaparaten; M.Deutsch, Hughes Aircraft; V.Gafni, Israel Aircraft Industries; B.Gliss, Max-Plank Institute, Stuttgart; S.Koenig, Tadiran; S.Kuehl, McDonnell Douglas; S.T.Levi, Israel Aircraft Industries; C.H.Poo, National University of Singapore; S.Tyberowitz, Tel-Aviv University.

The participants in the third working group, discussing how to establish and promote the discipline were B.Lang, Inria, Chairperson; A.Agrawala, University of Maryland; R.Buhr, Carleton University; L.Goldin, Rafael; V.Kadary, Israel Aircraft Industries; J.Kudish, Israel; J.Z.Lavi, Israel Aircraft Industries; L.Rudolf, Hebrew University.

B. Lang's pariticpation was partially supported by the Eureka Software Factory (ESF) project.

"Software Engineering Teaching Styles"

Moderator: Lionel Deimel
Software Engineering Institute

Teaching about Process Issues in Software Engineering
David Budgen and Chic Rattray
University of Stirling

A Layered Approach to Teaching Software Project Management
David Bustard
University of Ulster

Teaching about Process Issues in Software Engineering

David Budgen, Chic Rattray
Department of Computing Science
University of Stirling
Stirling
Scotland
FK9 4LA
Email: db@uk.ac.stir.cs

Abstract

Our experiences with teaching Software Engineering to Computing Science students are described, focusing mainly upon the use of two forms of teaching that have proved useful in helping students to learn about those *process* issues that are not well suited to the use of a conventional lecturing format. The first is the use of student presentations of technical papers in seminar sessions, which also introduces the students to the practice of reading and appraising technical papers. The second is the use of group projects in which the groups are required to produce specification and design documents, together with planning material, in order to form a 'feasibility study'. We discuss the way that the projects are structured, and the form of assessment used. For both techniques, we have summarised our experiences, and have made an assessment of their strengths and weaknesses.

1   Introduction

For the past nine years we have been teaching a course unit that provides a general introduction to Software Engineering, for a class which is made up of students in the Final Honours Year of the Computing Science degree programme [1], together with students who are on an advanced postgraduate conversion programme [3, 4]. Class sizes have generally been of the order of 30–50 students, with the undergraduates normally being the larger portion. The aim of this unit is to introduce the issues involved in *programming in the large*, and to describe some of the techniques and strategies that are used in large projects.

The unit itself is spread over twelve teaching weeks (the University of Stirling uses a two-semester system, rather than the conventional British academic year based upon three terms). Within this period, we seek to address both *product* issues and also *process* issues. As might be expected, the latter aspect provides the main difference between this course and the more conventional computing science courses that we teach to our students.

---

[1] Honours Degree programmes in Scotland require *four* years of study.

In teaching students about Software Engineering, it is an understanding of the *process* issues that is most difficult to convey effectively through conventional means such as lectures. In addition, we have not found the end of semester examination to be of much use in assessing the student's grasp of the main issues and techniques. So, over the period that this course has been running, we have therefore evolved a teaching style which is based upon using a combination of the following forms for delivery and assessment:

lectures are used to cover the technical (or 'product') themes such as design and specification techniques, testing strategies, cost modelling forms etc [2, 5];

student seminars provide access to examples of 'process' issues, by which we mean the 'management' issues such as productivity, working practices etc;

a group project is used to provide practical experience of some of the issues that arise during the specification and design tasks, and also helps the student to understand the interaction between the product and process aspects;

an individual assignment is used to highlight the difficulties in constructing formal specifications, and to assess the student's understanding of some of the *product* issues.

This course unit is assessed entirely by coursework. The group project counts for 60% of course marks, and the individual assignment provides for the remaining 40%. (The 'normal' balance in our course units is for 60% of assessment to be performed by means of an end of semester examination, and for the remaining 40% to be taken from assigned work.)

In this paper we have concentrated upon describing our experiences with the two forms that are used to teach about process issues. We describe our experiences with each form, the problems that we have encountered, and the benefits that their use has provided for the students. For the group projects, we also describe the way in which we have approached the vexed question of providing adequate individual gradings.

2 Student Seminars

In conjunction with its semester system, the University of Stirling runs courses on a 'modular' basis, with all courses having a fairly standard format of three lectures per week, together with one tutorial/laboratory class per week. In the early days of teaching this course, we realised that the small group tutorial system used in our other courses was not suited to the subject matter, and we switched to a scheme of reading research papers during the weekly session. This proved to be very effective, and over a period of time, these 'seminars' have evolved further into a much more structured format.

2.1 Organisation

For the seminars, the class is divided into groups of approximately sixteen students, and each such group is run as a separate seminar group (all of the groups undertake the same work in parallel). During the semester, each student in turn is required to give a presentation to their own seminar group, based on the contents of a selected research paper, and this is followed by a short group discussion of the theme which is generally led by the tutors. The one-hour seminar sessions are divided into two periods of twenty-five minutes, with each student being allocated one period, so that the group hears presentations on two papers each week. The actual presentation is expected to take between fifteen and twenty minutes, allowing about five to ten minutes for discussion.

The class tutors are normally present for all presentations. Apart from initiating discussion, it may also be important for the tutors to explain issues and to answer specific questions that may arise from the discussion or the papers themselves.

All of the students receive a handout which provides a description of the journals normally used as sources of papers, lists the papers for each week, and contains the abstract for each paper (where available). In addition, each student is loaned a copy of the paper which they are to present. We encourage students to read all of the papers being presented, but find that this is rarely practical in terms of time and workload.

2.2 Presentation Form

Quite apart from the benefit to the seminar group of receiving a good presentation of a topic, we believe that the ability to present technical ideas in a clear manner is an essential skill for an engineer. So although these seminars are not directly assessed for the purpose of the course, we do seek to give them a lot of emphasis within the course itself. We also find that the students are themselves aware of the importance of acquiring such skills, and that they appreciate the benefit of doing so within a generally supportive and sympathetic group.

Before the students begin their presentations, the first seminar session is used to discuss ways of presenting the material. As the students are required to use the overhead projector during their presentation, we examine some of the techniques appropriate to this. The introductory session emphasises the importance of such issues as giving a clear summary, having uncluttered viewfoils, making adequate notes, and of facing the audience while speaking. (Since introducing this session, we have noted a marked improvement in the quality of the presentations.)

Timing is apt to provide quite a problem, since for many students this will be their first experience of presenting to a group in this way. We encourage students to have a prior rehearsal with a timer, and as a result we generally find that it is unnecessary to 'cut' any presentations after the twenty minutes allocated.

2.3 Selection of papers

The papers used are selected by considering the following criteria:

- They must be reasonably short (usually between eight and fifteen pages), and it must be possible to make a précis of the contents that will fit into the available time slot.

- It should not be necessary to make use of the references cited in a paper, in order to obtain a general understanding of the paper. (We encourage students to look at some of the references to help them gain a better understanding of a paper, but it should not be *essential* for them to do so.)

- The topic should reinforce the subject matter of the course, usually by describing practical experience and experimental evidence (or lack of it) to support particular Software Engineering techniques. While a few papers cover technical (*product*) issues, we have concentrated on finding papers that describe *process* issues and experimental studies.

- The paper should be written in a readable style, not least because our classes usually include a number of overseas students for whom English is not necessarily the first language.

- The paper should be reasonably up to date (ie published within the last five or six years) unless it is a 'classic'.

As might be imagined, it is not possible to find very many papers that can meet all of these criteria! We seek to have a particular *theme* each week, generally concerned with 'process' aspects, but on occasion it does prove necessary to interpret the theme somewhat liberally. We have generally found that a mix of 'tutorial' papers (as published in such journals as *IEEE Computer* and *Information and Software Technology*) and of 'experience' papers (largely drawn from the 'heavy' journals) seems to meet our needs quite well.

Appendix A lists the papers that were used in the Autumn Semester 1990 (minus the abstracts) together with a brief note to indicate what we sought to obtain from each week's papers. The list changes a little from year to year as we find new papers or decide to change the themes themselves.

2.4   Observations on the Seminars

In general the standard of presentation is very high indeed, and clearly most students do put quite a lot of work into this. For many of them it is also something of an ordeal, since they may never have had the experience of speaking before a group, and so the tutors need to moderate the sessions according to the experience and confidence of the speaker. (As a matter of interest, one of the Spring Semester courses has now adopted a similar scheme, and both in this, and also in the presentations required on Final Year Projects, the effects of this earlier 'practice' is generally very noticeable.)

A significant benefit of using technical papers in this way, is that students come to realise that these issues are 'for real', and are not simply classroom concerns. It also encourages them to make their own assessment of the 'worth' of a paper, and to realise that the findings of researchers may be open to debate! The use of papers exposes them to a much wider spectrum of practical experience than we are able to do through lectures, and by drawing on our own experience, and this is particularly true for the 'process' topics. The involvement of the tutors in this discussion, helping the students to make assessments of the various issues, and to see how the various components of the course link together, is an important feature of the seminar structure.

The choice of papers remains a difficult one. Sometimes a paper that seems well suited turns out to be quite difficult for the students, and this is often because of one or more of the following reasons:

- the paper assumes a 'knowledge base' or 'experience base' that the students have not yet acquired;

- it proves difficult for a student to summarise the material adequately, within the time limits;

- the presenters fail to understand the extent to which complex ideas might be being abstracted within the paper.

The allocation of papers to students is performed by the course tutors. (At one time, students were allowed to choose a paper—but as they observed, they lacked the experience to make sensible choices!) The mixed nature of the class also allows us some scope for matching student experience to papers, and for ensuring that the initial presentations will set a high standard. However, despite this, and the experience of nine years of teaching this course unit, from time to time it still proves necessary to change a paper after a year's 'trial', because of one or more of the above reasons.

3 Group Projects

The use of *group projects* is quite widespread within the teaching of Software Engineering, and both the benefits and the problems associated with their use are well known [8]. However, the duration, form and assessment of such projects do vary quite considerably [15, 10, 1], with the great majority involving some form of implementation. In this section we concentrate therefore on those features of our group projects which are most likely to differ from other such projects that we are aware of, namely their emphasis on design and planning, and the form of assessment used.

3.1 Project format

The modular nature of the Stirling degree programme means that students undertake quite extensive practical work for each course unit. So in setting up our group projects we sought to avoid further programming and to concentrate upon the more unfamiliar domains of product *specification* and *design*. To support the teaching of process aspects, the students are also required to consider the *planning* aspects of a large project.

The project teams are relatively small. Our preferred size is four, but where necessary we use groups of three. We try to mix the undergraduate and postgraduates within the groups, since we have found that the two sections of the class have quite complementary expertise to offer. The undergraduates usually have much more practical programming knowledge, which is useful in the specification and design tasks—which require the group to identify technical solutions to a problem. For their part, many of the postgraduates have some external work experience, and so can provide useful inputs to the parts of the project which require the generation of plans and costings. The students themselves seem to regard this mixed format grouping as a useful strategy too.

For the project itself, each group is given the same 'requirements document' and is asked to perform a *feasibility study* for the implementation of the required system. The groups are considered to be in competition and in a tendering situation. Their study is required to generate a tender document which must provide the following sections:

An Introduction stating assumptions, techniques used etc.

A Requirements Specification which enlarges upon that originally given, adding the effects of any assumptions.

A System Design in the form of a mix of text and diagrams.

A Development Plan for the implementation of the system that they are proposing, including cost estimates and milestones.

A Test Plan to support the implementation of the system.

We impose limitations upon the size of each section (the actual documents are generally produced using a system such as LAT$_E$X), but leave the choice of techniques and forms for design representation to the groups.

In recent years the problems chosen for the group project have included the following systems.

- An *Air Traffic Control System*—which proved rather large, and we found that many of the postgraduates lacked the ideas about concurrency that were necessary. (We supplemented the basic information for this problem with material obtained from the Civil Aviation Authority!)

- An *Aircraft Autopilot*—which worked quite well. However, on two occasions the presence of a student who possessed a pilot's licence did cause their groups to get rather bogged down in the detail.

- A *Hospital Patient Monitoring System*—that was loosely based upon the example used in [6]. This problem proved to be quite successful and seemed to be of about the right size and degree of complexity for the time available.

The design representation forms that have been most widely used are the Yourdon notations of Data Flow Diagrams and Structure Charts [13], and the MASCOT notation [11], which is particularly well-suited for the description of concurrent systems.

The modular course structure at Stirling makes for highly decoupled course units. This in turn means that assigned work can rarely be set in the first two or three weeks of semester. As a result, the project generally runs over a period of about seven weeks. Like all assigned course work, it takes place in addition to the regular teaching component of the course, and so the group need to find their own times and places to meet. (The duration of this project is somewhat shorter than seems to be common elsewhere, and it does put a lot of pressure upon the students.)

Each group is assigned a member of staff as a 'monitoring officer', and is required to meet with them at least once per week during this period. We find that this ensures that no group goes too badly astray in terms of interpreting its task, and also provides a means of providing a degree of 'customer feedback' into the groups. We also encourage each group to maintain a 'lab book' [7], in which they record their decisions and the reasons for these, together with any other information that may be relevant. The lab book is then an important resource when they need to write their tender proposal over a very short period. (Currently we do not attempt to assess the lab book itself.)

Group Member:

Factor	Major Contribution	Some Contribution	Little Contribution
1. Organisation & Management			
2. Ideas & Suggestions			
3. Collecting source material			
4. Analysis & Design			
5. Compilation of Proposal			

Figure 1: Sample Voting Slip used for assessment

3.2 Project assessment

The 'tenders' generated are approximately the same size as Final Honours Dissertations (typically 70–90 pages of typescript and diagrams), and so the overall marking task is quite large. However, the use of a standard format for the 'tender documents' provides reasonable scope for applying a structured marking scheme, and as a further check, all projects are marked by two members of staff [2].

In common with most projects, the allocation of marks has a subjective element. In marking the design component, we generally give a greater weight to clarity of expression and presentation than to design 'quality', since the latter is difficult to assess in an objective manner [2]. (We also take the view that these are inexperienced designers, and that we are mainly looking for an ability to explain their ideas at this stage.) This accords well with the way in which student effort appears to be apportioned, since the students generally find it harder to describe the solutions than to develop them! Similarly, although the groups are encouraged to use standard design representations, we do not require that they follow a stylised design 'method'.

As with all group projects, the question of whether it is fair to give all members of a group the same mark is significant. Over the past two years we have applied a compensation mechanism which was derived from one of those suggested in Reference [9]. Using this scheme, each member of a group assesses the contributions made by the other members of the group in terms of five headings. For each heading, they are asked to state whether they considered the contribution of each member to be a major contribution, some contribution or little contribution. Figure 1 shows a typical 'voting slip' used for this part of the exercise.

The results of these votes are then tallied, and the individual mark for each student is computed by adjusting the common group mark. This adjustment is performed by using a scheme that considers only significant correlations in the votes, and allows some offset to compensate for the tendency to 'positive' voting. (Students tend to give more 'major' votes than 'little' votes.)

---

[2] Universities in the UK have a highly-developed mechanism for ensuring consistency of standards through a scheme of *External Examiners*. If the two internal examiners were to disagree significantly on grades, this would then be resolved by appeal to the external examiner.

Score	Adjustment Factor (points)
0 0 0	0
0 0 +1	0
0 0 -1	0
0 +1 -1	0
0 +1 +1	+2
0 -1 -1	-2
+1 +1 -1	0
+1 +1 +1	+3
-1 -1 +1	0
-1 -1 -1	-3

Figure 2: Translation Table for 'votes'

Total Points	Mark Adjustment
+14,15	+7
+12,13	+6
+10,11	+5
+8,9	+4
+6,7	+3
+4,5	+2
+2,3	+1
0,1	-1
-1,-2	-2
-3,-4	-3
-5,-6	-4
-7,-8	-5

Figure 3: Table used in converting points to marks.

Figure 2 shows the table that is used to convert votes into a numerical adjustment factor (in 'points'). In this table, a vote for *Major Contribution* will score +1, a vote for *Some Contribution* will score 0, and a vote for *Little Contribution* scores -1. Only significant trends are counted when assigning points. Fortunately such patterns as 0 +1 -1 and +1 +1 -1 occur only very infrequently. For groups of three students, the rather arbitrary adjustment that we make is to count the third vote each time as being 0.

The adjustment factor for each student is then totalled (in points) for the five headings, and further converted to a percentage mark adjustment. Figure 3 shows an example of a table used to make the conversion, with the offset being used to compensate for the students' tendency to vote 'positively' (there is usually a surplus of positive points).

In 1990, a further entry was added to each ballot paper, and the 'voter' was invited to assess their *own* contribution to the group. While we did not include these in the assessment, nor survey them in any systematic way, it was interesting to observe that while students often gave themselves a profile for the five headings that was in agreement with the assessment of their peers, the self-assessment was usually offset in a positive direction!

3.3 Observations

We have found that the standard of work in these group projects is very high, and the students themselves recognise the importance of the skills that they acquire from them. However, they are very time-consuming, and several aspects have to be handled rather carefully. Some particular issues needing care include:

- Selection of group membership. Our basic policy is to create groups that do not include groups of friends (where known). This then simulates the situation often encountered in industry, where members of a team may not be well acquainted before working together. Similarly, we seek to spread the overseas students among the groups, which gives them the experience of working more closely with native English speakers (and writers). These practices seem to conform well to those adopted elsewhere [15]. Inevitably a small number of students prove more difficult to fit into a group than others, but we have not found this problem to be insurmountable.

- The timescale is rather critical. Because the projects are quite intensive, we try to confine them to about six or seven weeks. This is also related to the subject matter, since like all design issues, there is no 'stopping rule' to determine when the project is complete [14], and so it is likely that allocating a longer period would simply increase the overall volume of effort, rather than reducing its intensity.

- The mixing of undergraduates and postgraduates has many positive benefits, but two significant problems that it creates are that:

  - the two types of student have different timetables, which may make it difficult for groups to meet during the daytime;

  - the undergraduates and postgraduates are differently motivated, in that the postgraduates are mainly concerned with *passing* the course, whereas the undergraduates are seeking a good classification towards their degree, leading to potential tensions within the group itself.

  Neither are major issues, but they need to be recognised. To assist with the former problem, we try to provide a bookable room in which groups can meet and use a whiteboard etc.

- It is generally difficult to cover all of the technical support material before the project begins. Some of the design technique issues, costing techniques etc tend to be covered while the project is in progress. (Again, this is a part-reflection of the problem of project duration that we have already discussed.)

- We have experimented with tool support, but find that the overhead of learning to use a relevant CASE tool such as Cadre's *Teamwork* offsets any benefits that it can offer. Access to general-purpose tools such as LaTeX and MacDraw seems to be the most useful level of provision for many purposes. Since this observation seems to run counter to our expectations, and to the observations of others [12], we can only conclude that the effective use of CASE tools needs good tutorial support (as was the case reported in [12], and was not the case for ourselves), as well as a longer project period. (As a further point, we do not expect students to necessarily follow a detailed 'design method' since they are largely performing architectural design tasks – and also because we do not believe that learning detailed design techniques is an appropriate way to learn about design itself.)

Overall, we believe that this form of group project reinforces the issues of *programming in the large* very effectively, and we are planning to expand this course further, within a syllabus revision programme that is currently under way within the Department.

4 Conclusions

The course unit described in this paper has been developed during a period in which ideas about Software Engineering have been evolving, and so the course unit has had to adapt its material to fit these ideas. We have generally found that our chosen format has helped with this evolution, as it provides a flexible framework for delivery of ideas and material. Although it is recognised by the students as being a valuable unit, there is no doubt that it does place a heavy load upon them during the semester. (In compensation of course, there is no exam!)

As we identified at the outset, it is the *process* issues (and their relationship with the *product* issues) that makes the teaching of Software Engineering different from most Computing Science topics. We believe that the process-centred techniques discussed here have proved useful and effective within our particular context, although still providing scope for further refinement.

With the greater importance of Software Engineering, we are planning to extend this course unit to become two sequential units, which undergraduates will then take in their third year. Our current thinking is that the first unit will be more conventional in form, using lectures and tutorials, and that the second will introduce the use of student seminars and group projects. By doing this, we hope to make some improvements, and to overcome some of the less satisfactory aspects of the present course unit, along the following lines:

- More of the technical groundwork can be covered before the group projects begin, and there will also be more scope to introduce the use of CASE tools in a more effective way, with supporting lectures and tutorials.

- The expanded timescale and increased lecture time will allow us to allocate some of the lecturing hours in the second course unit for group meetings, so helping to overcome the timetabling problems and to provide better means for monitoring group progress.

- A problem of the present structure is that we have to allocate students to groups within a few weeks of first meeting the postgraduate class. By moving the group projects to the Spring Semester, we will have had longer to assess them and so should be better able to construct balanced groups.

Overall, we believe that the use of a mix of teaching forms in this course unit has worked well for us over the past nine years. Only on a very few occasions have we had problems in placing students within a group, and none of these have been fatal to the effectiveness of the group. The seminars in particular, have proved to be very valuable in introducing students to more advanced study techniques, as well as in giving them experience with the presentation of technical ideas.

References

[1] M F Bott, *An Undergraduate Programme in Software Engineering*, 4th SEI Conference on Software Engineering Education,pp38–48, Published as *Lecture Notes in Computer Science 423*, Editor Lionel E Deimel, 1990

[2] David Budgen, *Introduction to Software Design*, Curriculum Module SEI-CM-2-2.1, Software Engineering Institute, Carnegie Mellon University, 1989.

[3] David Budgen, Peter Henderson, Chic Rattray, *Academic/Industrial Collaboration in a Postgraduate Master of Science Degree in Software Engineering*, in 'Software Engineering Education: The Educational Needs of the Software Community', Eds Norman E Gibbs & Richard E Fairley, pp201–211, Springer Verlag, 1987

[4] David Budgen, Peter Henderson, Chic Rattray, *Academic/Industrial Collaboration in a Postgraduate MSc Course in Software Engineering*, Journal of Systems and Software, 10, No 4, November 1989, pp261–266

[5] David Budgen, Norman E Gibbs, *The Education Programme of the Software Engineering Institute, Carnegie Mellon University*, Software Engineering Journal, 4(4), July 1989, pp176–185

[6] Allen Macro, John Buxton, *The Craft of Software Engineering*, Addison-Wesley, 1987

[7] D E Conway, S C Dunn, G S Hooper, *BCS and IEE accreditation of software engineering courses*, Software Engineering Journal, 4(4), July 1989, pp245–248

[8] P Garratt, *The group project anomaly*, University Computing, 11, 1989, 79–81

[9] G Gibbs, S Habeshaw, T Habeshaw, *Interesting Ways to Assess Your Students*, Technical & Educational Services Ltd, ISBN 0-947885-11-0

[10] Peter J B King, *Experiences with group projects in software engineering*, Software Engineering Journal, 4(4), July 1989, pp221–225

[11] Special Issue on MASCOT 3, *Software Engineering Journal*, 1(3), May 1986

[12] Barbee T Mynatt, Laura M Leventhal, *An Evaluation of a CASE-Based Approach to Teaching Undergraduate Software Engineering*, ACM SIGCSE Bulletin, 22(1), February 1990, pp48–52

[13] Meilir Page-Jones, *Practical Guide to Structured Systems Design*, Second Edition, Prentice-Hall, 1988

[14] H W J Rittel, M M Webber, *Planning Problems are Wicked Problems*, in 'Developments in Design Methodology', Ed Nigel Cross, John Wiley, 1984

[15] Brian Tompsett, *The System Cottage – a multidisciplinary engineering group practical*, Software Engineering Journal, 4(4), July 1989, pp209–220

A   Seminar Papers used in 1990

Week 1: Software Development

a) *Ease of Use : A System Design Challenge*, L M Branscomb, J C Thomas, IBM Sys Journal, **23**, 224–235, 1984
b) *A Spiral Model of Software Development and Enhancement*, Barry W Boehm, IEEE Computer, **21**, May 1988, 61–72

> These two papers provide a fairly useful introduction to the course themes. The first paper is concerned with the needs of the eventual user, and makes use of examples that the class can relate to quite easily, while the second looks at the software production process itself.

Week 2: How we work

a) *Factors affecting programmer productivity during application development*, A J Thadhani, IBM Sys Journal, **23**, 19–35, 1984
b) *The Role of Domain Experience in Software Design*, B Adelson, E Soloway, IEEE Trans on Software Eng., **SE-11**, No 11, 1351–1360, Nov 1985

> The first paper gives a survey of the nature of the tasks that programmers perform during a project (showing how little of a programmer's time involves actual code generation), and also demonstrates the difficulty of performing useful measurements in this area. The second paper describes some experimental work studying the nature of the design process, and introduces some interesting technical points.

Week 3: Design Issues

a) *A Rational Design Process: How and Why to Fake it*, D L Parnas, P C Clements, IEEE Trans on Software Eng., **SE-12**, February 1986, 251–257
b) *Designing Software for Ease of Extension and Contraction*, D L Parnas, IEEE Trans on Software Eng., **SE-5**, March 1979, 128–137,

> The paper by Parnas and Clements is concerned with bridging technical and process issues. If the presenter has any experience of industry, they may well be able to relate to it very well. The second paper is technically quite difficult, and is included as a 'classic' in the field. It really needs to be allocated to one of the stronger students in a class.

Week 4: Project Organisation

a) *Designing Complex Software*, A F Norcio, L J Chmura, Journal of Systems & Software, **8**, 165–184, 1988
b) *Managing and Predicting the Costs of Real-Time Software*, R D Warburton, IEEE Trans on Software Eng., **SE-9**, 562–569, 1983

> The first of these describes another study that involves the collection of data related to the software development process. It gives examples of lots of data collection forms, but this does not seem to lead to any problems in presentation, although it may help if the presenter produces a short handout with examples of these. The second paper has some rather nice experimental data and introduces the macro-modelling approach to costing.

Week 5: Programmer Productivity

a1) *The Parable of two programmers*, N W Rickert, ACM SigSoft SE Notes, **10**, 16–18, January 1985
a2) *The parable of two programmers - Continued/Still More*, W D Maurer, T E Barrios, ACM SigSoft SE Notes, **10**, 19–22, April 1985
b) *Reviews Walkthroughs and Inspections*, G M Weinberg, D P Freeman, IEEE Trans on Software Eng., **SE-10**, 68–72, 1984

> The two short papers making up the first session are actually quite difficult, since they need to be interpreted as parables in order to draw the conclusions. They really need to be allocated to an able student, who may also need some guidance. This item is *very* good for stimulating class discussion about the conclusions that should be drawn from the papers. The second paper provides a useful 'response' to the first session, and follows on rather nicely by discussing some practices that can help to overcome some of the problems identified in the first part.

Week 6: Quality Control

a) *Metrics, outlier analysis and the software design process*, M Shepperd, D Ince, Information & Software Technology, **31**, No 2, March 1989, 91–98
b) *The Impact of Programming Methodology on Program Complexity*, D L Carver, D B Simmons, J of Systems & S/W, **5**, 279–289, Nov 1985

> We have mainly used the paper by Shepperd and Ince as a means of enlarging upon the metrics issues covered in the lectures. This paper is a very well-written tutorial that can be used to stimulate a discussion about metrics and about design. The second paper takes a more 'classical' look at metrics, and is also concerned with trying to evaluate their worth.

Week 7: System Maintenance

a) *Mental Models and Software Maintenance*, D C Littman et al, Journal of Systems & Software, **7**, 342–355, 1987

This paper examines an area of the development cycle that lacks good papers. It reports on an experiment, and provides good scope for stimulating class discussion about both the problems of performing useful experiment, and also about the issues concerned in software maintenance.

A Layered Approach to
Teaching Software Project Management

David W Bustard
Department Of Computing Science
University of Ulster
Coleraine, BT52 1SA
Northern Ireland

Abstract. *The purpose of this paper is to present an approach to teaching project management that builds in layers up from general management concepts and techniques to those specific to software engineering. A course unit in this form has been presented to a class of final year undergraduates and some details of that experience are reported.*

1. Introduction

It is widely stated that the success of any software engineering project is largely dependent on the skills and experience of the project manager involved. Typical quotes [1] include:

Poor management can increase software costs more than any other factor (Boehm)

Poor management can decrease software productivity more rapidly than any other factor (Boehm)

The single most important factor in the success of a software project is the talent of its project manager (Brooks)

Given the acknowledged importance of project management it might be expected to have a central position in software engineering education. In practice, of course, it is usually technical issues that are given most attention, with management topics covered only towards the end of an undergraduate degree programme or perhaps even delayed to postgraduate level [3, 4]. This seems to arise because of a belief that:
1. Software management cannot be appreciated until the nature of software and its construction are both well understood.
2. The subtleties of management require a mature outlook and so the subject is better treated when students are physically older.

3. A degree course should reflect the fact that those entering the software engineering profession will initially have a technical role and only later take on management responsibilities.

These points do have some validity but there are counter-arguments:

1. Managing software production has much in common with management in general (e.g. preface to [5]) and so a substantial proportion of the activities involved can be appreciated with little or no knowledge of software development.

2. People effectively perform management tasks routinely in day to day living and so should be well prepared for a study of management concepts at any stage in a degree programme. For the same reason, management concepts are often easy to understand ("common sense") and so would seem to be better handled early on. Management issues are typically characterised by the uncertainly involved (risk management, cost estimation, etc.) and so it may appear preferable to first give students hard information (discrete mathematics, language semantics, hardware definitions etc.) before exposing them to the practice of working with guesses and approximations. In reality, however, such protection is unnecessary and has the unfortunate side-effect of placing more emphasis to the science rather than the engineering side of software production.

3. Management and technical staff work as a tightly knit team. Both groups have the same basic objectives: to complete each project on time, within budget and to a customer's satisfaction. Also, both groups need to be aware of each others responsibilities and activities so that they can be mutually supportive. This inter-dependence suggests that it might be best to teach project management in parallel with, or interleaved with technical material. It could even be argued that emphasis should be given initially to management activity as it provides the general framework in which the technical work proceeds.

The purpose of this paper is to suggest a way of ordering project management material that enables it to be taught flexibly with respect to technical software issues. The solution proposed is to cover the material in layers, dealing first with general management concepts and techniques before turning to those specific to software engineering. The next section discusses the details of this strategy and the following section reports on an early experience of developing and presenting a course unit in that form.

2. Project Management Layers

Having decided on a layered approach to project management, it then remains to determine the number and content of such layers. Managers are often described as "handlers of change" but perhaps more fundamentally they are *problem solvers*. With this assumption, a project management course can start by considering general material associated with problem solving before advancing to specific management topics. These topics can be divided into those relevant to any project and those specific to software. Problem solving itself is built on a collection of basic skills, the material for which can form the bottom layer of the hierarchy implied. This four layer structure is summarised in Figure 1, with each layer discussed in the sub-sections that follow.

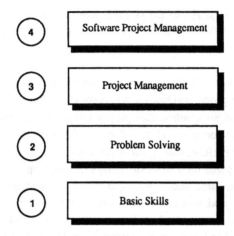

Figure 1: Four Layer Software Project Management Model

2.1 Basic Skills

Traditionally, a manager is expected to have adequate competence in three main skills [6]: conceptual thinking, administration and leadership. In this context, *conceptual thinking* essentially involves the generation and evaluation of ideas, *administration* is concerned with defining and implementing procedures and structures that bring order to all aspects of a project and *leadership* is the skill of achieving results through others. From these broad definitions it is then possible to identify more specific skills that can be considered directly. For example, conceptual thinking would involve *creative thinking* and *decision making* while administration would include *time management* and *delegation*. For each skill, there are then concepts and techniques that can be taught to aid its comprehension and development.

2.2 Problem Solving

The term *problem* is applied to the many difficulties that arise during the execution of a project. It also covers the concerns of the customer who commissions a project and indeed can be used to describe the project itself. Regardless of the scale of a problem, three definitions are sought in producing a solution: a definition of the *current situation* in which the problem resides, a definition of a more desirable *target situation* that alleviates the problem and a definition of the changes needed to transform the former into the latter.

Several informal procedural models for problem solving have been proposed [e.g. 7]. These identify a sequence of problem solving phases of the following general form:

1. *Identify problem*   what's going on?
2. *Gather information*   what are the facts?

3.	*Analyse information*	what are the root causes?
4.	*Generate solutions*	what can be done?
5.	*Select a solution*	what's the best thing to do?
6.	*Implement the solution*	how can it be done?
7.	*Verify the implementation*	has the problem been solved?

As with the software life cycle, some iteration among the phases is necessary when deriving and implementing a solution.

Problem solving models have also been produced specifically for projects [8]. One example is the *Soft Systems Methodology* (SSM), developed in the Department of Systems and Information Management at the University of Lancaster in England [9, 10, 11] over a period of more than twenty years. The main steps in SSM are summarised in Figure 2.

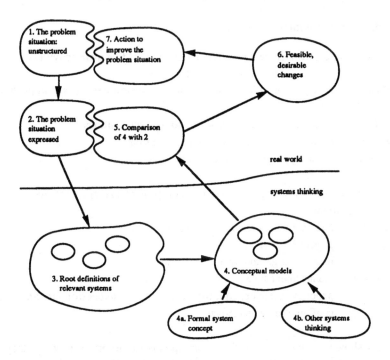

Figure 2: Soft Systems Methodology Outline

Stages 1 and 2 of the model deal with *problem expression*. Here a so-called *rich picture* is built up of the *problem situation* - "a situation in which there is perceived to be a mismatch between what is and what might, or could, or should be" [9]. Stage 3 deals with the definition of one or more viewpoints of the problem situation, each expressed as a *root definition*. For computing systems, for example, there would be a root definition for each different class of user of the system, representing their perspective of the problem situation. Stage 4 deals with the development and testing of *conceptual models*. A model is built by assembling the minimum list of verbs covering the activities which are necessary in a system defined in the *root definition*; this is essentially a data flow diagram. Phase 4a checks a model against a set of attributes which, from system theory [9], have to be present if a set of activities is to comprise a system capable of purposeful activity. For example, a system must contain a decision-taking process. Phase 4b involves the transformation of the model, if desired, into any other form appropriate to a particular problem. Again, in computing terms, this might be a formal description of a system expressed in an appropriate notation [e.g.12]. Phase 5 deals with the comparison of the conceptual models with the real-world to test them for adequacy. This phase is performed in collaboration with those involved in the problem situation to identify misunderstandings in the modeller's comprehension of the problem situation and to stimulate debate on possible changes to alleviate the problems present. The root definition and conceptual model may then be revised and the cycle repeated until a model has been produced that is satisfactory to all concerned. Implementation and verification are performed in phases 6 and 7, taking further revision cycles around the loop as necessary.

2.3 Project Management

Traditionally, project management is considered in terms of five main activities:
1. *planning*: predetermining a course of action
2. *organising*: arranging & relating work and responsibilities for accomplishment of objectives
3. *staffing*: selecting and preparing people for project positions
4. *directing*: bringing about purposeful action from staff
5. *controlling*: ensuring progress in line with the plan

These activities provide categories under which project management material can be covered. For example:
1. *planning*: task scheduling and cost estimation
2. *organising*: project team structures
3. *staffing*: interviewing, training and appraisal
4. *directing*: management styles
5. *controlling*: process metrics, quality assurance, inspection techniques and configuration management

The order shown for the five activities corresponds to the order in which they are of principal significance in a project: a project is planned, staff and management structures defined, people employed and the work tackled under management direction and control. In practice, however, most of the activities also have significance throughout a project and some of the procedures concerned are defined over many projects. For example, although cost estimation is most important at the beginning of a project when there may be competitive tendering for a contract, estimation must also be undertaken regularly during a project as a means of monitoring its progress. Also it is desirable to have cost estimation procedures that span several projects because the collective knowledge accumulated helps with future estimation [13]. The implication here is that studying some management activities at individual project level is too low. Instead that material should be presented from the point of view of the *environment* in which projects are undertaken. This suggests the following revised order of presentation: organising, controlling, planning, staffing and directing.

2.4 Software Project Management

All of the preceding material could be taught without reference to software as the ideas involved apply equally well to management in general. The order of coverage should be the same as that used in the project management component (i.e. organising, controlling, planning, staffing and directing) for the reasons given there, with a consideration of the software life cycle introduced when dealing with project control.

For software project management there are essentially no additional concepts to consider, only a need to investigate some specific management difficulties and to discuss supporting techniques and tools. In practice, however, this material is substantial because of the complexity of software projects. For example, any project will have a requirements definition phase but for computing applications the requirements can be very difficult to identify and also tend to evolve as a project proceeds. For particular types of computing problem, such as information processing, there are recognised methods and tools to support requirements identification and these can be examined in detail from a management point of view.

Other aspects of project management that are especially problematic for computing applications include cost estimation and configuration management. Here again, material particular to software projects can be presented, drawn from a rapidly growing body of knowledge and theory.

For the layered approach to be successful each layer should largely build on the one below. A discussion of software requirements in layer 4, for example, should build on a basic procedure for understanding the needs of customers established in layer 3 (dealing with general project management). That procedure, in turn, should build on some general problem solving strategy, such as SSM, covered in layer 2 - a strategy that involves the use of a range of basic skills, such as decision making, promoted in layer 1. Some basic skills may also be used directly in higher levels. For example, creative thinking can be discussed with respect to software project management for any type of open problem that has scope for an innovative solution.

3. The Layered Approach in Practice

The four layer project management model described in the previous section is a refinement to a course unit given to a final year undergraduate class for the first time in the academic year 1990-1991. The purpose of this section is to reflect on that experience. Some details of the material covered are presented and the discussion also partly serves as a justification for the layered approach.

The four layer model suggests a much greater separation of general and software management material than was actually attempted on the course. Only as the course proceeded did it become clear that such a separation was both desirable and practical. The actual order of material was as follows:

1. Introduction This component established a link between the management and technical sides of software production [42]. In particular, it included a summary of management activity with respect to a range of life cycle models [14, 15]. In the new proposal the introduction is much shorter, leaving technical software discussions to layer 4.

2. Basic Skills This component covered a range of concepts and techniques relevant to project management under four main headings: problem analysis, decision making, communication and organisation. *Problem analysis* discussed the general approach to problem solving along with a range of related techniques including brainstorming [7], lateral thinking [16, 17] and cause & effect analysis [18]. *Decision making* dealt mostly with the processing of information as an aid to making a decision. Examples of the techniques covered include impact analysis [15], cost benefit analysis [19] and risk analysis [20]. *Communication* dealt broadly with issues relating to the way in which people interact in a business context. The topics addressed included the means and principles of communication [21], ways of reaching consensus [22], the handling of meetings [23, 24] and the principles of negotiation [39]. *Organisation* dealt with time management, including delegation [23, 24]. In the new proposal, the base layer covers only the basic techniques, leaving problem solving to layer 2. All of the other topics remain, grouped under the three headings: conceptual thinking, administration and leadership.

3. Software Project Management This component followed the five management activities (planning, organising, staffing, directing and controlling) from the perspective of the software life cycle. *Planning* covered the Soft Systems Methodology (SSM) [9, 10, 11] as a requirements definition technique, project plans [25], task decomposition and representation [25, 26], planning tools [27, 28] and estimation methods [13]; *organising* dealt with management structures [29]; *staffing* dealt with interviewing [23], retraining [30], turnover [31] and appraisal [23]; *controlling* covered management styles of communication, staff motivation [32, 33] and configuration management [36, 37, 38]; *monitoring* dealt with metrics [19, 34], quality assurance [19, 35] and inspections [15, 19]. In the new proposal this component is divided into general and software project management issues, with SSM moved into the problem solving layer.

All management concepts were discussed with respect to software engineering issues (even though the presentation order made this unnecessary). In introducing most topics it proved convenient to motivate the material with a simple example from another area before looking in more detail at a computing application. For example, planning was introduced by considering what might be involved in arranging a Christmas party and cost estimation was illustrated by trying to price the repainting of a room.

The technical side of large scale software production was dealt with in a software engineering course unit run at the same time. As this unit involved software development, the project management unit was constrained to use exercises that largely focused on management topics. In this respect, the decision to start with basic techniques proved advantageous because it was then possible to have students begin practical work after one or two lectures. Some exercises, such as those involving brainstorming [7] and principled negotiation [39], were tackled by student groups. Attempting to evaluate student performance in these cases would have been detrimental to the exercise so only individual work was assessed.

A total of eight exercises of varying sizes were set, worth from 1% to 7% of the 30% total for the continuous assessment component of the course. The largest exercise required the students to present and assess an assigned project management paper to the rest of the class. The presentations were spread out over the three month period in which the course was given and were scheduled to appear just after the corresponding general area was covered in class. The papers were largely selected from standard publications in the field [2, 40].

Some exercises tackled traditional subjects such as risk management and the use of a planning tool but others were a little more experimental. The first, for example, asked the students to produce an assessment scheme for the presentation exercise. This introduced them to the concept of *soft* problems for which there is no right answer only a defensible position. Credit was given for identifying a suitable set of assessment criteria and for a well argued case in favour of a particular distribution of marks. The exercise also encouraged the students to think about the purpose of the presentation and could have been used to introduce a discussion of ways to resolve conflicting opinions.

Another unconventional exercise was one in creative thinking. It had four parts, thus
1. Suggest two names for a database holding records of children with cardiac problems
2. Suggest two new rules of project management
3. Use the brainstorming technique (as individuals) to identify ways of getting the best performance from staff
4. Evaluate the brainstorming ideas (produced in an earlier practical class) on how best to maintain good relations with customers

Such exercises are difficult to assess objectively but this task was eased by requiring the students to explain how they arrived at their answers and giving substantial credit for that discussion.

4. Conclusion

This paper has presented a four layer model for the organisation of software project management course material. The layers become progressively more specific, moving from basic skills in conceptual thinking, administration and leadership, through general management issues to a treatment of the management of software itself. This division of material seems to offer some flexibility in how and where project management is treated in a degree programme. In particular, it allows the material to be spread out over several academic years so that basic concepts can be covered early in much the same way as discrete mathematics is currently taught in support of technical software development [41]. One possibility would be to develop a foundation unit in "problem solving" that spanned the bottom two layers of the hierarchy, to be followed later by a project management unit covering the remaining two layers. The foundation unit would encourage a methodical approach to problem analysis in all areas of a computing course and not just those parts directly related to software production. Overall, the layered approach has shown that additional structure can be given to the basically fragmented material associated with management, thereby improving the coherence of any course in which the material is presented.

5. Acknowledgements

The ideas presented in this paper were developed during periods of sabbatical leave at the British Telecom Research Labs in Martlesham Heath and at the Software Engineering Institute in Pittsburgh. Many people at the two sites helped either directly or indirectly to shape the ideas, especially Peter Rigby and Huw Roberts at British Telecom and the Education Program Group (led by Professor Norm Gibbs) at the Software Engineering Institute. In the latter case, the education material developed by Jim Tomayko [1, 2] and the project management Continuing Education course material, produced under the guidance of Maribeth Carpenter and Harvey Hallman, were a particular influence.

Bibliography

1. Tomayko, J.E.: Software Project Management Video Course, Video Dissemination Project, Software Engineering Institute, Carnegie Mellon University, Pittsburgh, Pa., 1989
2. Tomayko, J.E.: *Software Project Management*, Curriculum Module SEI-CM-21-1.0, Software Engineering Institute, Carnegie Mellon University, Pittsburgh, Pa., July 1989
3. Ardis, M. & Ford, G.: *1989 SEI Report on Graduate Software Engineering Education*, Tech. Rep. CMU/SEI-89-TR-21, Software Engineering Institute, Carnegie Mellon University, Pittsburgh, Pa., June 1989
4. Ford, G.: *1990 SEI Report on Undergraduate Software Engineering Education*, Tech. Rep. CMU/SEI-90-TR-3, Software Engineering Institute, Carnegie Mellon University, Pittsburgh, Pa., March 1989
5. Brooks, F.P.: *The Mythical Man-Month*, Addison-Wesley, 1975
6. MacKenzie, F.P.: *The Management Process in 3-D*, in [40]
7. Osborn, A.: *Applied Imagination*, Scribners, New York, 1953
8. Rosenhead, J. (ed): *Rational Analysis For a Problematic World*, Wiley, 1989

9.   Checkland, P.B.: *System Thinking, System Practice*, Wiley, 1981
10. Checkland, P.B. & Scholes, J.: *Soft Systems Methodology in Action*, Wiley, 1990
11. Wilson, B.: *Systems: Concepts, Methodologies and Applications*, 2nd Edition, Wiley, 1990
12. Jones, C.B.: Systematic Software Development Using VDM, Prentice-Hall International, 1986
13. Londeix, B.: *Cost Estimation for Software Development*, Addison-Wesley, 1987
14. Boehm, B.W.: *A Spiral Model of Software Development and Enhancement*, in [40]
15. Gilb, T.: *Principles of Software Engineering Management*, Addison-Wesley, 1989
16. De Bono, E.: *Lateral Thinking For Management*, Penguin, 1971
17. De Bono, E.: *Six Thinking Hats*, Penguin, 1985
18. Ishikawa, K.: *Guide to Quality Control*, Asian Productivity Organisation, 1982
19. Pressman, R.S.: *Software Engineering - A Practitioner's Approach*, McGraw-Hill, 1987
20. Bunyard, J.M. & Coward, M.J.: *Today's Risks in Software Development - Can they be Significantly Reduced*, in [40]
21. Parkinson, C.N. & Rowe, N.: *Communicate*, Pan, 1977
22. Linstone, H. & Turoff, M.: *The Delphi Method - Techniques and Application*, Addison-Wesley, 1975
23. Video Arts: *So You Think You Can Manage?*, Methuen, 1984
24. Adair, J.: *Effective Time Management*, Pan, 1982
25. Fairley, R.E.: *A Guide for Preparing Software Management Project Plans*, in [40]
26. Cori, K.A.: *Fundamentals of Master Scheduling for the Project Manager*, in [40]
27. Computer Associates, *SuperProject Expert*, 1986
28. Claris Corporation, MacProject II, 1989
29. Fife, D.W.: *How to Know a Well-Organised Project When You Find One*, in [40]
30. McGill, J.P.: *The Software Engineering Shortage: A Third Choice*, in [40]
31. Bartol, K.M. & Martin, D.C.: *Managing the Consequences of DP Turnover*, in [40]
32. Blanchard, K. & Johnston, S.: *The One Minute Manager*, Berkley, 1983
33. Boehm, B.W.: *Theory-W Software Project Management: Principles and Examples*, IEEE Transactions of Software Engineering, Vol. 15, No. 7, July 1989
34. Mills, E.E.: *Metrics*, Curriculum Module SEI-CM-12-1.0, Software Engineering Institute, Carnegie Mellon University, Pittsburgh, Pa., December 1988
35. Brown, B.J.: *Assurance of Software Quality,* Curriculum Module SEI-CM-7-1.1, Software Engineering Institute, Carnegie Mellon University, Pittsburgh, Pa., July 1987
36. Tomayko, J.E.: *Software Configuration Management*, Curriculum Module SEI-CM-4-1.3, Software Engineering Institute, Carnegie Mellon University, Pittsburgh, Pa., July 1987
37. Feiler, P.H.: *Software Configuration Management: Advances in Software in Software Development Environments*, Tutorial Presentation, 12th ICSE, Nice, March 1990
38. Babich, W.A.: *Software Configuration Management - Coordination for Team Productivity*, Addison-Wesley, 1986
39. Fisher, R. & Ury, W.: *Getting to Yes - Negotiating Agreements Without Giving In*,

Arrow, 1987

40. Thayer, R.H. (ed): *Software Engineering Project Management*, IEEE Computer Society Press, 1988

41. Ince, D.C.: *An Introduction to Discrete Mathematics and Formal System Specification*, Clarendon Press, Oxford, 1988

42. Rook, P.: *Controlling Software Projects*, in [40]

Seven Lessons to Teach Design

J.P. Jacquot, J. Guyard

Université de Nancy I – ISIAL – CRIN

Campus V. Grignard — BP 239

F-54506 Vandœuvre-lès-Nancy, FRANCE

Key-Words

Software Engineering, Education , Teaching Design, Couarail

Abstract

Design is probably the most important topic to teach in a software engineering course, but it is also the most difficult. Beside trying to formalize the design activity, it seems equally important, from a pedagogical point of view, to understand why design is hard and what its prerequisites are. This paper presents an analysis of actual design errors found in students' projects. These errors fall into seven categories. Each category is analyzed in order to identify the root difficulty and to suggest some pedagogic solutions.

1 Introduction

A common debate among the software engineering community is where to draw the dividing line between "programmers" and "software engineers." To go beyond such ready made, and false, answers as "a software engineer is the team leader", "is one who uses XXX design formalism", or worse "is one who has followed a software engineering curriculum", we need to investigate deeper criteria.

A traditional criterion is to focus on the engineering part of the activity. An engineer is then a person who knows how to apply scientific results to produce artifacts and how to manage projects. Following this criterion, we have built a software engineering curriculum focusing on state of the art techniques and project management [Jacquot 90]. However, we constantly note at the end of each year that some of our students well deserve their qualification as "engineer" while others remain "high-level programmers". Although this judgement must be tempered by the fact that employers greatly appreciate our students, we still feel some kind of dissatisfaction.

An analysis of our judgement has shown that it is mostly motivated by the *design capabilities* of the students. In fact, a software engineer is a professional who knows how to *design* software. Then, the problem facing us is: "can we teach design?" Once again quick answers such as "oblige students to use Abstract Data Type techniques," or "teach them graphical design formalisms and tools" have proven insufficient. Examinations show that our students have a reasonably good theoretical knowledge of these matters but projects show they fail to instantiate and adapt this knowledge in practical situations. So, is teaching design hopeless?

We do not think so; but, to be honest, we do not presently see how to build a design course. The main reason is that design in general, and software design in particular, is not very well understood as an activity. Experimental studies, see [Hoc 88] [Visser 90] for instance, tend to indicate that current design formalisms, methods and tools are simple-minded when compared to the complexity of the design activity. In fact, *designing is very hard; and teaching design still harder.*

In this paper, we want to analyse where and why students' designs fail. Since our aim is mostly pragmatic — to improve our teaching of design — we have tried to track down actual difficulties through observation. This is by no means a rejection of "theoretical" studies aiming at defining design *methods*, but only a complementary point of view. In fact, writing this paper has made us discover that teaching design should focus equally on presenting (semi-)formal methods, and on promoting an adequate state of mind.

The remainder of the paper is organized as follows. The second section discusses the problem of getting data about designs. The main point is that written design documentation is a poor help in uncovering students' difficulties. Indeed, most design errors show up during maintenance time, i.e., just after students' projects stop! The third section presents our seven lessons. Each one introduces the problem, presents examples of failure, analyses the difficulty, and quickly discusses our present solution.

2 Collecting data

When we began to write this paper, we received a shock. The initial idea was simple: compile our shelf full of students' project documentation to extract common patterns of design errors. The verdict was soon brought in: we were unable to analyse those documents in depth. Indeed, qualities in a design, the best and the worst aspects often appear long after it has been written: in the delivered piece of software, during maintenance, and through its reuse in similar projects. This "discovery" tells us two things. First, the feedback we gave to students (through grades and comments) was too global and syntactic. Second, evaluation of a design requires an extensive knowledge of the software acquired by actually working with it.

So the kind of analytical study we want to do requires a software product:

- which has several actual users

- whose development process has been monitored

- which is maintained.

Fortunately, *Couarail* meets these requirements.

Couarail is a locally developed bulletin board system. Its first version was installed in 1984 on the UNIX machine of the Computer Science Laboratory (CRIN). Since then, it is by far the most popular tool among the researchers (around 200 people) who use it daily. Considered as a critical component of the CRIN communication organization, *Couarail* is regularly maintained by one of the authors of this paper. The current X version was prized at a national students' software contest organized by NCR-France.

From a pedagogical point of view *Couarail* is a very good project: the file management includes all the concurrent access difficulties, users are really hard to please on the interface quality, the size of code (around 13,000 lines of C) requires proper software engineering techniques while being still manageable. Since 1987, each software engineering class has had to work on a new version of *Couarail* (either in group or individual projects.)

All these projects enjoyed common organisation features:

- students are provided with all previous implementations of *Couarail* which are labeled as *prototypes*; these prototypes are the main "requirements."

- we impose backward compatibility for data; i.e., the new design is focused on the architecture, not on data organisation.

- portability on all the UNIX machines of the research and education networks is required.

- at the end of the project, we must be able to replace the current version used at CRIN by the new one.

The use of previous software as requirements is obviously a controversial point. Apart from the fact we lack a proper requirement document (writing it would be a project in itself and this point is treated elsewhere in the curriculum,) we think it gives students the opportunity to struggle with a not-so-uncommon real-life setting. Many students will be hired to work on existing projects, rarely conforming to state-of-the-art software engineering practices. Moreover, we feel that inducing requirements from existing software (either true prototype or old implementation) is essential when working on domains which are not well understood (as is electronic communication for our students.) Actually, this project is focused on *design quality* rather than on adequacy of an implementation with respect to a requirement document.

Couarail is now integrated to the common set of subjects proposed for the *professional projects*. These projects, realized by small teams, are aimed at providing students with an experience of a practical problem such as installing, porting, customizing, or maintaining a real software. Although *Couarail* was not initially planned to be focused on design activity, this multi-year project now proves to be a good source of information.

The observations which back up our analysis are all taken from the history of *Couarail*. They come from two main activities: bug-fighting during maintenance and monitoring of projects. This usage of a unique source of information raises the question of the generality of our analysis. Without denying the risk to be too anecdotal, we propose two answers to the objection. First, *Couarail* covers many types of programming problems (multi-user data-base, multi-processes, inter-process communication, user-interface, backward compatibility, ...) and at least 25 people have participated in the developments and maintenance. Moreover, we have screened all the symptoms, with the criterion that a symptom type must at least appear in two different versions and/or projects. Second, *Couarail* is the only piece of software for which we have records about *all* the life-cycle stages over seven years. Another project quite enjoys this property except for the maintenance stage: our teamwork project [Jacquot 90]. But, when we tried to extract clear symptoms and analysis, we found that our three-year experience has not given us a sufficiently deep knowledge of the design aspect of this project.

The last remark is very important since it explains partly why design is so difficult to teach: the feed-back loop, which is necessary to improve our design courses, takes many years to close effectively. By comparison, we have attained a satisfying teaching approach for complex activities such as requirement writing and project management in less than 2 years.

3 Seven lessons in teaching design

In this section, we discuss seven points which provide an explanation of numerous failures (either long-lasting bugs or unsuccessful projects) associated with *Couarail*. In naming them "lessons", we want to emphasize the idea that they must trigger questions about our teaching: what is presented and what remains?

Strikingly, most of the lessons appear quite naive. However, we have never seen them included in discussions about design. Indeed, they are generally considered as implicit prerequisites. From our view, building a design course without explicitly exploring those prerequisites and basic abilities is probably akin to building a house on sand.

3.1 Understanding the facilities

Building a software product implies using several complex facilities. The most prominent ones are the programming languages, the processors and the run-time environment. Many functionalities of theses facilities must be taken into account during the design stage, rather than only during the coding stage. Some services, or lack of, provided by the utilities will generate critical problems for exploiting and maintaining the application if they have not been clearly identified. As far as students are concerned, this kind of error originates in the fact they are not used to mistrust a tool a priori and to express the dependency from a tool. We have observed two failures associated with tools.

The first example is rather classical. The X version of *Couarail* suffered from erratic crashes. The cause, hard to identify, was a continuous growth of the allocated memory which ended up by violating the process fixed bounds. Fixing the bug was hard since it involved interaction between two concurrent processes (user-interface and data-base management.) Without exception, students omitted to integrate the constraint of a self-made memory management into their design, used as they were to more or less automatic memory managers.

The second example concerns the integration of two user-interface into *Couarail*: one for ASCII terminals and the other for bitmap terminals. The project failed because the students' design was a total mismatch with the object-oriented model supported by the *Sunview* library. In fact, students failed to realize that the facilities (curses and Sunview) implied two different dialogue structures: one, classical, driven by the application, and one by the user.

Such errors should not surprise us: students' whole previous experience prepare them to do so.

What can we do to teach students to include facilities into their design? Let us note that there is no straight answer for the two previous examples. A bare minimum is to force students to make explicit in their design what is considered as transparent and pushed down until the coding step. This can lead to prototype the use of a facility to specify its operational constraints and conditions. For instance, a recent design document written by our students indicated that LEX would be used, but considered this point as a simple implementation problem. To the question: "how LEX fits into the design?", the only answer was "LEX will do that."

One of the solutions to this pedagogic problem is to force students to be explicit and specify systematically the use of facilities. When a design document contains such a sentence as "this tool facility will do that for me", we must reply "Ok, we agree, but do specify it!"

3.2 Identifying the environment

Requirements indicate the functionalities expected from the application, but also the conditions of its use: an environment encompassing hardware, software and human. Meeting the constraints of the environment is an obvious goal of the designer. However, the next three failures show us this is not so obvious.

Although a great emphasis had been put on portability, we had a hard time to port the X version of *Couarail* from the education network to the research network although both are based on UNIX machines and Ethernet. A first problem, never really elucidated, probably arose from window managers (a great idea of X but which leads to unreasonable difficulties!) A second problem was the impossibility of launching *Couarail* through the "remote shell" command of UNIX. The cure has consisted in a complete rework of the initialisation procedure. In each case, students forgot to enquire about the typical use of *Couarail*.

A second failure was more subtle. One of the brightest designs of *Couarail* included a true data-base server which should run as a deamon to which interface managers should connect. The major restriction was a bound of about 15 simultaneous connections. Indeed, this is really short for a bulletin board system servicing a community of 200 people!

A third failure is the loss of an apparently innocuous feature between the first versions and the current versions: users can no more specify a board to go on the command line running *Couarail*. Although this feature disappeared in 1988, people regularly try to use it nowadays! Reintroducing it is impossible except by making an awful "hack."

The common denominator of these three failures is overlooking important environmental constraints. It could be argued that the requirements were faulty. Indeed, but we think that one of the *fundamental qualities of a good designer is to identify such flaws* (ambiguity or lack of information) as earlier as possible. Once again, we do not think that traditional curricula suitably prepare students to this kind of systematic criticism: typical programming assignments are focused on a technical point (algorithmic construct, data-structure, programming tool, ...), not on the production of a real-life software.

Then, our pedagogical problem is to induce a state of mind in which constructive criticism and analysis become natural. The main difficulty with such an objective is due to time constraints. On the one hand a project which exemplifies environmental constraints is by necessity of important size, and so will require several months to be fulfilled; we think that any project must go until implementation. On the other hand, forbiding development work until a "good" design has been produced requires many iterations between student and staff and so, will consume a lot of time. Our current solution is to use two projects and stress the environment problem as a by-product. The first project is associated with the Graphic User Interface course, requirements and design are quickly made with the help of a staff member and the final software is criticized by stressing design inconsistencies. The second project is the teamwork project where a more intensive work on requirement writing is required from the students.

3.3 Using design formalisms

When being presented with software life-cycle models, students agree on the necessity of a clearly identified stage for the design. Unfortunately, when working on a project, they seem unable to insulate this fundamental activity from others.

A typical failure with respect to this point concerns the documentation of the current version of *Couarail*. This application is architectured on two processes which communicate through UNIX *pipes*. The communication is complex and involves several types of data, commands and error messages. Defining a communication protocol is an obviously critical design activity. Although we urged students to write down this protocol, we never got any useful description.

There are two possible causes for this kind of failure: students did not understand *why* it was so important to have a paper description different from their program code, and they did not know *how* to write such a description. We think the second cause is the major one. As a justification, we just note that the many activities of an informatician are always taught with an associated formalism, except design.

It could be argued that teaching a design formalism (say VDM [Jones 86], or LARCH [Liskov 88], or anything else) would be a remedy. We do not agree since the difficulty is more subtle than that. A designer must be able to use several formalisms because no single one could serve all parts of a complex software. For instance, in the case of *Couarail*, three different formalism types must be used: a user-interface specification formalism for the external interface, a grammar for the communication protocol, and a functional design formalism for the data-base management component.

Our point is that students must not necessarily learn new formalisms to design but learn how to use already known formalisms in a new context. Our current solution lies midway between using new or old formalisms. For the teamwork project, we require that a student studies [Liskov 88] and writes a synthetic document presenting the design method and proposing an instance of the presentation framework adapted to the project. This framework must be used by the whole team to present their designs when applicable, other presentations (with automaton and grammars) being also required when best suited. The main idea is to replace the *passive* attitude of just using a formalism, by an *active* attitude of elaborating an adequate framework.

3.4 Prototyping is not designing

Convincing students to build a prototype is difficult. But more difficult is to convince them to throw away a prototype, be it self-built or given, to design an architecture. In fact, an early prototype is a substitute for requirement documents, not a model of the final architecture. A typical error is to extend the prototype to produce the software.

The current version of *Couarail* suffers badly from this kind of error: many critical pieces of code dealing with file access are simply duplicated in each procedure using them. Obviously, a good design should define specific file access procedures, only to make a coherent error recovery scheme possible. Our aborted tentatives to clean the code unambiguously show that it is a major design decision.

The cause of this failure is easy to trace back. We gave the students a version of *Couarail*, stressing its prototype nature. Unfortunately, they did not understand what this nature exactly means: keeping the ideas but putting the code in the waste-basket!

More generally, the main problem with prototyping is to decide when to stop. This is indeed the critical issue but it seems foreign to our students. As we already pinpointed in a previous paper, students are only used to develop prototypes. Academic assignments are aimed at understanding a technical concept by its practical use, not at using it to design software. So the design of delivered programs is a result, not a starting point, of the projects.

Teaching our students the good use of prototypes is of primary importance. However, it is difficult in practice. Once again, time plays against us since the need to develop a prototype appears only with sufficiently complex projects but then its development can last too long. Using fast prototyping systems could be a good answer to the difficulty but requires the student to be fluent with them.

We try to overcome the difficulty by two means. The first one is to suggest the development of some "paper prototype" for the teamwork project. The idea is to get the benefit of a true prototype (by working with examples) without the cost of programming. The second one is to propose projects for small groups during which an operational software must be produced from a given prototype. Neither solution is by any means perfect but they are a reasonable first approximation.

3.5 Reusing designs

One of the current curses in software production is the tendency to build each new project from bare ground. The problem is mostly due to the incapacity of present programming technology to provide us with off-the-shelf components. In [Santhanam 90], an interesting solution is presented. Unfortunately, such ideas are unpractical in our present curriculum organization. Our approach is then to promote reuse at the higher level of design. This is achieved by systematically giving students pieces of software close to the project they have to realize. This simple idea should not mask the following difficulty.

The very first version of *Couarail* (called *continuum* at the time) contained a very big bug: users were never assured that a posted message would not be lost. The reason was that users worked on temporary personal copies of message files which were then pushed back in the common repository; in case of simultaneous postings, the last user to finish was the winner! The explanation for the bug was very clear when it appears that *continuum* was a straightforward reuse and adaptation of a mail reader: mail files are not shared by several users.

Our lesson of this story is that reusing design is effective provided that all the differences between the existing software and the new project have been identified and analysed. Such work requires two basic capabilities:

- reverse engineering up to the *rationales* for design decisions (even good design documentation is generally terse on the subject)

- deduction of implementation constraints from implicit requirements.

How to teach these capabilities remains an open question for us.

3.6 Designing a design strategy

Design is a complex activity which must be planned to be successful. Unfortunately, no general technique exists yet. The apprentice designer has then a first, difficult, problem to solve: "What can I do now?" Two answers, equally bad, use to appear.

The first answer is to rush to program "obvious" components. If not useless, these components will probably be the sources of many problems hereafter. Most of the crashes of *Couarail* are attributable to over-optimistic assumptions on the data presentation (fixed number of blanks, user name only in lower case letters, ...) The cure always follows the same pattern: to replace the offending simple code by a more general one. The missing strategical design decision has been to "program defensively": i.e., to systematically list potential data malformations and accommodate them.

The second answer is to rush to write a design document conforming to a given standard syntax. Each year, the teamwork project offers us the opportunity to read a perfectly structured design document whose content consists only of a paraphrase of the requirements and of nice diagrams but which are void of meaning!

Learning to plan design activity should be a fundamental aim of a software engineering curriculum. Teaching intensively a well formalized design method is probably necessary, but we are not convinced it is sufficient. The current methods provide a much needed syntax and some useful hints, but fail to give universal guidelines. In fact, recent works on design strategies (see [Visser 90] for instance) tend to comfort Shneiderman [Shneiderman 80] when he claims that nearly nothing is known in this area. When confronted with such an absence of knowledge, we can only resort to training for which the academic structure is not well suited.

3.7 Measuring design

Overdue projects or useless products are common in the computing community. While it is tempting to blame bad practices, it should not be forgotten that software engineering has a unique feature: there is no formal tool to assess the quality of a design before completion of the project – [Sommerville 89] is unambiguous about the poor practical value of current design metrics for instance.– Other engineering fields have mathematical or analogical models which can be used early in the design to reject unrealistic design decisions.

A failed *Couarail* project offers us a typical example of the problem. The bright design of a data-base server (already cited) led to a prototype which demonstrated the feasibility of the approach only, but could not be considered as usable product (this was a requirement of the project.) The main problem was a misjudgment of the development time implied by the design.

Computer scientists have very few tools to assess the quality of a design. Students have less so! Moreover, it is difficult to induce a critical attitude toward the design stage, because they are used to "patch" their design while coding. Students become conscious of the problem only when they must abandon a project because of a design which leads to unreasonable development time. This kind of failure is generally badly resented.

A possible solution is to run a "cross-project" where two teams work on the same project, both writing a design document but implementing the design of the other.

4 Conclusion

At the end of this study, we have been convinced that the design ability requires two different capabilities.

The first one is architectural sense: identifying functions, drawing modules, establishing interfaces, ... This capability is the visible tip of design since it appears in the document. Teaching it is not easy due to the lack of formal models, but existing rules of thumb and good sense allow to show students pragmatic methods.

The second capability is systematic critics. It requires an alert state of mind in which nothing is considered as granted a priori. Teaching such an attitude is probably impossible, but we can prepare the ground on which it can develop. At least, we must teach them that a deep critical analysis of the requirements for a software is the key to a successful design.

We hope that this analysis will help to build an effective design course. Although we do not pretend to be exhaustive or to have uncovered all the secrets of the design activity, we have now a good starting point to tackle the problem.

Acknowledgements

We wish to address our most grateful thanks to all people who have helped us in writing this paper. First are Peter King and the anonymous referees who have greatly contributed to bring the text to a readable state. Next are all our colleagues who have always kindly accepted the inconvenience to use new versions of *Couarail*. And, obviously, all students and colleagues who have participated, in one way or another, to the development of this application.

References

[Hoc 88] J.M. Hoc. *Cognitive Psychology of Planning.* Academic Press, London, 1988.

[Jacquot 90] J.P. Jacquot, J. Guyard, and L. Boidot. Modeling teamwork in an academic environment. In L. Deimel, editor, *Proc. of SEI'90 Conference*, pages 110–122. SEI, Lecture Notes in Computer Science, 1990.

[Jones 86] C.B. Jones. *Systematic Software Development Using VDM.* Prentice-Hall, 1986.

[Liskov 88] B. Liskov and J. Guttag. *Abstraction and Specification in Program Development.* MIT-Press, cambridge – mass. edition, 1988.

[Santhanam 90] V. Santhanam. Teaching reuse early. In L. Deimel, editor, *Proc. of SEI'90 Conference*, pages 77–84. SEI, Lecture Notes in Computer Science, 1990.

[Shneiderman 80] B. Shneiderman. *Software Psychology. Human Factors in Computer and Information Systems.* Winthrop Publisher Inc., Cambridge – Mass., 1980.

[Sommerville 89] I. Sommerville. *Software Engineering.* Addison-Wesley, third edition, 1989.

[Visser 90] W. Visser. More or less following a plan during design: oportunistic deviations in specification. *International Journal of Man-Machine Studies*, 33(3):247–278, September 1990.

Design Evolution:
Implications for Academia and Industry

Linda M. Northrop

William E. Richardson

Department of Computer Science

United States Air Force Academy

Abstract

Design technology has grown over the last thirty years in response to improved programming languages and a rapidly expanding software problem domain. Faced with rapidly developing design approaches, it is vital that a meta-study of design be accomplished periodically in order to keep this growth in perspective. Such a study is necessary to determine how design can be most effectively integrated into undergraduate computer science programs and how design should be taught and applied in industry.

This paper represents a brief summary of a recent meta-study of design. In this study, design growth, seen as an evolution, was charted and a taxonomy of design approaches was produced. From this taxonomy, design approaches were analyzed in terms of their underlying theory and were categorized into generations. The results of this study, as presented here, are recommendations for the integration of design into undergraduate computer science programs with a software engineering component and recommendations for the training and use of design in the industrial sector.

Introduction

Design is inherently difficult and inherently difficult to teach. During the past thirty years several design approaches have been documented and practiced. Design technology has grown in response to both a rapidly expanding software problem domain and improved programming languages. The problem domain has gone from small, sequential, data processing systems to very large, real time, distributed systems. Maintenance problems and the software crisis have precipitated a cry for reuse of tested components and for greater system modularization. Design methods which have sufficed for years are in many instances now ineffective.[MEY88] At the same time, language research is increasingly centered on non-procedural, object-oriented languages. Although the books and tools for these languages lag the requirement, these languages have undoubtedly spawned the current leading edge design approach. Previous design approaches are simply not satisfactory for object-oriented implementation. [HEN90]

The change from one design approach to the next has not involved revolution, but rather, has been a natural evolution. Analysis of this design evolution reveals some interesting findings about the importance of the theory of design and similarities and differences among the various design approaches. These discoveries have direct ramifications on the teaching of design and the application of design methods in industry.

In this paper we first present the history of software design approaches and discuss a taxonomy for these approaches. We then provide, in table form, an in-depth analysis and comparison of these approaches followed by a brief summary of the table contents. Based on this analysis, we conclude with several recommendations for the inclusion of design in computer science curricula and the advancement of design applications in the industrial setting.

Taxonomy of Design Approaches

The design approaches which have endured have been precipitated by both programming language developments and increased sophistication and breadth in the problem domains for which software systems are being designed. Indeed, the very idea of a design approach was an anathema until the late 1960's when people began to think about programming techniques. No one would have conceived of creating abstract data types if the only mode of expression was assembly language. And so, while the design process ideally precedes implementation, it is the language inventions which have necessitated new approaches to design. Language evolution in turn has been a natural response to enhanced architecture capabilities and the ever increasingly sophisticated needs of programming systems. We have identified five distinct design approaches which impacted the software design discipline: function-oriented design, data flow-oriented design, data structure-oriented design, object-based design, and object-oriented design. We have chosen in this discussion to exclude the few formal design approaches which fall outside this framework.

For purposes of this paper we have differentiated among design approaches, design methods, and design attributes. Design approaches are the general categories of design (e.g., data flow-oriented). A design method is a specific instance of a design approach (e.g., Yourdon's Structured Design). Design attributes are fundamental characteristics that are apparent in almost every design approach (e.g., abstraction).

Function-Oriented Design

The first notable design approach, which we will call the function-oriented approach, was essentially an outgrowth of the structured programming movement. It began in the early 1970's as a problem solving technique prescribed to precede structured programming; the function-oriented approach involves step-wise refinement of processing steps.[WIR71],[PAR72] Using this top down technique the functionality of the system is progressively designed and proceduralized. The data involved has little impact on the design and is actually a consequence of the procedures. This approach was a natural design technique for systems which would be implemented in the early high-level procedural languages and has been proven successful for number crunching applications and for simple sequential logic systems typical of those early programming years.

Data Flow-Oriented Design

As languages began to include data structures and language techniques began to concentrate on parameter interfaces, design approaches which concentrated solely on procedures were not adequate. Moreover, the increasingly prevalent information system applications dictated that input and output be addressed as well as the process. In response, the data flow-oriented approach, as exemplified in both the Structured Design Method promoted by Yourdon, Myers and Constantine and the Structured Analysis and Design Technique (SADT), moves beyond simply heuristics for functional procedure design. [MYE78], [ROS77], [CON79] The focus in this much more systematic approach is the flow of information between processes. The processes themselves are designed after the data flows into and out of the processes have been defined. The defined processes become the basis for the design structure which is depicted using structure charts. The structure is then refined using the modularization criteria coupling and cohesion. The data flow-oriented design approach has met with documented success in its targeted area of application, namely, sequential information systems with non-hierarchical data.

Data Structure-Oriented Design

In the late 1970's and early 1980's, as database applications grew in number, and database languages became available, the focus in these domains accordingly shifted from functionality to data. From these movements grew new design methods which likewise switched emphasis from the functionality of the programs to the structure of information; that is, to the data structures. The data structure-oriented approaches are based on the tenet that data structure drives program structure. As typified in the Jackson Structured Programming (JCP), the Jackson System Development (JSD), and the Logical Construction of Programs (LSP) design methods, the data structure approaches begin with the design of entities which model the problem.[CAM86], [JAC75], [JAC83] Actions, or functionality, are defined in terms of these entities. These techniques are soundly applicable in the database domains and systems with highly structured data for which they were targeted, but fail to adequately address functionality issues in other systems.

Object-Based Design

As systems grew in size and complexity, as applications shifted from information systems to real time and distributed systems, and as maintenance became an insurmountable problem, modularity and reusability became increasingly important. Language experts developed the concept of encapsulating data structure and behavior in abstract data types (ADTs). A whole family of languages, including CLU, Ada and Modula, which supported both abstract data types and separately compilable modules was developed. This new abstract data type perspective once again necessitated a fresh look at design. The methods described by Booch and Liskov in the 1980's are characteristic of the design approaches which address implementation using abstract data types.[BOO83], [LIS86] We will call these techniques object-based design approaches to correspond with the title given the languages which prompted them. The early object-based design approaches (e.g., derived from CLU) were predominantly academic inventions and have not been fine tuned to an industrial strength. However, the Ada design approaches built on these early foundations with reported success in the development of medium scale systems, especially embedded systems. Most significantly, however, the research behind object-based methods was the precursor for the latest advancement in design approaches - namely, object-oriented design.

Object-Oriented Design

Object-oriented design approaches have been described as the natural result of design technique evolution and the culmination of functional and data structure views into a single approach. In the object-oriented model, systems are viewed as cooperating objects which encapsulate structure and behavior and which belong to classes which are hierarchically constructed. All functionality is achieved by messages which are passed to and from objects. The language support for the needed encapsulation, inheritance and polymorphism is readily available in C++, Eiffel, Smalltalk, Objective Pascal, CLOS and others. The boundaries between analysis and design in the object-oriented paradigm are extremely fuzzy. The whole process is inherently incremental and relies heavily upon prototyping. Recent books on object-oriented design by Meyer, Booch, Coad and Yourdon as well as the recent flood of articles in software engineering and computer science literature suggest that the object-oriented model is clearly the new frontier in software development.[MEY88], [BOO90], [COA90] The object-oriented approaches are touted as being capable of making great strides in yielding the much needed maintenance support and reusability. While it appears to be too soon to clearly identify application areas best suited to object-oriented design approaches, the early evidence suggests that the development of real time, large scale and distributed systems will be significantly impacted.

Analysis of the Design Approaches

The taxonomy of design approaches is further elaborated on the comparison chart in Table 1 below. This chart aids analysis of the design approaches in terms of major design attributes, problem domains, and other design issues. These major design attributes have also been called "design concepts." [FAI85], [PRE87] Such analysis provides the necessary perspective for serious consideration of design education and use.

Design Evolution

A review of Table 1 shows that the five design approaches yield a continuum in the major design attributes from the earliest (leftmost) to the most recent (rightmost). For example, functionality becomes decreasingly important as we proceed to the right on the chart. Accordingly, the concepts of data and data encapsulation increasingly become the more important issues as the functionality declines in importance. This evolutionary rather than revolutionary change of emphasis in design approaches is extremely significant because of what it means in terms of design education and application. These conclusions include:

First, this continuum of values for the various design attributes makes a very strong appeal to the need to understand the theory of design. With a solid understanding of design theory, including the significance of the design attributes, understanding a particular design approach will be straightforward. A thorough grasp of the attributes of design also serves as an excellent foundation for advancement to new design approaches as they are created.

Table 1

Comparison of the Five Design Approaches

	Function-Oriented Design	Data Flow-Oriented Design	Data Structure-Oriented Design
Major Design Attributes:			
Abstraction	Functional	Functional	Data
Modularity	Procedure	Process	Process
Refinement	Functional	Functional, Data	Data, Functional
Hierarchy	Functional	Functional	Data
Strategy	Functional Decomposition	Functional Decomposition	Data Decomposition
Language Targets	Procedural	Procedural	Procedural with Data Structuring
Reused Components	Procedures	Processes	Data Structures
Design Reuse Amount	Very Low	Low	Low
Information Hiding	No	No	No
Inheritance	No	No	No
Problem Domain:			
Scale	Small	Medium	Medium
Information System	Simple	Simple	Database
Real Time System	No	Some Extentions	No
Concurrent System	No	No	No
Other Design Issues:			
Life Cycle	Waterfall	Iterated Waterfall	Modified Waterfall
Direction	Top Down	Top Down	Top Down
Notations	HIPO, Flowcharts	DFDs, Structure Charts	Jackson, Warnier Diagrams

Table 1 (continued)

Comparison of the Five Design Approaches

	Object-Based Design	Object-Oriented Design
Major Design Attributes:		
Abstraction	ADT	Object
Modularity	Separately Compiled ADT	Groups of Classes
Refinement	ADT	Classification, Behavior in Classes
Hierarchy	ADT	Class
Strategy	ADT Decomposition	Object Decomposition
Language Targets	Object-Based	Object-Oriented, Object-Based
Reused Components	ADTs	Classes
Design Reuse Amount	Medium	High
Information Hiding	ADT Implementation	Class Implementation
Inheritance	No	Class
Problem Domain:		
Scale	Academic/Medium	Large
Information System	Academic/No	Database
Real Time System	Academic/Embedded	Good
Concurrent System	Academic/No	Good
Other Design Issues:		
Life Cycle	Modified Waterfall	Prototype Spiral, Water Fountain
Direction	Bottom Up	Modified Bottom Up
Notations	Boochgrams	Class, Category, Object Diagrams

Further, this continuum indicates that learning the specifics of one design approach will be beneficial rather than debilitating in applying other approaches which are closely aligned on the chart. However, there is other evidence which indicates that understanding one design method, without a real understanding of either design attributes or the design approach represented by that method, is of little help in making the transition to a new design approach.[PRE87]

Finally, if this evolutionary pattern continues at the rate it has been occurring over the last three decades, our current students can expect to see at least four new approaches to software design in their software development careers. This means that they must have a firm understanding of the basics of design so they can react to these changes, and, furthermore, they should have experience as close to the leading edge of this evolution as possible so they do not have so much ground to make up as they attempt to survive the transitions to even newer approaches.

Design Approach Generations

Further analysis of the chart in Table 1 indicates there exists great similarities among the first three design approaches (which we call the first generation design approaches). These similarities can potentially be used to benefit the individual learning various design approaches. Obviously, as you scan down the columns for these three approaches, there are several issues which are unimportant, for example, information hiding, inheritance, and large scale implementations. Likewise, there are some issues that are fundamental, such as process modularity, top down design, the waterfall life cycle, and procedural target languages.

Similarly, there are correlations between object-based and object-oriented design (which we call the second generation software design approaches). The object-based design approach has, for the most part, not been formalized beyond the academic approach described in the literature. However, the object-based approach can essentially be melded into the object-oriented approach by ignoring inheritance and making the reasonable correlation between abstract data types and classes. [BOO91]

Even though there is a moderate jump in the evolution between the first and second generation design approaches, the thread of the design attributes remains unbroken from generation to generation. Additionally, many of the techniques developed in the first generation are still necessary and incorporated at the lower levels of the second generation. For example, even in the object-oriented approach, the smaller scale concerns of data flow-orientation, like coupling and cohesion, are very relevant. [BOO91] Similarly, the behavior within objects of the object-oriented approach will ultimately require a function-oriented design approach. Consequently, in addition to pointing out the evolutionary nature of the software design taxonomy, analysis of Table 1 suggests that each succeeding generation depends upon the tenets of the previous generations to solve the simpler portions of the design. The generations truly build upon each other.

Integration of the Design Approaches

Based on the above taxonomy of design and the subsequent analysis, some generalizations can be made concerning the integration of design approaches into both the academic and industrial communities. Obviously, factors other than strictly design issues (for example, analysis approaches used, implementation language mandated, software problem domain encountered, etc.), will impact the integration of design approaches into these communities. Nonetheless, the following are reasonable guidelines for review of a curriculum or industrial program.

Academia: Function-Oriented Design First

The majority of undergraduate programs currently enter the design continuum from the function-oriented end because this is where most educators are comfortable, because the designs done in the early courses are simple and small, and because typical procedural languages like Pascal support this approach. Additionally, as noted above, all subsequent design approaches build on the function-oriented approach to some extent. If a successful software component is part of the agenda of these programs, there are concerns regarding how far down the spectrum they need to progress and how they get there in the limited time available. The above analysis demonstrated that it is imperative that software students be exposed to both the theory of design and several design approaches in the continuum, especially those on the leading edge.

These requirements would suggest that the theory of design should be introduced as early as possible in the curriculum. Furthermore, because of the inherent benefit to transitions between approaches derived from this theoretic underpinning, design theory should precede any attempt to introduce a different design approach. Naturally, the most obvious plan from here would be to transition in order down the design approach continuum until object-oriented design is studied. Unfortunately, few curricula will have the flexibility and time to proceed in this step-by-step fashion. Fortunately, there are some short cuts that will help ease the crunch.

First, it is important to note that some supporting issues, such as management of design (e.g., configuration management, quality assurance, etc.) and CASE tools, are relatively unchanging between design approaches. Further, experience has shown that it is possible to skip one of the data-oriented approaches without harm. [RIC88], [NOR89] Finally, because of the noted overlap and natural evolution, many second generation concepts and mind sets can be taught concurrently with first generation ideas.

With these short cuts in mind, an appropriate curriculum would contain the following ordered components:

1. Procedural language with function-oriented design.

2. Design theory.

3. Comparison of function-oriented design approach with object-based design approach.

4. Data-oriented design approach with a complete data-oriented method (including management and CASE issues).

5. Object oriented design approach.

Components one and two are obvious. From our experience, component three can be accomplished in several ways. In CS2 type courses, simple designs done in the functional style can be redone using object decomposition as the strategy. Additionally, ADTs fit very naturally into data structure courses and programming languages courses (when discussing object-based languages) which typically precede software engineering courses.

Component four is a standard software engineering project course using a data-oriented design method. [TOM87] Component five is a new course which is based on the rising technology of object-oriented design. Since the object-based approach will have been studied previously, this course can concentrate on issues like classes and inheritance which are unique to object-oriented development. Since the object-oriented approach can, with some compromise, be implemented using object-based languages, staying with procedural languages used in previous design approaches which are extendable to object-based languages (e.g., Ada, Pascal, or C) further reduces the overhead of this approach. Obviously, the use of object-oriented language to implement object-oriented designs is preferred, but until better compilers, books, and environments are more widely available for these languages, this may be too much to ask of a curriculum.

Academia: Object-Based Design First

A smaller number of undergraduate programs have chosen to start their students in non-procedural languages (e.g., Lisp, Smalltalk) or languages which are object-based (e.g., Ada). [FRA90], [CLA90], [PUG90] Such object-based and object-oriented beginnings are based upon recent discussions that the object model is a more natural mode of expression, that students can get an earlier acquaintance with larger scale problems via reuse of provided classes or packages, and that students will be spared the sometimes painful transition to this approach later in their academic careers. The concern with these programs, unlike those previously discussed, is not how far down the spectrum to progress, but how much, if any, of what preceded the second generation should they be conversant in.

As described earlier, the object-oriented design approaches borrow heavily from the earlier approaches. Students who don't bring that evolutionary perspective may lack some of the maturity needed to succeed in large scale object-oriented design. Also, the object model has not reached sufficient maturity to include management counterparts and automated tools nor a comprehensive method which systematically addresses the other phases of software development such as analysis, and testing. The object-oriented approaches seem not to be particularly well suited for information systems applications where the data flow-oriented approaches have succeeded. Since many software practitioners' work currently involves information systems, it seems important that students be acquainted with these techniques as well. Finally, based upon our analysis of design trends, the second generation approaches will undoubtedly pave the way for a yet unknown third generation. In order to make future transitions, students need to have a firm grasp of design theory.

These arguments suggest that at this point in order to present a successful software component, these programs must include both theory of design and some transition education to previous design approaches; applications remain diverse enough to warrant more than knowledge of strictly an object-oriented or object-based approach. Given these requirements, an appropriate curriculum would contain the following ordered components:

1. Non-procedural, object-based or object-oriented language with object-based or object-oriented design (respectively).

2. Design theory.

3. Comparison of function-oriented approach with object-based (or object-oriented) approach.

4. Object-oriented design approach.

5. Management issues and how they are addressed in other design approaches.

Components one and two are again obvious. Component three can again be accomplished in CS2 type courses and programming language courses where comparison methods would naturally fit. Components four and five would both be part of a software engineering course or sequence. The object-oriented approach would be practiced, but other approaches and management issues would be, at a minimum, carefully studied.

Industry: From First Generation Design

Unlike academia, industry is ultimately much more interested in a specific design method than in an understanding of the general concepts of design and design approaches. To generalize further about industry is difficult because many industrial designers are interested in a very small segment of the software problem domain. Therefore, it is necessary to divide the industrial software world into at least two groups. The first group, those who deal strictly with the design of data process or information systems, will likely not move into the second generation of design approaches. These companies will more likely take advantage of the development in fourth generation languages and new methods within the first generation of design approaches.

For the second group of industrial software developers, those doing large scale, real time, and/or distributed software systems, a move to the second generation is warranted, either now or in the near future. The question is "how to proceed?" The authors' experience has shown that people in the industrial setting have a firm grasp of, and are narrowly focused on, the particular design method espoused by their company. Too often this means that these software designers are far removed from their study of design attributes and design approaches. It would be possible to simply retrain these designers to an object-oriented design method without any education about the underlying attributes or approach. (We assume that since the object-based approach is, for the most part academic and a relatively minor degeneration of object-oriented approach, it would be unnecessary and unproductive for a company to transition through this intermediate step.) And to do so, would perhaps be faster in the short run. However, our analysis has suggested that prefacing the transition to the new method with study of the object-oriented design approach (and a study of the significant design attributes) would be of significant long term benefit to the company. [NOR90] This implies that transition to a new design method is best viewed as education first(design attributes and the object-oriented approach), followed by training (the specific object-oriented method required by the company.)

Conclusions

Design becomes more important as software systems become larger and when the software is embedded in other systems. Design has progressed from the simple functional decomposition methods that sufficed for very small sequential programs, through several stages where data gained in importance. Each of these design approaches resulted from gains in program language sophistication and an increase in the software problem domain, often brought about by advances in hardware technology.

Analysis of the advancement of the design approaches shows that the change in design, while rapid, has been evolutionary rather than revolutionary. There is no evidence that the factors causing these advancements in design are any less emphatic today than they have been for the last thirty years. Therefore, we must expect continued evolution in the discipline of software design.

Further analysis of the various design approaches gives rise to some interesting results about design, which can be summarized as follows:

1. An understanding of the underlying theory of the attributes of design is imperative as the foundation for advancing to new design approaches as they are created.

2. Knowing one design approach is useful in learning another approach, especially if they are adjacent in the design continuum. However, understanding one design **method** without an understanding of the design approach is not beneficial in a similar transition.

3. New design approaches are created every seven years on the average. This means software professionals must be able to move from one software design approach to another with relative ease if they are going to remain proficient in the field.

4. New generations of design approaches appear to depend upon understanding the previous generation for solution of the simpler portions of the design.

The application of this analysis suggests the importance of multiple design approaches in both the academic and industrial sectors. Specifically, the traditional university computer science program will start by teaching a procedural language and a simple function-oriented design approach. Transition to other approaches will be required to develop a software professional. Indeed, transition all the way through the approaches to object-oriented approach is recommended. However, this is possible only after the students are literate in the theory of design as the recommended curriculum for this transition indicated.

Other university programs will start with non-procedural languages and an object-based approach to design. The result is similar, however, this program will need to transition in both directions on the design approach continuum.

Finally, for those companies in the industrial sector designing software which is large scale, real time, and/or distributed, a transition to an object-oriented method is appropriate. This transition should not be simply a retraining from one design method to another, but should also include design education to derive the long term benefit from the required transition.

Design is a very dynamic skill with ever changing approaches. Constant review and analysis of the framework of software design will be necessary to force our university curricula and industrial training programs to take fullest advantage of new design technology.

BIBLIOGRAPHY

[BOO83]   Grady Booch, **Software Engineering with Ada**, Benjamin/Cummings Publishing Company, 1983.

[BOO91]   Grady Booch, **Object Oriented Design with Applications**, Benjamin/Cummings Publishing Company, 1991.

[CAM86]   J. R. Cameron, "An Overview of JSD," *IEEE Transactions on Software Engineering*, February 1986.

[CLA90]   Michael J. Clancy and Marcia C. Linn, "Functional Fun," *SIGCSE Bulletin*, Vol 22, Feb 1990.

[COA90]   Peter Coad and Edward Yourdon, **Object Oriented Analysis**, Prentice-Hall, Inc., 1990.

[CON79]   L. L. Constantine and E. Yourdon, **Structured Design, Prentice-Hall**, Inc., 1979.

[FAI85]   Richard Fairley, **Software Engineering Concepts**, McGraw-Hill, Inc., 1985.

[FRA90]   Thomas S. Frank and James F. Smith, "Ada as a CS1-CS2 Language," *SIGCSE Bulletin*, Vol 22, June 1990.

[HEN90]   Brian Henderson-Sellers and Julian M. Edwards, "The Object-Oriented Systems Life Cycle," *Communications of the ACM*, September 1990.

[JAC75]   M. A. Jackson, **Principles of Program Design**, Academic Press, Inc., 1975.

[JAC83]   M. A. Jackson, **System Development**, Prentice-Hall, Inc., 1983.

[LIS86]   Barbara Liskov and John Guttag, **Abstraction and Specification in Program Development**, McGraw-Hill, Inc., 1986.

[MEY88]   B. Meyer, **Object-Oriented Software Construction**, Prentice-Hall, Inc., 1988.

[MYE78]   Glenford J. Myers, **Composite/Structured Design**, Van Nostrand Reinhold Company, 1978.

[NOR89]   Linda Northrop, "Success with the Project-Intensive Model for an Undergraduate Software Engineering Course," *SIGCSE Bulletin*, Vol 21, Feb 1989

[NOR90]   Linda Northrop, *Software Engineering*, Product Software Engineering Training, Eastman Kodak Company, Rochester, New York, 1990.

[PAR72]   D. L. Parnas, "On the Criteria To Be Used in Decomposing Systems into Modules," *Communications of the ACM*, December 1972.

[PUG90]   John Pugh, "Object-Oriented Programming in the Computer Science Curriculum," *SIGCSE Bulletin*, Vol 22, Feb 1990

[PRE87]   Roger S. Pressman, **Software Engineering: A Practitioner's Approach**,Second Edition, McGraw-Hill, Inc., 1982.

[RIC88]   William E. Richardson, "Undergraduate Software Engineering Education" in *Software Engineering Education*, edited by G. Ford, Springer-Verlag, New York, 1988.

[ROS77]   Douglas T. Ross and Kenneth E. Schoman, Jr., "Structured Analysis for Requirements Definition," *IEEE Transactions on Software Engineering*, January 1977.

[TOM87]   James Tomayko, *Teaching a Project-Intensive Introduction to Software Engineering*, Special Report, Software Engineering Institute, Carnegie-Melon University, March 1987.

[WAR85]   P. Ward and S. Mellor, **Structured Development for Real-Time Systems**, Prentice-Hall, Inc., 1985.

[WIR71]   Niklaus Wirth, "Program Development by Stepwise Refinement," *Communications of the ACM*, April 1971.

[WIR86]   Niklaus Wirth, **Algorithms and Data Structures**, Prentice-Hall, Inc., 1986.

Teaching Software Design in the Freshman Year

Keith Pierce, Linda Deneen, Gary Shute
Department of Computer Science
University of Minnesota, Duluth
Duluth, Minnesota 55812-2496

Abstract. *Designing high-quality software is difficult, and therefore instruction in design should hold prominence in educating future software engineers, just as in other engineering disciplines. Nearly all software engineers receive their education within programs in computer science, but these programs typically provide inadequate instruction in design. The missing ingredient is instruction in the making of intelligent choices among design alternatives. We must increase the emphasis on the teaching of design principles for guiding the choice-making, not just in senior or graduate courses in software engineering, but throughout the undergraduate curriculum. In particular, the teaching of design in the introductory programming sequence can be improved. We present some examples of how instruction in design can be incorporated into the first courses in programming.*

1 The Design Phase of Software Engineering

It is not hard to defend the thesis that the design phase of a software product's life cycle is the single most important activity that determines the ultimate quality and profitability of that product. Good design leads to software that is robust and maintainable, has few bugs, is less expensive to develop, and has a long lifetime; bad design begets a product that is expensive to maintain, requires frequent bug fixes, and in the worst case is abandoned early in its life cycle, perhaps even before its initial release.

The design process is both highly creative and difficult, so it is not surprising that exceptionally gifted designers are scarce. However, more artifacts wait to be designed than those few gifted designers have time for. Therefore each traditional architectural and engineering field has developed a set of principles that guide designers of average ability in devising solutions of acceptable quality. Software engineering is the youngest engineering field, one that seems to require tools and techniques radically different from traditional engineering disciplines, and thus the underlying principles of good software design are not yet well understood. Nevertheless, in the generation or so of the field's existence we have acquired a body of knowledge (albeit smaller than those of traditional engineering fields) of how to go about design. All software engineers ought to obtain this knowledge, and therefore instruction in design should be an integral part of their education, as it is in all other engineering disciplines.

2 Deficiencies within the Undergraduate Computer Science Curriculum

Nearly all professionals entering the field of software engineering have graduated from computer science programs, and few receive graduate training. Thus, if instruction in design is to be improved, we must concentrate on the undergraduate curriculum in computer science. In preparation for the discussion we examine typical computer science curricula for the presence of instruction in design.

In the course sequence that typically begins the computer science program (CS1 and CS2) the major emphasis is on top-down functional decomposition using stepwise refinement. There also we find careful discussion of recursion, as well as increasing emphasis on data abstraction and the natural extension to object-oriented design and programming. But beyond the freshman year we find little instruction in the tools and techniques of design. A curriculum may include a senior course in software engineering that discusses other design methods such as data-flow design and object-oriented design [Sommerville 89]. But most courses focus narrowly on some particular domain of knowledge. If there is any discussion of design, it is in the context of observing the design of a particular class of products (e.g., compilers) or algorithms (e.g., file processing). Absent is any discussion of the intellectual activity that led to the discovery of their design.

The developers of a typical undergraduate curriculum seem to believe that design is so difficult that it should be avoided. It is easier to concentrate on safer subjects like compilers or file processing, where software designs are set in concrete and there ensues little discussion of the decisions that went into their design. But the overwhelming majority of graduates of computer science programs obtain employment involving some aspect of software development. Lack of literacy in design requires these employees to undergo extensive on-the-job training, which undoubtedly contributes to the increasing criticism by employers of the education received in the traditional computer science curriculum.

3 Teaching Design Means Teaching Choices

Texts for the introductory sequence in computer science concentrate on presenting the mechanics of top-down functional decomposition through stepwise refinement. Senior-level courses in software engineering may present the mechanics of Jackson Structured Programming. One should ask whether this approach teaches design as a creative activity. Some pessimists would argue that creativity cannot be taught and, therefore, neither can design. Rather than continue this rhetorical and nonproductive line of questioning, we turn for guidance to traditional, more mature engineering fields, where design *is* taught. One finds, for example, in the stated criteria of the Accreditation Board for Engineering and Technology (ABET) "... when *choices and decisions* must be made, engineering design is involved [italics ours]." This, to us, is the key to teaching design: the teaching of how to make rational choice among alternative solutions.

When one looks at instruction within computer science, one finds missing the teaching of design as the making of choices. When design is taught, it is systematically presented as a body of methods, not as a body of rational alternatives. It seems to us that instruction in design would improve dramatically by making this single modification in how we teach: presenting alternative design strategies and alternative solutions derived using these strategies, presenting the criteria for judging the quality of the alternatives, and forcing students in laboratory exercises to make and justify a choice among them.

We claim that this can be carried out effectively in the introductory sequence, and indeed ought to be, to impress on neophytes the need for decision-making during the development process.

4   Curricular Alternatives for Improving Design Instruction

Accepting the premise of the need for improved instruction in design within the undergraduate curriculum, we turn to strategies for implementation. Possible strategies are (a) proposing a completely new curriculum, (b) adding new courses in design, and (c) revising existing courses within the traditional computer science curriculum.

The Education Division of the Software Engineering Institute (SEI) has tackled (a) by proposing an undergraduate degree in software engineering [Ford 90]. In this proposal the entire undergraduate program is revamped in order to focus less on the science of computing and more on the engineering of software products. The degree emphasizes the software development process in general, and design techniques in particular, and presumably would correct the criticisms we have posed. The degree has merit and we support its serious discussion, but economic, personnel and bureaucratic factors will discourage many such programs from emerging soon.

Therefore, if the education of future software developers is to improve quickly, we must modify the curriculum and instruction within existing computer science programs. Proposal (b), to add courses in design, also has been considered by the SEI in its series of curriculum modules that aid in the creation of courses in software engineering. One of these [Budgen 89] is an excellent source for establishing a course in software design. The course (and the focus of nearly all other SEI curriculum modules) is intended to be at the graduate or senior level. While such a course is commendable, design cannot be taught in just one course near the end of a student's education; there must be repeated emphasis throughout the undergraduate curriculum.

We are led, then, to the thesis of this paper: that existing courses throughout traditional computer science programs be modified to incorporate instruction in design as often as possible, and that instruction in design be modified to include presentation of alternatives and the tools to analyze and make rational choices among the alternatives. Starting from the bottom up, we propose some modifications to the traditional introductory course that will improve the instruction in software design.

5   Design Methods and Strategies

To lay the groundwork for the discussion of specific recommendations, we first present an overview of software design. The following list comprises the best-known design methods and strategies, but is not intended to be exhaustive. The methods are intended to be generic; elaborate structured methods such as the Jackson Development System (JSD) are omitted.

5.1   Low-Level Design Strategies

Some common strategies employed in the design of small modules are:

1. Choice of basic programming constructs: sequence, selection, and iteration.
2. Count-controlled iteration versus event-controlled iteration.
3. Static versus dynamic data structures.
4. Recursion versus iteration.

5.2   High-level Design Methods

High-level design involves making decisions about the organization of modules. Some well-established methods are:

1. *Function-oriented design,* in which the design is decomposed into a set of interacting units having a clearly defined function.

2. *Object-oriented design,* in which a software system is viewed as a set of interacting objects having a private state.

3. *Data-flow design,* a method of arriving at a hierarchical functional decomposition, in which the hierarchy is derived from a data-flow diagram.

4. *Concurrent systems design,* in which an object-oriented or function-oriented design is realized as a set of parallel communicating processes.

5.3   Higher-level Architectural Design Strategies

The increased size and complexity of current software systems have introduced additional complexity to the design process. Mary Shaw contends that such complexity requires "architectural level" design strategies that capture essential properties of major subsystems and the ways that they interact [Shaw 89]. Although some overlap occurs with the list in the previous section, the list that Shaw presents is important enough to be repeated in its entirety.

1. *Pipes and filters,* in which modules are strung together, one module's output becoming the next module's input.

2. *Data abstraction,* in which a number of independent objects invoke each other's operations. (With the addition of inheritance, this is known as object-oriented programming.)

3. *Layered Systems,* in which the system is organized hierarchically, each layer providing services to the layer above it, each descending layer involved with a lower level of abstraction.

4. *Rule-based Systems,* arising from artificial intelligence applications, in which computation is organized as an unordered collection of rules, each of which gives a condition under which the rule applies and an action to take when it applies.

5. *Blackboard Systems,* used in knowledge organization applications, in which a central data structure represents the current state of computation, and a collection of independent processes check the state and update it if they can.

6 Low-Level Design Strategies for the Introductory Sequence

There are some aspects of design that are taught very well in introductory courses, such as top-down design, data abstraction, and the low-level design strategies outlined in section 5.1. However, we can do better. We must enforce at each opportunity the notion that the process of design is the process of making choices by providing examples of alternative designs and by encouraging analysis of their relative merits. In the following subsections we present several examples. We begin with suggestions for improving the instruction in two low-level design strategies: use of arrays and recursion.

6.1 Arrays: Incremental versus Non-incremental Design Strategies

Many textbooks present an excellent discourse on alternative memory management schemes (see [Helman et al. 90] for an excellent exposition). Tradeoffs are carefully discussed among the alternatives of using arrays, linked lists, binary trees, and so forth. But these texts may omit discussion of a more fundamental design choice, namely, whether to store data at all.

For instance, how many of us teach the use of arrays as a conscious choice of *design strategy*? More likely, we introduce the syntax and semantics of arrays, present a few simple examples, and then send students away with a programming exercise in which they are *required* to use arrays; the question of whether arrays are actually needed to solve the problem is immaterial. However, by making the choice to use an array in the solution to a problem, one has made a top-level design decision that affects the fundamental nature of the solution.

Guttag and Liskov lucidly illustrate this in their discussion of the design of a text formatter [Guttag, Liskov 86, page 274]:

> A good way to study the problem structure is to make a list of the tasks that must be accomplished. Here is a list for *format*:
>
> 1. Read input.
> 2. Interpret input.
> 3. Produce output.
>
> ... Although we have listed the tasks in approximately the order in which they might be carried out, we do not assume that this order will exist in the final program. In fact, for the tasks just given we have a major choice to make. We could complete each task before starting the next, but this problem does not require that all input be interpreted before output can be produced. We can thus do the job incrementally, interpreting the input and producing output as we go. Since an incremental solution is needed to satisfy our space constraints, we shall make this choice.

Thus, by making the choice to not use an array to store input, we have chosen to process input incrementally, either because the problem does not require reading the entire input stream prior to producing output, or because space constraints prohibit reading and storing the entire stream. This is a fundamental design choice that we should emphasize when arrays are introduced. Unfortunately, some textbooks don't help. For example, one text used as the prime motivation for introducing arrays the problem of finding the average of input values [Kay 85]. A perusal of other introductory texts yields little in the way of guidance.

One of the authors has used the following examination question to test the kind of thought process needed in order to make the general choice between incremental and non-incremental processing:

> Which of the following problems require the use of arrays for their solution? Explain.
>
> 1. Determine the mean of a large collection of numbers.
> 2. Determine the median of a large collection of numbers.
> 3. Determine the most frequently occurring value in a large collection of exam scores.
> 4. Given a collection of 200 numbers, input in the order 1st, 2nd, 3rd, ..., print the collection as a table in the following format:
>
> | | | | |
> |---|---|---|---|
> | 1st | 2nd | 3rd | 4th |
> | 5th | 6th | 7th | 8th |
> | ... | | | |
> | 197th | 198th | 199th | 200th |
>
> 5. Given a collection of 200 numbers, input in the order 1st, 2nd, 3rd, ..., print the collection as a table in the following format:
>
> | | | | |
> |---|---|---|---|
> | 1st | 51st | 101st | 151st |
> | 2nd | 52nd | 102nd | 152nd |
> | ... | | | |
> | 50th | 100th | 150th | 200th |

It has been our experience that without prior discussion of the concept, students do not score highly on such questions, leading us to the conclusion that designers (i.e., intelligent-choice makers) are made, not born.

6.2 To Recur or Not to Recur?

Serious discussions of choice-making also should be initiated when recursion is introduced. Problems having recursive solutions tend to fall into four categories:

1. The recursive solution, although conceptually simpler than an iterative solution, incurs a significant penalty in performance.

2. The recursive solution is primarily an artifice used to illustrate recursion, most likely using trivial tail recursion, but the problem is most naturally solved iteratively.

3. The recursive solution is simple and very expressive and incurs only the minor performance penalty associated with procedure calls and returns, but simple iterative solutions can be found with minimal effort.

4. The problem is recursive by nature — the recursive solution is conceptually simple, and iterative solutions are very difficult to discover.

The issue of when one should use recursion is complex, but the decision is clearer if one first categorizes the problem as above. One might argue that one should never use recursion as a design strategy for problems of type 1 or 2, should always use recursion for problems of type 4, and probably ought to use recursion for problems of type 3 only when it is critical to trade expressive simplicity for the small improvement in performance. The following question can be used on an examination or for in-class discussion to drive this point home.

> Classify each of the following problems into one of the four categories given above. Explain.
>
> 1. Tower of Hanoi.
> 2. Computing binomial coefficients.
> 3. Printing the contents of an array.
> 4. Tree search and traversal.
> 5. Finding the nth Fibonacci number.
> 6. Quicksort.
> 7. Recursive descent parsing.

When recursion is taught, we should emphasize the importance of categorizing the problem, and the significance of the tradeoffs that ensue from the choice to develop a recursive implementation. In particular, students should be brought to realize the misuse of recursion. However, a perusal of many popular texts shows a general lack of instruction in making choices for or against recursion. One text [Koffman 89] mentions tradeoffs, but frequently uses examples of type 2. Another text [Naps et al. 89] asks students to derive a recursive algorithm that finds the nth Fibonacci number without mentioning the horrible cost of such a solution. This text also seems to imply that the exponential complexity of the recursive solution of the "Towers of Hanoi" problem is caused by the recursion.

7 High-Level Design Strategies for the Introductory Sequence

We turn now to a discussion of higher-level design strategies in the introductory sequence. When the design of a typical problem is presented, a "correct" functionally decomposed solution is presented without consideration of alternatives. But any problem will have several reasonable designs that can be discovered either by taking a different tack during functional decomposition, or by using different design strategies such as object-oriented design or concurrency. The background needed to discover such alternative designs is accessible to students in the introductory sequence.

In the first subsection below we present a problem and three design solutions based on data-flow analysis. In the second subsection we give a solution to the same problem using pipes and filters. The third subsection describes yet another solution to the same problem, this time using concurrent design. Finally in the fourth subsection we introduce the design strategy of layered systems and give a different problem to illustrate it.

7.1 Data Flow Analysis: Creating Hierarchy from Dataflow

The goal of functional decomposition is to produce a hierarchical structure for all of the functions required to solve a problem, but seldom is there a discussion either of the rationale for selecting a particular hierarchy or of the fact that there are choices for organizing the design. Data-flow design is a powerful method for deriving the hierarchy from a data-flow diagram [Pressman 88, chapter 6]. In a standard curriculum, the method is not introduced until a senior course in software engineering, but an appropriately simplified strategy can be discussed in the introductory course. Plauger illustrates this dramatically using as an example the problem of writing a text formatter [Plauger 87]. Drawing heavily from his article, we present the problem and three alternative solutions derived from data flow analysis.

A simple text formatter reads lines of unformatted text and composes and outputs lines of approximately uniform width. Assuming that we avoid complexities such as hyphenation, a solution is presented by the data-flow diagram in Figure 1.

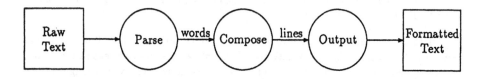

Figure 1: Data flow network for the text formatting problem

Each bubble represents a transformation in which an input data flow is transformed into an output. The first transformation reads text characters, building and outputting words. The next transform composes words into justified lines and delivers them to the last transform, which sends the justified lines to the caller.

Data-flow diagrams impose no control hierarchy on the tasks comprising the transformation bubbles. The goal of data-flow design is to produce such a hierarchical control structure. Oversimplifying greatly, one can impose such a structure by choosing a bubble to be "main", lifting up the diagram by that bubble and "shaking it" into a tree shape. The design strategy comes in picking the correct main bubble. Thus, in our example one obtains three distinct structure diagrams depending on which bubble is chosen as "main". See Figure 2.

Each of the three hierarchies in the figure gives rise to a legitimate solution to the problem:

1. *Compose*, the main function, is built around a loop, repeatedly calling *Parse* for a word, building a justified line. When the line is full, *Compose* calls *Output* to send the line to the justified text file.

2. *Output*, the main function, repeatedly calls *Compose* to request a justified line, which it uses to build the output text file. *Compose*, when called, repeatedly calls *Parse* to get words until a justified line is built, at which time it delivers the line and returns control to *Output*.

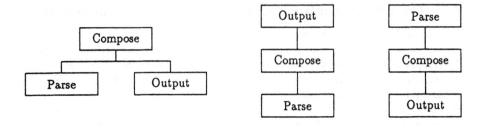

Figure 2: Alternative structures derived from the data flow network

3. *Parse*, the main program, repeatedly reads characters from the unjustified text file, building words. Whenever a complete word is built, *Parse* calls *Compose*, sending the word. *Compose*, maintaining enough private static memory to hold a partially filled line between activations, adds the word to the line. When a call results in a filled line, *Compose* ships it to *Output* and then returns control to *Parse*.

All three are reasonable solutions that introduce no more data flow than that present in the original data-flow network. The first two are in some sense simpler and less baroque than the third, which cannot be programmed cleanly in a language like Pascal that does not implement private static memory. The second solution might also require private memory of *Parse* if any look-ahead or push-back is required by the complexities of parsing. So we are led to the usual solution in which the middle bubble is chosen to be main. But instead of design by dogma, we are led to the best solution by logical analysis of the effects on the complexity of solutions arising from other choices. Furthermore the example has introduced beginning students to the powerful method of data flow design.

7.2 Pipes and Filters: An Alternative to Hierarchical Organization

As Plauger points out [Plauger 87], the implementation of a transformation in a data-flow diagram is simplest when it is chosen as the main module. This leads naturally to a design in which every transformation is main, via the organization of a program as a sequence of independent processes, each receiving input from its predecessor and sending output to its successor. This, of course, is the "pipes-and-filters" paradigm of system architectural organization [Shaw 89]. UNIX pipelines are easy to code and maintain, and the technique is valuable in building prototype software. For these reasons, design-by-pipes is an important technique that should be taught to our majors. It may be introduced in intermediate or advanced systems courses, but can it be successfully introduced in the freshman year as an alternative design paradigm.

A fourth solution of the text formatting problem above arises by implementing the three bubbles as filters. If one has a UNIX-based system on hand, then one can actually implement the solution as three autonomous programs that communicate via standard input and output and that are connected by the UNIX pipe operator. In a sense this is an extension of data-flow design, since we are letting each bubble play the role of "main".

This solution illustrates the concept of pipe but is rather artificial and inefficient, since each filter has to repack input (compose a string from character input) produced by the predecessor's output. A more realistic example that is accessible to freshmen is the problem of building a cross-reference table for a Pascal program — that is, a list of identifiers found in the program together with a list of line numbers where each identifier occurs. Presented to freshmen without any accompanying hints, the problem is formidable and likely will lead to failure. However, an elegant solution, stated in terms of data flow, is to view the solution as flow of data through three transformations. The first scans the program, writing to output each occurrence of an identifier as it is scanned, together with the number of the line on which it is found. The second filters out any reserved words. The third reads the identifiers, builds the cross-reference table, and eventually prints it. See Figure 3.

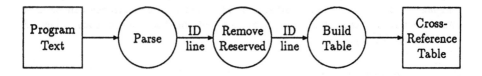

Figure 3: Data flow network for the cross referencing program

One can have students build and test a pipeline solution to this program in three independent stages, corresponding to the three transformations. Once written, the three are put together with a UNIX pipe, and the problem is solved, simply and elegantly. Moreover, the student has added another strategy to his or her bag of design tools.

7.3   Concurrent Design: An Alternative to Sequential Execution

With the growing popularity of multiprocessor and distributed systems, it is becoming ever more important that students not only have some familiarity with the concept of concurrency, but also recognize concurrency as a design alternative. A typical curriculum may introduce concurrency in a senior course in operating systems. There are several disadvantages to such an approach. First, the emphasis is restricted to using concurrency to build operating systems. Second, by putting off instruction in concurrency we ingrain in students a sequential mindset, difficult to undo. Third, students are not taught early on to consider concurrent solutions of problems outside the domain of operating systems.

A major obstacle that must be hurdled in order to teach concurrency early in the curriculum is the difficulty of programming concurrent solutions. This problem is gradually being overcome by the increased use in the introductory sequence of programming languages such as Ada. This language implements a conceptually simple, syntactically clean model of concurrency using tasks. With the introduction of such languages, concurrency can be taught in the freshman year, and indeed it has been at several institutions.

The pipes-and-filters solution of the formatter problem is a concurrent solution, since Unix implements pipes by activating the filters as concurrent processes. However, such a solution is unsatisfying as an introduction to concurrency since it hides such complexities as synchronization, mutual exclusion, and buffering. A better solution is one written in Ada in which the transforms are written as tasks. This forms the fifth in our sequence of alternative solutions to the formatter problem. For brevity we omit the Ada implementation of this solution.

Although the introduction of concurrency as a design alternative in the introductory sequence is feasible, it is not without its pedagogical difficulties. For example, Ada's tasking model requires synchronous communication via the rendezvous, but maximum use of concurrency is achieved by asynchronous communication combined with buffering of data transmission. In order to obtain this in Ada, one must introduce additional "mailbox" tasks that uncouple the transform tasks and buffer the data transmission [Burns et al. 87, page 35]. Students struggling with conceptual issues may be overwhelmed by the added complexity of the implementation. Perhaps other languages that implement conceptually simpler models of concurrency can be used more effectively in the introductory sequence, but the discussion of such is beyond the scope of this paper.

7.4   Layered Design

Nearly all introductory textbooks — at least for CS2 — now thoroughly cover data abstraction as a design technique. The method promotes such positive design attributes as information hiding and modularity. A natural extension of this concept is that of a layered system in which each layer provides services to the next higher layer and implements a lower level of abstraction. Such systems are commonly found in operating systems and network systems.

We contend that it is important to introduce the concept of layered systems early, and not to wait until a senior course in operating systems or networks. Although it may be unrealistic to expect freshmen to learn the concept sufficiently well to make design decisions based on the concept, an early introduction plants the seed of understanding for later use in synthesizing design solutions.

Although our previous example of the text formatter does not lend itself well to the layered-systems approach, examples of layered systems that are accessible to freshmen do exist. One example [Gilbert 83] poses the problem of computing π to several hundred decimal places. Although overwhelmingly complex in the eyes of freshmen, a careful exposition on the solution as a layered system renders the solution manageable, with students able to fill in the details. The levels are

1. The series approximation to π, using only basic arithmetical operations applied to arbitrary-precision integers.

2. The arithmetic of arbitrary precision integers.

3. The implementation of big integers as sequences of digits.

4. The storage allocation routines that are called to produce or extend sequences when necessary.

8   Summary

In order to better educate future software engineers, computer science programs must improve the quality of instruction in design of software systems, and in particular they must incorporate this instruction throughout the undergraduate curriculum. It is desirable, and indeed quite possible, to introduce at the freshman level examples, techniques, and tools that illustrate nontrivial design strategies and give students the skills to make intelligent design decisions. We have demonstrated that the design strategies of data-flow design, pipes-and-filters, concurrent design, and layered design are accessible to freshmen, and have presented sample problems that illustrate these alternatives.

References

[Budgen 89]   David Budgen, *Introduction to Software Design*, SEI Curriculum Module SEI-CM-2-2.1, Software Engineering Institute, Pittsburgh, 1989.

[Burns et al. 87]   Alan Burns, Andrew M. Lister, Andrew J. Wellings, *A Review of Ada Tasking*, Lecture Notes in Computer Science, volume 262, Springer Verlag, 1987.

[Ford 90]   Gary Ford, *1990 SEI Report on Undergraduate Software Engineering Education*, Tech. Report CMU/SEI-90-TR-3, Software Engineering Institute, Pittsburgh, 1990.

[Gilbert 83]   John G. Gilbert, unpublished programming assignment from the Institute for Retraining in Computer Science, Clarkson University, 1983.

[Guttag, Liskov 86]   Barbara Liskov, John Guttag, *Abstraction and Specification in Program Development*, MIT Press, 1986.

[Helman et al. 90]   Paul Helman, Robert Veroff, Frank R. Carrano, *Intermediate Problem Solving and Data Structures: Walls and Mirrors*, Benjamin/Cummings, 1991.

[Kay 85]   David G. Kay, *Programming for People/Pascal*, Mayfield, 1985.

[Koffman 89]   Elliot B. Koffman, *Pascal: Problem Solving and Program Design*, Third Edition, Addison-Wesley, 1989.

[Naps et al. 89]   Thomas L. Naps, Douglas W. Nance, Bhagat Singh, *Introduction to Computer Science: Programming, Problem Solving, and Data Structures*, Alternate Edition, West, 1989.

[Plauger 87]   P. L. Plauger, "Who's the Boss?", *Computer Language*, July, 1987, pp 17–22.

[Pressman 88]   Roger S. Pressman, *Software Engineering, A Practitioner's Approach*, Second Edition, McGraw-Hill, 1982.

[Shaw 89]   Mary Shaw, "Larger Scale Systems Require Higher-Level Abstractions", *Proceedings of the Fifth International Workshop on Software Specification and Design*, 1989, pp 143–146, IEEE Computer Society.

[Sommerville 89] Ian Sommerville, *Software Engineering*, Addison-Wesley, 1989.

"Special Topics
in Real Time and Environments"

Moderator: Norman E. Gibbs
Software Engineering Institute

Teaching Software Engineering
for Real-Time Design
Conni Goodman Marchewka
Texas Instruments Incorporated

Industry-Academia Collaboration to Provide
CASE Tools for Software Engineering Classes
Laurie Honour Werth
University of Texas

Teaching Software Engineering for Real-Time Design

Conni Goodman Marchewka
Texas Instruments Incorporated

Abstract. *Designing software for real-time systems continues to be a challenge. In addition to functional requirements, real-time systems typically have strict requirements in the areas of performance, size, and the need for concurrency which complicates the design process[PRE87]. The best design will depend on the particular requirements of a system. A designer must learn to apply principles for determining which design will best fit the needs. Teaching students skills in real-time design becomes more difficult because of the many design issues. Although software engineering principles must be expanded to handle the complexity of real-time systems, these principles should still be applied to real-time design. Since TI develops many real-time systems, TI teaches an "Introduction to Real-Time Software" course to improve the design skills of novice real-time designers. This paper describes the content of the real-time course and how software engineering principles are applied to real-time design. It also describes how real-time design concepts are reinforced through examples and exercises.*

1. Introduction

Good software design continues to get increased attention. Transferring creative solutions generated from within the mind into an implementation without errors has been difficult [BRO75]. Applying software engineering principles improves this transfer. Many of the design principles and methods that have grown over the years are based on *sequential* software making them more difficult to apply to real-time, multi-tasking systems. Pressman [PRE87] states "The design of real-time software encompasses all aspects of conventional design while at the same time introducing a new set of design criteria and concerns. Because real-time software must respond to real-world events in a time frame dictated by those events, all classes of design (architectural, procedural, and data design) become more complex." These principles must therefore be adapted and expanded for real-time, multi-tasking systems.

The Defense Systems & Electronics Group (DSEG) of Texas Instruments develops software for military contracts and much of the development is in the area of embedded real-time systems. Even software systems used to test hardware components, testing missiles for example, may be real-time. The "Introduction to Real-Time Software" course, designed to handle the special issues of real-time systems, is part of a larger software engineering curriculum. DSEG developed the course because many software design engineers do not receive enough training in school to be immediately proficient in real-time design. To improve real-time design skills, the objectives of the course are to teach students to:

- identify the characteristics of a real-time system
- determine when an application requires a real-time solution
- develop alternative design approaches
- estimate performance
- evaluate designs against system performance, requirements, and criteria for good design
- evaluate impacts of processor selections
- apply these principles on the job

Training is most effective when the tasks can be proceduralized, making it easier for students to apply the training on the job [HAR88]. Unfortunately, there is no *cookbook* formula which can be given for real-time design since it is a creative process and each project will have unique characteristics and requirements. To affect on the job behavior, the course teaches students the underlying concepts and principles and how to apply them for their specific circumstances. The course focuses on teaching software design engineers the skills of evaluating their specific situation and selecting the best design. Wherever possible, job aids are included to aid students in applying principles and evaluating designs on the job.

For better skill transfer, the course is organized around the software development lifecycle. The case study and examples are derived from the DSEG environment. The course is task oriented, training the student to answer common questions such as:

- How can we interface with external devices?
- How can we respond to multiple, asynchronous events?
- How do we handle errors?
- What is the criteria for deciding whether a unit should be a task?
- How can we communicate between tasks?
- How much processing should be allocated to a task?
- How many tasks should we have?
- How do we estimate, handle, and evaluate performance/timing requirements?
- What features does an operating system need?
- How do we avoid deadlock?
- How do we test our system?
- How should processing be allocated to a processor?
- How can we interface between processors?

The "Introduction to Real-Time Software" course was developed and is taught by the author who is a member of the Computer Systems Training Branch (CST). CST is DSEG's primary software training organization and offers a wide-spread curriculum to handle the variety of training needs. A detailed description of DSEG's training curriculum is described in a previous paper [MOO88], but a brief overview of related courses includes:

- Software Engineering Workshop: a three-day course which introduces the DSEG software engineering process, DSEG practices and standards, the DOD-STD-2167A life cycle, software engineering principles, and evaluation criteria.
- Real-Time Structured Analysis and Software Design: currently two five day versions are offered. The first course is based on the Ward and Mellor methodology [WAR85]. The other course is based on work done by Hatley/Pirbhai [HAT88].
- Processor Architecture Courses: a variety of courses covering the architecture of different processors used within DSEG such as the MIL-STD-1750A, Intel 80x86 series, and the TMS320-C30.
- Language and Operating Systems Courses: Courses covering software design and implementation for Ada, C, assembly languages, etc. and operating systems courses such as Unix

The "Introduction to Real-Time Software" is the second course in the curriculum and builds on the concepts that were taught in the Software Engineering Workshop. The three-day real-time course gives the students important skills to apply in designing software for real-time systems. It provides the foundation for other courses.

Real-time software design is complex and there are many issues which need to be addressed in the training. The remainder of this paper discusses how the course is designed to give students the proper foundation and practice in applying the principles, for a variety of situations, through exercises and discussion. Where possible, the students receive checklists and job aids which can be used on the job.

2. Course Design

Software engineering requires applying a disciplined approach to software design. In addition to meeting requirements, since requirements often change, the goals of software engineering are modifiability, efficiency, reliability, and understandability [BOO87]. The course teaches students software engineering principles such as abstraction, information hiding, modularity, localization, uniformity, completeness, confirmability [BOO87], cohesion, and coupling. It then teaches them how to apply these principles to real-time software design. A major course goal is to teach students how to design to *avoid errors*. Alerting students to the common problems of real-time systems, such as deadlock, mutual exclusion, and synchronization [FAI85], and teaching them early defect-detection techniques, such as evaluation, helps them prevent errors in their designs.

The course focuses on designing software for real-time systems. In order for students to understand real-time design, background concepts must be introduced such as concurrency, inter-task synchronization and communication, and interfacing to input/output devices. Organizing the course around the software development life-cycle ties the concepts more directly to their jobs. The course is composed of seven major modules (with approximate course times):

- Course Introduction (1 hour)
- Requirements Analysis (2 hours)
- Computer Architecture (2 hours)
- Preliminary Design (6 hours)
- Detailed Design (9 hours)
- Implementation (1 hour)
- Integration and Test (3 hours)

The underlying concepts are introduced where appropriate, built-upon, practiced, and discussed. The students practice applying the real-time principles by designing a case study, evaluating those designs, and raising the important issues in each phase of the life-cycle.

The following sections describe the course modules to show how the real-time principles are taught. Common threads used throughout the course include:

- identification of what should be done during each phase of development,
- exercises using a case study based on an actual project,
- project examples which demonstrate a variety of real-time issues and solutions,
- checklists of common defects introduced during each phase of development, and
- class discussions allowing students to expand on their experiences and lessons learned.

2.1. Course Introduction

The complexities of real-time systems are numerous. Real-time systems may monitor or control multiple external interfaces. System processing may be driven by data and/or events which must be responded to within strict timing constraints. The data arrival times are often unpredictable. Multiple events may occur simultaneously. They may need to run in different modes, depending on the ever changing external environment. Reliability may be crucial. And in addition, they may have constraints on throughput and memory since they are often implemented on microprocessors.

These characteristics are amplified through the discussion of example systems that were developed within DSEG. During the review exercise, students practice recognizing real-time characteristics in example systems.

2.2. Requirements Analysis

Although requirements analysis is not a focus of this course, the phase is reviewed to put design into context. This section reinforces the training the students received in the Software Engineering Workshop on the criteria for good requirements. It continues to stress the importance of writing complete, testable requirements (including real-time requirements) to promote the early detection of defects. Students receive a checklist of typical defects introduced during the requirements phase.

The first case study exercise gives the students practice with identifying real-time requirements. The purpose of the exercise is to bring up real-time issues that will be discussed during the course and to raise questions in the minds of the students on how they would handle these requirements. The students read the case study Statement of Work (SOW) which is a subset of the Light Armored Vehicle Air-Defense (LAV-AD), a system developed in DSEG. The LAV-AD system displays all of the real-time characteristics discussed during the course introduction, thus providing an example for many real-time design issues. For example, LAV-AD has many external interfaces which it monitors and controls including a weapons subsystem, a primary sight subsystem, and operators through handgrips, a turret control panel, and an interactive display unit. LAV-AD has multiple modes of operation (e.g., manual tracking or auto tracking) and is driven by data and events which must be responded to within strict timing constraints (e.g., operator choosing to fire weapons).

Timing requirements from the case study are used to demonstrate the need for predicting performance during and after allocating requirements. The students are given an overview of the methods that can be applied to predict performance. Although the students practice reading LAV-AD Structured Analysis and Design diagrams, the methodology is covered in a different course.

2.3. Computer Architecture

Real-time systems are often implemented on microprocessors and must interface with special devices. The real-time designer can not treat the hardware as a *black-box* since the processor selection, the number of processors, the types of interfaces, and the estimated performance impact design choices. This module introduces the student to options in Input/Output (I/O) interfacing, computer architecture, the real-time clock, program-controlled I/O, estimating software timing, and benchmarking. The students practice estimating the processing time of some simple examples. They also receive and discuss a job aid for processor selection issues. Processor architecture is discussed in general, since specific processor training is handled in other CST courses.

2.4. Preliminary Design

Before beginning the real-time preliminary design discussion, a section is included to reinforce general design concepts. Since a course goal is *good* design, this section provides background information on the scientific process, software engineering principles, and design evaluation criteria. These principles are then emphasized throughout the course during discussions and exercises for evaluating the design choices. An overview of the different design methodologies is provided, and these methods are contrasted during discussion of examples. A formal design method is not taught, since different projects may select different methods.

It is common for real-time systems to have performance requirements as well as functional requirements. "The problem for real-time systems is proper allocation. Real-time performance is often as important as function, yet allocation decisions that relate to performance are often difficult to make with assurance." [PRE87] Since handling performance requirements is difficult, performance often becomes the driving factor at the expense of other design goals.

For example, inexperienced designers may become concerned with micro-efficiency issues such as the efficiency of a particular language construct or the passing of parameters. Global data may be chosen to improve efficiency yet it sacrifices reliability and makes understandability, testing, and maintenance more difficult. Micro-efficiency may be chosen because:

(1) the efficiency of one's own unit is easier to understand than system efficiency and

(2) it is perceived that if all units are as efficient as possible, the system will also be efficient.

Unfortunately, this second premise is not necessarily true for multiple reasons. First, it is typical for 10% of the code in the system to run 90% of the time [OGD78]. It is the efficiency of that 10% of the code which is of utmost priority. Second, the decomposition of the software requirements can have a significant effect on the performance. Multi-tasking and interrupt handling have been used to get the most out of the processor throughput by using the *idle* time that would otherwise exist.

A goal of this module is to teach students broader meanings of efficiency, or efficiency at the macro level. Macro-efficiency can be achieved through the *careful* use of concurrency. Careful, because poor task design can degrade efficiency due to excessive context switching. Excessive context switching can occur if a task polls or otherwise runs when not necessary, a task is complex or contains excess processing, or there are too many tasks in the system. If concurrency is underused, cycles are wasted and events may be missed. Task design is a careful balancing act between task overhead (the number of tasks and context switching), event recognition, idle processor time, and creating a design which is testable.

Therefore, when decomposing a real-time system, one of the common issues is multi-tasking. Should multi-tasking be used? Which units should be tasks, and which should be procedures? The students receive background information on concurrency such as what is a task, task states, scheduling, and priorities. Next, they practice decomposing the case study requirements into Computer Software Components (CSCs). First, the students individually determine the CSCs and interfaces. Next, the team discusses each answer and develops a group decomposition on a flip chart. The discussion of each student's solution helps demonstrate that many potential solutions exist. The team evaluates those solutions to determine the team's solution. During the exercise, the instructor acts as consultant to answer questions, raise important issues, and verify the students' understanding of preliminary design. Each team describes their solution which is contrasted to the LAV-AD CSC decomposition.

Once the students have developed the preliminary design, they determine what processing should occur concurrently and whether or not a CSC will contain a task. For tasks, the students examine performance and scheduling issues. Is the task data driven, event driven, or periodic? What should the relative priorities be? Examining the need for concurrency reinforces that a task should run only when absolutely necessary to allow the processor to run potentially more critical tasks.

2.5. Detailed Design

During detailed design, the designer will start looking at *how* a unit will be implemented. The scientific process is again reiterated, focusing on the steps of developing multiple potential solutions, and choosing the best solution. The purpose of this module is to introduce the student to a variety of design solutions and show how to contrast those solutions through evaluation. This is the largest module and is divided into multiple sections:

- Inter-task synchronization and communication
- Handling external interfaces
- Performance estimation and considerations
- Designing for reliability
- Operating system and task design considerations

The first section covers inter-task synchronization and communication techniques, such as the semaphore and message passing. To simplify the detailed design, the exercises use a monitoring sensors example which is less complex than the case study. The students practice developing multiple designs for the same set of requirements. The series of exercises are designed to give students practice in applying each of the interface techniques, designing the same example in a variety of ways, and evaluating designs to select the best design for the circumstances. The students first design the example as a sequential system, with a driver calling the main functions. Next, they design it using multiple tasks which communicate using semaphore-protected global memory. In order to use multiple tasks, the students must examine what processing can occur concurrently and the inter-task dependencies. Finally, they design the tasks to communicate through message passing. These designs are then compared and evaluated against the software engineering principles, the requirements, and performance. Ada tasking issues and the rendezvous are covered in the Ada course, but an example Ada rendezvous solution is handed out to the students.

In addition to discussing which units should be tasks, the students learn how much processing should be in a task. Some of the engineering concepts can be applied directly at the task level. An example is cohesion: Have a task perform a single, well-defined function. If a task tries to do too much, chances are it will run more often than necessary. The students are asked for design options to improve on the following design:

> A task ran periodically because it read data from two queues. The
> data could arrive in any order therefore it could not afford to sleep
> on either queue.

The students are first asked to identify potential problems with the design, after reminding them that a task should be suspended (not running) whenever possible. In this case, it was far better to split the task into two tasks which suspended on their respective queues waiting for data. The savings in context switching caused by polling the queues every 100 milliseconds far outweighed the extra overhead caused by adding a task. The data arrival for these tasks was asynchronous and infrequent. By splitting the tasks, they may be suspended for hours rather than waking up every 100 milliseconds to check the queues.

Design options for handling external interfaces, such as interrupt handling, polling, and memory mapped I/O, are also discussed. The case study is then divided into smaller pieces, with each team designing a portion of the system using the LAV-AD Software Requirements Specification (SRS), Interface Requirements Specification (IRS), and Preliminary Software Design Document (SDD). The teams prepare for a design review using a checklist of topics which should be considered such as the requirements, interfaces, data, potential errors, and decomposition. During the design reviews, the other students practice evaluating the proposed designs.

2.6. Implementation

Since most students have had experience in the implementation (code and unit test) phase, this module is an overview which provides a link to other courses which cover implementation issues more specifically (e.g. a particular language, programming standards, etc.). This module raises common language issues and reviews DSEG practices and standards in the areas of structured programming and code walkthrough techniques. This module emphasizes the importance of thorough unit testing since errors are harder to find at integration. A successful test is defined as one which has a high probability of finding a new error [MYE79] and shows that the unit meets its requirements. Unit test approaches and common errors are discussed and practiced. An overview of test tools useful at the unit level is included.

2.7. Integration And Test

Deciding which test cases to run during integration and testing is a very creative task. This module begins with a discussion based on a quote from Myers that testing is more creative than design [MYE79]. Unfortunately if a structured process is not followed, the success of the tests (finding errors) depends on the experience of the tester. To improve the success of integration testing, this module teaches a process for planning and integrating a real-time system. To help students determine the types of integration tests which should be run, this module provides checklists of common types of errors and the types of tests which should be run (e.g., stress testing).

Although the planning for integration should be done earlier in the lifecycle, the students now have the background concepts necessary to do this. They practice planning the integration and test phase for the case study by determining the order of integration, the types of tests which should be run, and potential risks. Each team presents their integration plan and the reasons for selecting their approach.

3. Lessons Learned

Choosing an appropriate case study was difficult. The case study needed to be small enough for classroom work, yet have enough real-time features to raise the critical issues. A sub-set of the LAV-AD project was chosen since it demonstrated common real-time issues and constraints. The scope of the case study was narrowed to focus on key concepts for more complicated exercises. At times, such as during detailed design, it was necessary to use a simpler example for the exercises.

If a designer does not understand the system (hardware, operating system, other tasks), they may select a poor design because they did not consider all relevant issues. Since the requirements for systems vary, it was important to include a variety of examples and exercises to give students practice in applying the design principles for different situations. Because there are so many real-time issues, each module contains a list of suggested readings to help students research topics in more detail (e.g., the specifics of a particular interface). The course job aids are useful during the exercises, with the added benefit of providing an on-the-job reference.

DSEG develops a variety of real-time systems (e.g., weapons systems, electro-optics, avionics) and has many small projects which use different languages or processors. The course could be simplified by limiting the scope and decreasing the number of underlying concepts. If the course was based on a specific language, operating system, and processor, the students could implement their designs. Rather than teaching many versions of the course, DSEG decided to teach a concepts course which serves as a prerequisite to other courses. If a company develops similar systems using only a few languages and processors, then it may be desirable to teach a machine-based course.

Typically, a few of the students attending each class have had some real-time experience. Encouraging those students to contribute to class discussion benefits everyone. It gives them an opportunity to share their experiences and provides additional real-time issues and examples. Course evaluations have shown that even those students with real-time experience benefit from the course through an increase in skills for developing and evaluating design options.

4. Summary

Designing the real-time course was challenging due to the complexities of real-time design. For training to be successful, students must be able to apply what they have learned to their specific project. Since the requirements vary between projects, it is important for students to practice applying principles and evaluating designs for a variety of applications. Project examples from DSEG are useful for discussing variations in requirements. During the discussion of examples and exercises, *what if* questions help demonstrate variations in design selection. For example, changing certain requirements or assumptions (e.g., different timing requirements or processor) can make a different design solution preferable. Many of the exercises were designed to demonstrate different design solutions. For example, having students work individually and in teams allows them to see different solutions. In addition, the students practice evaluating those solutions against the requirements and the software engineering principles to determine the team solution. After evaluating designs, students agree that software engineering principles are useful and should be applied to the design of real-time systems.

References

[BOO83] Booch, Grady, *Software Engineering with Ada*, Benjamin Cummings, 1983

[BRO75] Brooks, Fredrick P., *The Mythical Man-Month, Essays on Software Engineering*, Addison-Wesley Publishing Company, Inc., 1975

[FAI85] Fairley, Richard E., *Software Engineering Concepts*, McGraw-Hill, Inc., 1985

[HAR88] Harless, Joe H., *Job Aids Workshop*, P.O. Box 1903, Newnan, GA 30364, Harless Performance Guild, Inc., 1988

[HAT88] Hatley, Derek J, and Imtiaz A. Pirbhai, *Strategies for Real-Time System Specification*, Dorset House Publishing Co, Inc., 1988

[MOO88] Moore, Freeman L., and Phillip R. Purvis, "Meeting the Training Needs of Practicing Software Engineers at Texas Instruments", *Lecture Notes in Computer Science*, vol. 327, Software Engineering Education, Springer-Verlag, 1988, pp. 32-44

[MYE79] Myers, Glenford J., *The Art of Software Testing*, John Wiley & Sons, Inc., 1979

[OGD78] Ogdin, Carol Anne, *Microcomputer Design*, Prentice-Hall, Inc., 1987

[PRE87] Pressman, Roger S., *Software Engineering: A Practitioner's Approach*, second edition, McGraw-Hill, Inc., 1987

[WAR86] Ward, Paul T., and Stephen J. Mellor, *Structured Development for Real-Time Systems*, vols. 1-3, Prentice-Hall, 1985

Industry-Academia Collaboration
To Provide CASE Tools for
Software Engineering Classes

Laurie Honour Werth
Department of Computer Sciences
The University of Texas at Austin
Austin, Texas 78712
lwerth@cs.utexas.edu

Abstract. The University of Texas' project-based Software Engineering class for undergraduates has used software tools for development and as final products for several years. When the opportunity arose to use Electronic Data Systems' (EDS) in-house development tool, INCASE, in the class, it was a natural extension to earlier work.

The major change is the emphasis on data rather than process modelling. With a CASE tool, students are able to concentrate on requirements elicitation, prototyping, screen design and other more modern topics than are usually covered in a one semester software engineering course. The project is large enough that the software engineering techniques and tools are seen as valuable. The course and CASE tool are described, together with lessons learned and suggestions for similar collaborative efforts.

Introduction

CS373 is a typical project-based Software Engineering class for seniors [Wer87; Wer88]. We have used commercial CASE tools such as HP's *TeamWork* both for design and as enhancement projects [Wer89b], Object-Oriented packages such as MacApp to develop graphic interface programs such as software costing models and configuration management tools [Wer89a], and have written our own CASE tools using HyperCard and Oracle [Wer90a;b]. When Electronic Data Systems' (EDS) offered to collaborate in using their in-house development tool, INCASE, it seemed a good opportunity to expose the students to an industrial-strength CASE tool, as well as to introduce data modelling into the curriculum.

With a CASE tool to generate the code, students were able to concentrate on analysis and design, using and evaluating software tools, code and specification reuse; rather than spending most of their time and energy on programming. They were able to work with a large enough system that software engineering helped, rather than appearing to be a tiresome requirement to an otherwise uneventful coding task. Students learned leading edge topics such as data modelling and code generation to which undergraduates are rarely exposed. Both industry and academic instructors benefitted from exposure to different learning environments. We all worked hard to make this project a success. Students and instructors were well rewarded.

The course and INCASE system are described together with a report of the training, laboratory facilities and project. A summary of the project highlights and lessons learned includes an evaluation of the INCASE environment. Finally, suggestions for similar future efforts and conclusions are presented.

The Old Course

In the past, the course had covered a variety of analysis and design techniques along with basic implementation, testing and maintenance concepts, using Pressman's text [Pre87]. Structured Analysis and Design techniques were expanded to encompass object oriented programming and applied to a team project. Projects have included an assortment of software engineering tools for software engineering students using a variety of graphic interface software packages on Macintosh IIs.

Each week the instructor holds a walkthrough with each team to inspect the current project document: System Definition, User's Manual, System Requirements, three Design Documents, Prototype Demonstration, Test Plan, Code Demonstration, Test Results, Response to Software Trouble Reports, and Project Legacy. All documents are collected in a project notebook which is made available to future classes. At the end of the semester, each team evaluates one of the other teams' project and fills out Software Trouble Reports. During the maintenance phase, all STRs must be acknowledged and some changes must be implemented.

The average of the weekly document, demonstration and presentation grades is the team project score. This represents half of each team members grade while the two examination scores account for the remaining half. Students also complete an evaluation of each team member's contribution to the project; this becomes an possible adjustment to each member's project grade.

Software tools and code reuse are featured for development and in the final product for several reasons. They enable students to work with a larger project than they could develop from scratch during a single semester, and they reduce the "Not Invented Here" syndrome so prevalent in universities and industry today. By reducing the emphasis on programming, students can focus on analysis and design, particularly on the prototyping approach and interactive computer human interface design. Students have coded vigorously for three or four years by the time they get to this course. There is only one semester to try to convince them that tools, teamwork, configuration management and standards are an important and necessary part of any engineered software.

The New Course

After a general introduction to Software Engineering, the class began as usual with a description of life cycle models and analysis/design techniques. Incorporating the CASE tool involved several changes to the course organization. Because of the complexity of the tool, more time was required for training and for implementation of the project. Students constructed a rudimentary project individually during a training session and then modelled and generated code for subsystems of an existing EDS system as their team project. EDS provided an expert user who held interviews and walkthroughs with the teams on Friday afternoons.

At the end of the semester, students evaluated the INCASE software, project, and training. They were encouraged to keep individual journals of their experiences which were compiled into the project legacy. Each team made a formal presentation on their project results and their assessment of the CASE tool.

The INCASE training classes and laboratory support are described below, together with a description of the EDS system which was used for the team projects.

INCASE Training

The head of EDS's new research facility in Austin, a recent University of Texas PhD graduate, first proposed the collaborative effort to provide EDS' CASE tool for use by Software Engineering students. Enthusiastic support was provided by the Vice President for Research and Development of the Dallas-based EDS corporation. Legal issues were resolved and the course format was developed: four weeks of training, together with a class project to design a subset of an existing system for an EDS subsidiary, a computer hardware and software distribution firm.

The Head of the EDS R&D training organization came to Austin from Dallas each week to teach the classes, following the usual academic format of 50 minutes, three days a week. The course was condensed from EDS' normal 21 eight-hour class days to twelve one hour classes with the in-class exercises assigned as homework, but there were still two large binders of course materials and exercises to cover.

One hands-on session was given on INCASE. The EDS instructor held office hours each afternoon and made himself available in the laboratory in the evenings, often well past midnight. As part of the training, students individually implemented a simple CCP inventory control system, (Computer Clone Pros, a medium size manufacturing company) from E-R diagram through screen design to working code. After the classes were completed, a staff member came from EDS Dallas two or three days a week to troubleshoot and help students resolve both INCASE and project problems.

Lab Facilities

EDS provided and installed six SUN SPARC stations for the students' use. One machine was used as a server with five systems available to the students in one of the regular UT Computer Sciences Department laboratories. A signup sheet was used to balance machine usage and to encourage off-line development.

The EDS instructor also brought his personal Mac II system for developing new course handouts, course critique etc. He was provided an office with telephone and copy support.

The CASE Tool

INCASE development began in 1984 and is currently in Release 10.0 [EDS90]. Data modelling became a major focus by August 1987 in Release 5.0 with the full integration of the data modeling tool with the screen, report, transaction and record design tools. All of these tools reside on a UNIX workstation and are integrated through a central repository. The ultimate goal is automatic generation of a program satisfying the users' requirements. A communications link is established to transfer the products of code generation to the mainframe source libraries, to compile and link edit the programs and to perform system testing.

The data-centered approach is based on the premise that a business' data is more stable than its processes. The data model provides a foundation upon which the process model can be built. Experience has shown that at least 80 percent of processing in most business data processing applications involves relatively straightforward add, change, delete and inquiry functions. The logic to support these basic processes is stored as reusable specifications and is automatically supplied during code generation.

Consolidated Data Modeling (CDM), based on Chen's notation (Che85) is the heart of the INCASE system (Zue89). CDM provides a three level designer's view of the logical data requirements for a

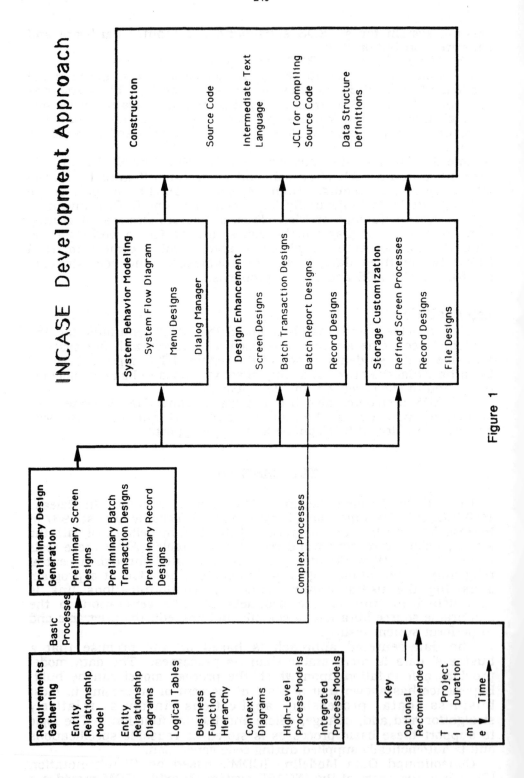

INCASE Development Approach

Figure 1

business. It combines the *entity-relationship* model (a blueprint of the things a business deals with and how they interrelate), the *logical table* model (which collects relevant attributes of entities and relationships) and a common dictionary or *repository*. CDM was included beginning with release 9.0 of INCASE.

The Project

The TPD project was divided into two subsystems: order entry and warehouse. The class was divided into four teams of six or seven students. Each team had a co-team with whom it cooperated on the entire project. The result was two parallel implementations of the project.

Each team assigned one student the major subsystem interface responsibility. Another student on each team volunteered to learn and take over some system administrator tasks which the EDS instructor had been providing. The Teaching Assistant also functioned as a system administrator. Short training classes were held for these students.

On Fridays, an EDS staff member arrived from Dallas to take the role of expert user for the TPD (EDS' Technical Products Division) Sales Order Entry and Warehouse subsystems. Iterations of the design were turned in on Wednesday and critiqued at the customer interview and walkthrough on Friday. The extended entity-relationship diagram (ERD) was the major tool used to structure and record the results of each week's user interview. We had discussed interviewing techniques, but the subject of the project, the CASE tool and the data modeling techniques were so far removed from the students' experience that the first few weeks were spent mastering these basics.

The expert user patiently went over and over the systems while subtly convincing the students that the data model really could reflect the business policies they were trying to implement and that the simpler the ERD they used, the more flexible their design would be. Toward the end of the semester, after the training and the practice exercises had been completed, the project jelled quickly.

Lessons Learned

Due to scheduling constraints, one team contained most of the full-time professionals enrolled as students in the class. Even though they were working at least 40 hours a week, their experience helped them master the CASE tool and define the project more easily than the typical undergraduate student. They were more organized and kept minutes of their meetings and tape recordings of the walkthroughs. Their team journal included the following, fairly typical, summary of lessons learned.

Technical Lessons
- Introduction to the data process development paradigm
- Use of a state-of-the-art professional CASE system
- Exposure to typical business data processing applications

- Direct experience interviewing users to determine requirements and deliverables
- Evaluation of both software systems and people

Managerial Lessons
- Importance of initial planning and division of labor
- Establishing and scheduling priorities on projects
- Clarification of goals needed to determine team's core mission
- Pro and cons of the democratic team organization
- Techniques and experience giving presentations

Team Experiences

Most of the students were concerned about the fear of individual failure and pleasantly surprised to find that their team members were more enthusiastic, mature and responsible than originally expected.

While the regular undergraduates, only a few of whom had software development experience, had a harder time getting started, they came into the project with fewer preconceived notions. Their designs were not quite as polished but demonstrated more of a departure from the original system as implemented at EDS. Being forced to rethink several aspects of their design due to problems with the CASE tool, while frustrating, actually helped them to better understand both INCASE and the project. They particularly came to appreciate DeMarco's advice: Be prepared to start over.

One team had fairly severe organizational and non-participation problems. In the end however, they developed an improved user interface, using some of the more advanced INCASE features. One of the students had become very interested in the these issues during the summer Computer Human Interface class, and it was nice to see the positive effects on this project.

The EDS experienced user was very impressed with the teams innovative approaches and the deep understanding of the system, even though the students were not able to completely implement the project during the semester. Students averaged about 20 hours per week on the project with some students working considerably more and few somewhat less.

Student Evaluation of the CASE Tool and Project

To help assimilate the deluge of course materials and project, at the end of the course students were asked to evaluate the INCASE environment, training and project and to summarize their experiences for EDS and for future classes. Weiderman [Wei88] and Shneiderman [Shn86] were the primary evaluation models provided to the students.

Areas evaluated included: Interface, Functionality, Performance, Support, Learnability and Help facilities. Students developed and completed Likert evaluation forms based on a scale of one to ten, with one being a low or negative rating and ten being a very high or positive rating. Individual comments were also solicited. Overall, average scores were in the middle of the range, though considerable variation between various aspects was found. These will be reported in detail elsewhere.

Interface aspects evaluated included statements such as "Consistent use of mouse buttons," "Font was clear and readable". Suggestions for a more friendly interface included suggestions for improving the screen partitioning and design, the possible inclusion of color, and a more meaningful wait icon. Another proposal was to include X Window interfaces for several places where the UNIX command shell was needed.

The *Functionality* provided, interaction between tools, support for version control, project management and documentation were considered in the second category. Students detailed major problems encountered with the tool using standard Software Trouble Report forms. Ease of system use and reliability were not as good as they wanted. Until the code was actually produced, students didn't fully grasp the magnitude of the task of generating interactive, windowing project code automatically.

Students generally felt that *performance* would have been better if a more powerful network/repository manager server, an additional print/batch manager server and more disk storage had been used. Problems due to the original network hardware connections need to be remedied in the future. Most of the students were familiar with UNIX, C and X Windows-based systems before the class, but felt that additional expertise would have been helpful.

Evaluation of INCASE *learnability* included training and the formidable learning curve. The course work and lab support received generally high ratings. The instructor was prepared and the lectures well organized. More time to permit a deeper treatment of the design tools was recommended. The lab was essential, but students felt that a dedicated system administrator - other than the instructor - was needed. Students felt that using a CASE tool and data modeling require a large amount of training and a strong commitment from the software engineer. They correctly surmised that attitude has a major influence on the effective use of software engineering tools and methodologies. Once over the steep learning curve, students felt that the tool's payback exceeded the investment cost many times over.

They were less enthusiastic about the *Help* available. The online help facility was not installed on our system, so help was limited to "large, dry documentation manuals." Error messages were seen as very database specific and needed to include instructions on how to resolve the problem.

Advice for the Future

Many general issues related to this topic are discussed in [Wer88] "Software Tools at the University: Why, What and How". The following is a survey of key points for this particular effort:

* Planning
* Resources
* Training the trainers
* Reducing learning curves

A great deal of up-front *planning* is required. Resolving legal issues is the most time-consuming. We were fortunate that EDS was committed enough to expedite project start-up in what must have been record-setting time. The Computer Sciences department chair was supportive as well, but bureaucratic wheels at most large companies and universities grind exceeding slowly, and this can doom many projects before they even start.

It would have been convenient to have used the Computer Sciences department's *hardware*, but system incompatibilities, heavy departmental machine usage and security problems made it necessary for EDS to provide SPARC stations for the project. In the end, the six workstation network was inadequate for the 26 member class. In effect, only four workstations were available because one was reserved as a file server and a second as the print server. This was intensified by the students waiting until the last minute to work and by their desire to work together at the same time, using most, if not all, of the available machines simultaneously.

Many of the usual problems of lack of project life cycle tool coverage and *software* incompatibilities were neatly sidestepped by the completeness of the INCASE system. However, the tool's complexity and the shortage of training time resulted in several major problems. Student needed someone available at all time they were working to help diagnose and repair problems. While large numbers of INCASE Software Trouble Reports were generated, many of the problems experienced were still not understood well enough to be remedied by the end of the semester. A number of the smaller problems were related to configuration problems causing the C/SYBASE connection to return errors on the execution of the generated code. Tool rigidity and inconsistency caused more trouble than necessary and created a fear of database corruption, while slow response time inhibited experimentation and learning. However, the students developed many real-world skills such as kicking the network connectors, re-booting the system and clearing the print queue. An average of 325,000 total lines of generated code was created by each group.

While the help feature was not functional, copious system *documentation* and training materials were provided. High level and summary documentation as well as cook-book "closed lab" exercises were generated by the EDS instructor for the students. These materials and more have been included in the new version of the training materials. It was felt that in future classes, time should be allowed to give the students an overall view of the system before jumping into the details of data modelling.

Training the *professor and teaching assistant* would have been expedited had they been provided some knowledge of the system before the training began, but there was neither time, nor a convenient mechanism to do this. Making experienced industry personnel available reduced the time required to get the academic instructor and teaching assistant converted to the joys of data modelling, without the necessity of learning the details of complex tool operation. Team teaching and learning together with the students may not appeal to instructors with "high control needs" but the collaboration was especially appreciated in this instance.

As has often been observed, it is not possible to compress projects indefinitely time-wise. The INCASE environment is complex enough that it probably merits its own project-based course. With a goal of generating working systems, it is difficult to partition or *reduce the learning curve*. As an alternative, the course could be limited to specification or data modelling aspects only, or the students could be more experienced coming into the course. Too much time was spent learning to use the tools and not enough time was available to understand the concepts being presented. Some reduction of work will be needed in any future undergraduate offering. Either the entire course needs to be dedicated to the task or the material needs to be inserted at appropriate points in a sequence of software engineering courses.

It was helpful to work through the tiny example before starting the project. The size of the project should have been reduced, or a more familiar and well-specified domain such as the library problem should have been adopted as the project. This would have greatly decreased the students' work load, permitting better mastery of the conceptual material.

Everyone worked hard and we all learned a lot. While the students had cogent suggestions on improving the software, and the learning environment can be improved on the next iteration, the effort was well repaid. Students were especially gratified by the positive response to the project from the companies with which they were interviewing. One graduating senior went to work on the INCASE project.

EDS has benefited from the exposure which translated into increase INCASE marketability and recruiting opportunities. If undergraduate students can learn to use the tool, design and implement a functional real system in a single semester then they feel, INCASE has emerged as a viable business solution.

Conclusions

The basic analysis and design-based course and project organization were retained in this industry-academia collaboration effort to provide CASE tools for software engineering students. While process modeling techniques such as data flow diagrams and state transition diagrams were covered, the major emphasis was on data modeling using extended entity-relationship diagrams. This represents a fundamental shift from software design and process modelling to requirements gathering and the user interview, one of the most significant pedagogic aspects of the undertaking.

Students worked in an iterative prototyping environment, at an abstract level. As the system's entity-relationship diagram was entered, a working window-based system was generated. The learning curve was steep, but as students began producing working code, concepts of code reuse and application generation were concretely realized, and their appreciation of the CASE tool grew exponentially. Indeed, the use of CASE tools may be the most effective way to concentrate students' efforts on front-end analysis and/or design skills.

Data modelling is often taught in information systems departments, but computer science departments still emphasize process modelling, despite the increasing importance of object oriented design and domain modelling at the graduate level. A book which combines data modelling, together with data flow diagrams and state transition diagrams in a methodology developed at GE, *Object Oriented Modeling* and *Design Techniques* [Rum91], might be a good text for such a course. Several of the microprocessor-based CASE tools support entity-relationship diagrams and there is at least one code-generating CASE tool, MicroStep by Syscorp [Bru88; BYTE89; Park90] Beside being less expensive and more available, these tools are more robust and consistent for easier student learning in a single semester.

The respective instructors profited greatly from their interaction. Exposure to industrial-strength training materials and techniques was beneficial to both academic instructor and students while the necessity to compress the training into a short time period yielded a more top-down or conceptual approach as well as a number of short-cut "cookbooks" and graphical learning aids for use in future EDS presentations of the course material. Where instructors and students are less dedicated, it may be preferable to offer this opportunity as part of a masters program or as a project course following a software engineering theory course(s).

The class recognized the effort and expense invested by EDS on their behalf. They worked hard and cheerfully to overcome the severely compressed learning cycle, unfamiliar application domain, hardware and software constraints inherent in the situation. Their evaluations were mature and constructive. EDS personnel more than merited the letters and speeches of appreciation made by the students. The students, in turn, surely deserved the beautifully framed certificates and accolades awarded by the EDS Vice President after their final presentations.

Acknowledgements

Support provided by the following EDS staff members is gratefully acknowledged: Glenn Self (Head of EDS Research and Development), Neil Iscoe (Head of Austin EDS Research and Development), Tom Barrett (instructor), Joel Davis (expert user), Dawn Ebanks (staff support), Jason Grant, and Bruce Cocek and Harold Hanson. We were all inspired by the dedication shown by the EDS participants.

This endeavor could not have been successful without our teaching assistant, Dan Clancy, and the four hard-working student teams: The Night Owls (Kim Bass, Ken Einhorn, Susie Elliott, Marcus Kierschbaum, Daryl Le, Ron Perez), The BEARCATS-Always on top of things (Keith Landau, Rodney Walters, Debbie Yang, Chris Campbell, Anju Bansal, Jimmy Jusuf, Doug Raschke), Team2 (Richard Everett, Mona Karia, Clay Rayborn, Raul Rutiage, Maggie Walczynski, JoJo Wong); The Conquistadors (Chris Braband, Jim Jones, Bach Nguyen, Sang Tran, Rich Villareal, Kevin Walters).

Bibliography

[Bru88]   Bruce, T. "CASE Brought Down to Earth". *Database Programming & Design*, Oct. 1988.

[BYTE90] "Making a Case for CASE". *BYTE*, Dec 1989.

[Che85]   Chen, P. "Database Design Based on Entity and Relationship". *Principals of Data Base Design*. Englewood Cliffs, New Jersey: Prentice-Hall Publishing Company, 1985.

[Cran89]   Crandall, V. "The Development of an Industry-Education Relationship in the the Test Environment: The Novell-Brigham Young University Experience". *Sixth International Conference on Testing Computer Software*, Washington, DC. May 22-24, 1989.

[EDS90]   Electronic Data Systems. *INCASE Product Overview. Release 9.5.* July 1990.

[Mac90]   Mach, R. "Information Engineers Wanted to Build Enterprise Models". *Software Magazine*, September, 1990.

[Park90]   Parker, T. "CASE on the PC: The state of the art". *Computer Language*, Jan 1990.

[Pre87]   Pressman, R. *Software Engineering: A Practitioner's Approach*. 2nd ed. McGraw-Hill, 1987.

[Rum91]   Rumbaugh, J., M. Blaha, W. Premerlani, F. Eddy, and W. Lorensen. *Object-Oriented Modeling and Design*. Prentice Hall, 1991.

[Shn87]   Shneidermann, B. *Designing the User Interface*. Addison-Wesley, 1987.

[Wei88]   Weiderman, N., N. Habermann, M. Borger, M. Klein. "A Methodology and Criteria for Evaluating Ada Programming Support Environments". *Software Engineering Institute Annual Report*, Carnegie Mellon University, 1988.

[Wer90a] Werth, L. H. "Object Oriented Programming and Design Class Projects - Macintosh User Interface Tools." *Journal of Object Oriented Programming*, Nov/Dec 1990.

[Wer90b] Werth, L. H. "Graphical Interfaces as Software Engineering Projects." *Proceedings of the Twenty-First Symposium on Computer Science Education*, Feb, 1990.

[Wer89a] Werth, L. H. "Teaching Object-Oriented Programming Using MPW/MacApp on the Macintosh." July, 1989 at the Software Engineering Institute in *Software Engineering Education*, L. Deimel (Ed). Springer-Verlag, 1989.

[Wer89b] Werth, L. H. "Preparing Students for Programming-In-The-Large." *Proceedings of the Twentieth Symposium on Computer Science Education*, Feb, 1989.

[Wer88]   Werth, L. H. "Software Tools at the University: Why, What and How." April, 1988 at the Software Engineering Institute in *Software Engineering Education*, G. Ford (Ed). Springer-Verlag, 1988.

[Wer87]   Werth, L. H. "A Survey of Software Engineering Education". *SIGSOFT Software Engineering Notes*, Oct. 1987.

[Zue98]   Zuehow, T. "Introducing EDS Consolidated Data Modeling". *EDS Technical Journal*, Vol. 3, No. 2, 1989.

Session 7

Developing Software Engineering Expertise

Moderator: Nancy R. Mead
Software Engineering Institute

Developing SE Expertise
Julian S. Weitzenfeld, Software Quality Services

What We have Learned about Software Engineering Expertise
Thomas R. Riedl, Software Quality Services
Julian S. Weitzenfeld, Software Quality Services
Jared T. Freeman, Software Quality Services
Gary A. Klein, Klein Associates
John Musa, AT&T Bell Laboratories

Instruction for Software Engineering Expertise
Jared T. Freeman, Software Quality Services
Thomas R. Riedl, Software Quality Services
Julian S. Weitzenfeld, Software Quality Services
Gary A. Klein, Klein Associates
John Musa, AT&T Bell Laboratories

Knowledge Elicitation for Software Engineering Expertise
Julian S. Weitzenfeld, Software Quality Services
Thomas R. Riedl, Software Quality Services
Jared T. Freeman, Software Quality Services
Gary A. Klein, Klein Associates
John Musa, A&T Bell Laboratories

Developing SE Expertise

Julian S. Weitzenfeld
Software Quality Services
East Windsor, N.J.

The following three papers are about different aspects of the same project: the development of a course at AT&T Bell Laboratories to accelerate the professional growth of software developers by teaching debugging skills. Although the project phases overlapped in time considerably, the sequence of the papers follows the sequence of the project: data collection, conclusions about professional expertise, design of the course. The authors took advantage of this to avoid redundancy in the papers; questions that occur to a reader while reading the methodology paper may very well be answered in one of the subsequent papers.

The papers could have been arranged in term of two broader issues they approach. The first and third papers -- the research methodology and course design -- comprise an approach to training that I call "training for expertise." There is by now an extensive literature documenting in many fields that expert performance differs from novice performance. However, there have been relatively few non-military attempts to accelerate the rate of growth of expertise. If it can be done for software development skills, it most likely can be done for many other forms of expertise. The first and third of our papers are concerned with issues that will arise in any such project of training for expertise.

The second paper in this set focuses particularly on software engineering skills. It is generalizable in a different way. The findings about the nature of expertise in software engineering have implications for the design of the work environment, job definitions, career paths, etc. The current slogan here is to focus on performance enhancement, not on training. Although our team's assignment was to design a course, that objective is too narrow to utilize these results fully.

One last point -- I refer to "our team." Although the papers have different lead authors, the order of authorship should not be taken too seriously. The papers and the project itself reflected a genuine team effort at all stages. It is more helpful, perhaps, to identify the primary roles played by the various members of the development team. John Musa of Bell Laboratories and Charles Kirschenmann, now of AT&T Corporate Education and Training, sponsored and supported the project; Tom Riedl initiated it, was the project manager, and provided familiarity with software engineering environments; I was the primary methodological consultant -- recommending research and analysis strategies and designing research instruments; Klein Associates, represented by Gary Klein and Marvin Thordsen, had developed the Critical Decision Method, conducted most of the interviews, and provided experience with knowledge elicitation for performance improvement; Jared Freeman and Charles Chubb, an Assistant Professor of Psychology at Rutgers, were the primary course designers and have been delivering the course. In addition, Michael Cassidy, of Bell Laboratories sponsored my time on the project; James Fritsch and Malcolm Conway, as Bell Laboratories' internal reviewers for the papers, provided timely and helpful comments.

What we have learned about software engineering expertise

Thomas R. Riedl
Julian S. Weitzenfeld
Jared T. Freeman
Software Quality Services
East Windsor, NJ

Gary A. Klein
Klein Associates, Yellow Springs OH

John Musa
AT&T Bell Laboratories, Murray Hill

ABSTRACT

A knowledge elicitation project was conducted to provide material for a course in software system debugging skills. Although the results confirmed aspects of the general model of human expertise in the cognitive science literature, focusing on the critical role of strategy, of creating a cognitive model of the problem domain, and of metacognition, there also were less expected findings. In particular, the importance of social skills was highlighted, even for so technical a task as code reading. In the industrial environment, expert debuggers are aware of the social contexts both of the environment in which the original code was written and in which the debugging is being done. This knowledge is useful in selecting paths of investigation and also in making efficient use of human resources in debugging.

INTRODUCTION

We conducted a study of software debugging in AT&T Bell Laboratories environments in order to generate requirements and class material for a course in expert debugging. Our results significantly altered our view of what ought to be in such a course. In this paper, we wish to review some of these shifts of salience.

If we look for guidelines regarding what makes a good software developer, we might look at university and continuing education curricula, including the SEI-developed curricula, and to the academic research on productivity and programming skill. These curricula are designed as introductions to processes, languages, systems, etc. By and large, these curricula focus on the objects and procedures in the developers' environment (e.g. tools, methodologies, technologies), not on what the developer does with them. In the cognitive sciences, on the other hand, studies of developers focus inside the developer with a vengeance. Typically they strip the programmer or developer of any of the support mechanisms and disturbances of a commercial environment and present an "abstracted" task to the subject[1].

A typical experiment in the psychology of code reading, for example, will present subjects with short unfamiliar code (with or without bugs) and ask them to debug, reproduce, or describe it. Such experiments almost never provide documentation and absolutely never provide a telephone, email facility or neighbor. Do these simplifications affect the relevance of these studies? We have some data that suggests that they do. The content of debugging expertise is far more diverse than is generally believed. We would like to describe some aspects of this enlarged view of technical competence.

METHOD

The methods we used in this study included emailed and paper surveys, Critical Decision Method (CDM) interviews[2], a day-long group discussion on debugging, and prototyping of training materials with several expert reviews, as well as customer feedback in postcourse evaluations. The data is drawn primarily from a sample of 15 developers from three Bell Laboratories facilities and five different projects[3]. These included both large and small, and both development and maintenance projects, and informants included both male and female developers. Less formal corroboration of the findings come from the reactions of experienced developers who have taken the expert debugging course since it was introduced. To our surprise, such veteran developers have comprised approximately a tenth of the students in the first offerings. Apparently, there is a population of experts who make it their business to check out materials such as ours. (Some of their motivation, aside from intellectual curiosity, will be made clear at the end of the present paper.) This group, representing a more diverse population than the formal informants, has also endorsed our findings and priorities. (We believe the high proportion of experienced developers taking this course is itself worthy of further study.)

We should issue a few cautionary notes first. What we will describe is not our full findings because they are too extensive and because some are proprietary. A second caveat is that our findings were based upon a relatively small sample of experts and were done within one company. Although we diversified our sample within our constraints, we are presenting these results as an invitation to further study. We expect them to focus attention on important and hitherto neglected aspects of software engineering expertise; we do not expect all of them to be accepted as true of all software engineers in all contexts.

FINDINGS

Strategy Our first finding is that like experts in other fields[4], our experts began by thinking about the problem extensively before moving ahead. They reported that their mentees and others in their labs often did not do this.

A particular problem among software developers is related to the focus on debugging tools. Those tools, powerful as they are in the course of a search for something specific, create temptations to explore a system at too specific a level or with too great a fixation on the single tool being used. Many of our informants reported that they were slower to go to the lab (to employ tools) than many of their colleagues. We have not quantified this result, but it fits extensive anecdotal data.

Our informants gave the impression of always knowing what they were looking for, even when what they were looking for was how to proceed with the search. That is, if they didn't have a clear idea of what information they needed next, they would focus on finding this out rather than engage in a hopeful but poorly directed search. In interviews, less expert debuggers described periods of "thrashing" - not explicitly using that term. Our informants indicated that stopping for strategic reflection when one doesn't know what one is looking for is not as common as it ought to be.

How do you look for what question to ask? There are several ways, but one good way is to talk to someone else about the problem. Occasionally, our informants did this. We shall return to this strategy shortly. More often, however, they were aware of alternative search paths and were confident in their ability to estimate the cost of pursuing each path, as well as estimate the likelihood that the fault would be located on each path. Decision strategies were based upon these expert judgments. Search for a fault in a system consisting of hundreds of thousands or millions of lines of code is a series of heuristic cost/benefit judgments about where to look next. There is no efficient search algorithm. Consequently, the strategic planning that expert debuggers do is in large part dependent upon their judgments of the likelihood that a particular search path contains the fault and of what effort and resources it will take to search that path.

CODE READING

In code reading skills, distinct from searching code for a bug, we again found performance characteristic of experts in any field. Expert debuggers sometimes perceive code in terms of chunks that are individuated by high-level principles, such as chunks related to the symptoms of certain types of problems. However, these are quite specific to particular systems. It would have been possible to begin mapping separate perceptual training curricula for different systems, but we focused our first effort at generic training, which would have a broader application. Some of our more general findings pertain to levels of intensity of reading code, the issue of comments and documentation in code reading, and the issue of human resources to avoid reading code.

Levels of intensity. There is a difference between reading code to determine its intent (i.e. functionality), its style, and reading code "closely" to understand the implementation. Reading code closely is a line by line reading, examining the assumptions of the code and mentally modelling its operation in your head, thinking about the past history of each piece of data it handles. This may be done in several passes.

At least one informant thought that until people have spent 5 years or so with the same system, they do not know what it means to read code closely. That is, there is a feeling that new developers don't realize what they don't know about code that they have read. There are two reasons for this. One is that is requires a good model of the rest of the system; the second is that it is so labor-intensive that a developer only does it when he or she is very confident that the error lies in a particular block of code. Inexperienced developers rarely reach this level of confidence.

Use of comments and documentation. Some of what we discovered about expert code reading surprised us. Let us focus on what might look like no skill at all: reading code comments (the stuff in English that is supposed to help you by telling you what the code is doing). Novices often believe the comments. There is a dilemma here. It is, of course, much easier to read code when you know what it is supposed to be doing. It is much easier to find out what it is supposed to be doing when someone tells you in English than when you have to infer it from the code itself. So, one piece of advice we got is to review all the available documentation about the code, including the comments. However, novices often accept what the documentation says as true., e.g. they are not sufficiently skeptical

The next piece of advice we got on this topic was never to accept the documentation as gospel, including the comments. In light of the need to know design level information, this would be a real dilemma. Read it, but don't necessarily believe it. What then? Certainly we were generally told to be skeptical of documentation. Experienced programmers from any environment generally know this.

But our expert programmers showed a rather different approach to code comments. They treated code comments as evidence. They inferred from the comments information about how many people wrote the code, and about what kind of people they were. Under what kind of conditions did they work? Are there signs of carelessness or haste? A person who forgets to mention certain things in the comments is likely also to forget certain things in the coding. Poor comments can even mislead the program designer. (And knowing how may help you locate the error.)

The comments tell about revisions. How many people have revised the code. When? Under what conditions? Does it look as though they might have been less than fully aware of the presuppositions and intent? In general, expert debuggers look at code commentary to tell them about the task context and about the kind of people who have touched the code. But comments don't say this; they show it. (There are overtones of Wittgenstein's Tractatus here: some things can only be shown, not said. Consider: "Do not believe what I say.")

Why is this important? Because judgments about the costs and benefits of various search paths are informed by a much larger body of information than we had thought, and, judging from the literature, more than anybody else has thought. It is clear that information about the characteristics of the original programmer would improve the validity of likelihood judgments. What is surprising is that software developers are able to get it from code comments and coding style.

It is interesting to contrast this expertise with the stereotype of the developer. At Bell Laboratories, they are typically people with both bachelors and masters degrees in computer science or engineering. The stereotype has it that they earned high grade point averages by concentrating on their major (engineering) subject curriculum; that they are relatively poor in verbal and social skills; and that they like to solve problems alone. They have little patience with nontechnical people or with fools, two categories they may not always distinguish. Contrast this stereotype with the population identified to us as expert debuggers.

Our experts approached code comments much the way a clinical psychologist approaches a patient. That is, all the products of the programmer in his or her social situation constitute evidence. This evidence can be read to support conclusions about the competence and resources that have gone into the code. Of course, the range of conclusions that can be drawn depend upon the evidence in any particular case. However, at least in some cases the evidence will tell you the nature of a fault as well as the likelihood of finding it in a particular place. This information is only there, however, to someone who looks for it with a rich understanding of the variety of work conditions and the variety of people who are doing development in them[5].

Use of human resources. We found an even more striking contrast between our original expectations about code reading and our data. As we mentioned at the outset, most studies of programming or debugging focus on code reading. Our experts preferred not to read code at all, if they could help it; certainly not to read unfamiliar code without assistance, the situation typically presented to subjects in academic research. Recall that we are dealing with projects that can reach millions of lines of code. The situation is qualitatively different from anything that can be presented in an experimental situation. It is simply unwise and inefficient to try to approach new code if there someone else already familiar with that code. Our experts' first choice, if at all possible, was to go for help.

Going for help is not a skill that technical employers consider when hiring programmers, nor is it an activity supported by management mechanisms. Going for help is, nonetheless, a skilled behavior that experts value, and at which they excel.

Experts know to whom to turn for help. In a large system, that means knowing who is responsible for each module of code. Of course, if they do not know this, they find out. If more than one expert is available, more subtle questions of team selection arise. There is the "favor bank," an informal accounting of who has been drawing upon whose expertise. One aspect of expertise is monitoring and using the favor bank accounts. Another aspect is considering each individual's strengths and weaknesses against the particular task at hand, as well as their availability at the right time and place. And yet another aspect is considering the interpersonal dynamics between oneself and the others.

OTHER INTERPERSONAL SKILLS

These interpersonal relations also are managed by our experts, sometimes in quite deliberatively manipulative ways. One factor mentioned again and again in our data was the clumsy way in which new developers often approached someone from who they needed help, e.g. "There's a problem in your code!." The most self-confident of our expert developers knew how to subdue their egos in order to involve someone else in the project. This means knowing what kind of approach works best with different people; it means appearing puzzled and confused, if necessary, to arouse their interest; it means managing the approach so it doesn't infringe on their other obligations. A whole range of social and interpersonal skills goes into asking for help. According to our informants, these skills do not come naturally to new developers, and often they did not learn them in kindergarten. Simple politeness turns out to be a social skill that is underdeveloped in many Bell Laboratories new hires. This represents a functional deficiency.

We have spoken of forming ad hoc teams. That is just the beginning of the teamwork skills that may be called upon in fault finding and correction. The skills we have mentioned are relevant even for a single session together in the lab. If more than two people are involved or the problem extends over a longer period of time, more negotiation and interpersonal skill is involved: matching tasks and roles to people, allocation of resources, decision-making methods, fitting the work into assigned work-loads, learning from one another.

Another aspect of interpersonal skill is getting information from non-experts. When a fault is manifested in a field situation, often technical people are called upon to fix it without making a trip to the field site. Bell Laboratories has courses in interviewing skills, of course, and some developers take these courses. Their debugging may become more efficient as a result. However, we found that they confront special situations that are not treated in any interviewing course with which we are familiar. For example, we have some reason to believe that the experts require special skills in extracting information from non-experts in telephone conversations.

In short, the kind of strategic planning that characterizes expert debuggers is greatly aided by a thorough understanding of the person and context that produced the code and often also of the customer who is experiencing the problem. These understandings appear to be guided by a sensitivity to signs and symptoms that develops with experience. In addition, acquiring and managing the resources that make for efficient debugging also requires psychological and social judgment, and negotiating skills.

A software system is (among other things) a social construction. In fact, what distinguishes software engineering from computer science is in large part the social dimension that necessarily arises when a software-based system reaches a certain size. This social dimension is not added onto or peripheral to the technical dimension. Social and psychological factors permeate the technical ones.

STRATEGY AGAIN

We have classified the components of expertise into skill at getting information from documents, getting it from systems, and getting it from people, in addition to strategic competence. In the first of these categories, we encountered technical code search strategies: forward, backward, and Boolean search. We were told when they were most useful, and we have good examples of their use in very complex problems. Getting information from systems, includes considerable expertise in managing verbosity and tracing techniques, using breakpoints, testing, etc. These are technical skills that also often develop with experience.

For pedagogical purposes, all of these dimensions of expertise are relevant. However, our informants also made a point of telling us that teaching these methods had a much lower priority than did the "non-technical" strategies we shall be reporting. In our course evaluations, we have found more divergence of opinion among the less expert developers, an indication of a training need.

If we look at the psychology of debugging, we can consider the entire process to be a sequence of queries of the form, "What should I do next?" Some of these are low level questions, answered simply by knowing the procedure one is executing. Others are higher level questions - strategic questions - that arise when there is no subgoal operating for which there is an algorithm or when there are a variety of subgoals and no algorithm for choosing. Our claim is that answering many of these questions requires gathering and evaluating social and psychological information as well as technical information.

Self-monitoring, which is also characteristic of expert performance in general[6], is another important component of the psychological knowledge that constitutes part of debugging expertise. Judgments about the cost/benefit ratio of a search path requires knowledge of oneself as well as knowledge of the system. This includes knowledge of one's strengths and weaknesses, knowledge of the other demands on one's time. Our metaphor for our experts knowledge is that it is a map of the system. Our experts' maps are coded in several ways. One way, which we have discussed, is the extent to which a component is reliable. However, the maps are also coded as to the degree of the expert's familiarity with them. Our suspicion, from some of the anecdotal evidence, is that new developers are much less able to distinguish code that they know from code they do not know. Consequently, they are likely to act themselves where a more experience developer would know to ask for help.

Our experts also are very clear that they have learned from experience that the problem can always be in their code. It is certainly not that they have less self confidence than novices. However, they tell us that they are much more ready than are less experienced staff to consider the possibility that an error is theirs. This is hard won self knowledge, part of the metaknowledge that comprises their expertise.

KNOWLEDGE OF NOVICES

This brings us to another area of unexpected social knowledge. Our informants proved to have a very rich model of novice behavior. Some of our interview probes are based upon a comparison of ones' own behavior with that of a less experienced person. Since our informants had all served as mentors, it was natural to ask them what their mentees might have done. This probe often produced quite definite and emotionally charged accounts of mentee behavior. It appears that one of the major incentives our informants had for cooperating with us was to remove some of the mentoring load that they typically carry. On several occasions in our group discussion, participants would be eager to chime in with their own testimony about novice behavior. Their extensive and frustrating contact with less expert developers has produced this unexpected body of expertise about how people act. It is quite a different aspect of the demand for social competence in their job.

CONCLUSION

In summary, we are struck by the extent to which expertise in debugging is social and psychological expertise. Moreover, it is likely that much of this skill is used by developers in other applications other than debugging. Debugging requires interpersonal skills because software systems are social products; given the ever-increasing size and complexity of software systems, these skills become more and more necessary.

We are concerned that the prevalent stereotype of a "computer person" may be discouraging people with the proper balance of skills from appropriate engineering majors. Moreover, the structure of university courses, with an emphasis on individual competition, technical innovation, and coding problems devoid of social context, may promote inappropriate attitudes and sub-optimal work habits. The structure of most departmental requirements and the prevailing culture in most universities leads engineering majors to the belief that courses in the social sciences and humanities are not relevant to their performance as software engineers. We have no way of knowing, of course, how much this environment delays the learning of the requisite interpersonal skills when graduates enter the work environment. Nor do we yet have any measure of what proportion of new hires eventually acquire these skills. By making their relevance clear in the debugging course, we hope to contribute to students' development as software engineers. By making the relevance clear to professional trainers and educators in this paper, we hope to provoke more research into the extent and the significance of this component of software engineering expertise across sub-disciplines.

NOTES

1. See Freeman, J. et al (1991) for a more extensive discussion.

2. Klein, G. A. et al (1989). CDM is a variant of the Critical Incident Technique, cf. Flanagan, J. (1954).

3. See Weitzenfeld, J.S. et al (1991) for a more extensive methodological discussion.

4. See Glaser, R. & Chi, M. T. H. (1988), pp. xix-xx.

5. One useful model of what expert debuggers are doing is the explanation-based decision making model of Pennington & Hastie (1986).

6. Glaser & Chi (1988), p. xx.

BIBLIOGRAPHY

Glaser, R. & Chi, M. T. H. 1988. Overview. in Chi, M. T. H., Glaser, R., & Farr, M.J. *The nature of expertise*, Hillsdale, N.J.:Erlbaum.

Flanagan. J. C. 1954. The critical incident technique. *Psychological Bulletin*. 51.4:327-358.

Freeman, J., Riedl, T., Weitzenfeld, J. S. & Musa, J. 1991. Instruction for Software Engineering Expertise. *Fifth SEI Conference of Software Engineering Education*.

Klein, G. A. 1989. Utility of the Critical Decision Method for eliciting knowledge from expert C debuggers. Proprietary to Klein Associates and Bell laboratories.

Klein, G.A., Calderwood, R., & MacGregor, D. 1989. Critical Decision Method for eliciting knowledge. *IEEE Transactions on systems, man, and cybernetics.* **19**.462-472.

Pennington, N., & Hastie, R. 1976. Evidence evaluation in complex decision making. *Journal of Personality and Social Psychology.* 51:242-258.

Weitzenfeld, J.S., Klein, G. A., Riedl, T., Freeman, J. T., Musa, J. 1991. Knowledge elicitation for software engineering expertise. *Fifth SEI Conference of Software Engineering Education.*

Instruction for Software Engineering Expertise

Jared T. Freeman
Thomas R. Riedl
Julian S. Weitzenfeld
Software Quality Services
East Windsor, NJ

Gary A. Klein
Klein Associates, Yellow Springs OH

John Musa
AT&T Bell Laboratories, Murray Hill

ABSTRACT

Research, development and delivery of a course concerning how experts debug complex software systems raised questions about how to teach expert software skills -- including interpersonal skills -- to software professionals. For example: How can we teach students the metacognitive monitoring and control skills that experts exhibit? How can we help students identify what knowledge they lack concerning the specific systems for which they are responsible? Are cognitive models useful instructional tools? Answers to these and other questions are proposed.

Introduction

Researchers concerned with the psychology of computer programming have made great strides in the past two decades. However, their findings are of limited value in teaching software engineering skills, particularly to experienced professionals.

Studies of programming language variables (goto, nested loops, variable typing, and visual programming) as well as code style (indentation, comments, and variable names) have clearly and, most argue, beneficially influenced programming education. However, some contend that the findings concerning these variables are equivocal (Sheil, 1981; Pennington, 1982); thus, current curricula based on these findings may be unsound.

Text-processing research (Atwood and Ramsey, 1978; Pennington, 1987) concerning program comprehension does not confront the potentially overwhelming influence of strategy in selecting what code to read in the first place.

Theories that explain program comprehension as a process relying on recognition of plans and stylistic conventions (Black, Kay, and Soloway, 1987; Brooks, 1983; Ehrlich and Soloway, 1984; Rist, 1986) do not contend with the significant influence of application- or program-specific knowledge (Gould and Drongowski, 1974; Robertson and Yu, 1990; Gould, 1975).

Research that approaches program comprehension at the highest level -- as a strategic process -- is in a nascent state (Robertson, Davis, Okabe, and Fitz-Randolf, D., 1990).

Finally, all of the psychological studies of computer program comprehension severely restrict in the laboratory large sources of variance with which students must contend in the real world (Brooks, 1980; Sheil, 1981). Programming studies are typically conducted with individual undergraduate- or graduate-level programmers reading short (25 - 500 lines) bodies of unfamiliar code without the aid of documents or tools. Interviews with fifteen expert software debuggers in Bell Laboratory, across several projects at several worksites (Riedl, Weitzenfeld, Klein, and Freeman, 1990) indicated that these conditions are disturbingly unrealistic. Debugging in this professional environment generally involves teams of programmers -- each with graduate training in computer science and eight to 30 years of on-the-job experience -- analyzing enormous (500 to 1,000,000 lines) bodies of familiar code with support from reference materials, tools, and runtime versions of the systems being debugged.

Thus, the psychological research on programming expertise is of limited value to corporate trainers because it does not grapple with major sources of variance in real-world tasks. Thus, the research fails to point educators toward significant gaps in software curricula.

For example, the interpersonal aspects of programming comprise an all but virgin territory in software education. The debugging research mentioned above (and described elsewhere at this conference) highlighted the importance of social skills in gathering information critical to locating system errors. Yet, skills such as interviewing and small-group management are absent from undergraduate and graduate computer science curricula. Similarly, industry hiring practices focus almost exclusively on the technical proficiency of candidates, and (at least at Bell Laboratories) on-the-job honors and in-house publication opportunities are awarded strictly on technical grounds.

This paper raises several educational questions related to issues such as this, and it proposes solutions that may be of value to software engineering educators. The thoughts that follow are one product of a training research, development and delivery program aimed at teaching programming professionals how experts debug complex systems. Bell Laboratories is the program's sponsor. The course developed from this research is now entering its second year. Though there are few empirical data concerning the course, the offering has been well-enrolled and students have reviewed it well. We also draw here on our roles as software educators and researchers on other projects.

Specifically, this paper will address the following issues:

1. Expertise requires system-specific knowledge. How can we help students identify what they need to learn as individuals, without customizing courses to particular software systems?

2. Expertise requires practice. How can we help students learn skills that must be developed over the long term?

3. Expertise requires strategic flexibility. How can we teach programming students the metacognitive monitoring and control skills that experts exhibit?

4. Expertise requires interpersonal skills. Given that technical professionals often undervalue these skills, how can we teach them?

5. How and when should software engineering courses employ hi-tech instructional tools?

6. How can we tap the research opportunities in software education to further knowledge concerning software engineering?

Issue #1: Expertise requires system-specific knowledge. How can we help students identify what they need to learn as individuals, without customizing courses to particular software systems?

System-specific knowledge consists of factual knowledge and procedural knowledge, which we will discuss in that order. Factual knowledge is, for example, the ability to list the keywords in a computer language. Procedural knowledge is the ability to write a program in that language.

Factual Knowledge

Expert knowledge in fields studied to date (Ericsson and Polson, 1988; Staszewski, 1988; Chase and Simon, 1973; Chase and Ericsson, 1981) depends heavily on domain-specific knowledge. Though there are some expert debugging strategies that appear to span systems (Riedl, Weitzenfeld, Klein, and Freeman, 1990), much of what students need to develop debugging expertise is simply more knowledge about the systems for which they are responsible. It is reasonable to extrapolate that developing expertise in software development and programming, probably requires that students learn more about the applications on which they work. Unfortunately, educational economies of scale dictate that software engineering courses focus on knowledge that applies across systems. How can training developers resolve this conflict between students' needs for task-specific knowledge and the administrative demands for generalizable lessons?

One method, which has been well-received in the debugging course, is to have students identify for themselves the areas of system knowledge about which they feel ignorant. In class, students break into small groups to describe their recent debugging experiences. Working by themselves, they then draw a map (a variant of a semantic network) of the system components considered in that episode, and allow a classmate (generally a co-worker) to critique it. The students individually flag components and component relations that they feel they understand poorly. They then list one or two of these weak areas for the class. The instructor, the class, and the student propose ways to learn the needed information.

Thus, there is an ad hoc peer review of system knowledge and of students' educational plans. Both represent system-specific activities in a domain-general debugging course.

A second strategy used in the course is to highlight the breadth of system knowledge that experts apply to debugging software and to provide a taxonomy of that knowledge (knowledge about the code, the operating environment, system history, etc.). The taxonomy gives students a structure within which to test their knowledge of their own systems.

Procedural Knowledge

It is somewhat more difficult to identify students' deficiencies of skills. On-line exercises are not feasible where, as in the debugging course, students do not share knowledge of a single system.

Thus, we employ a simple and successful, though somewhat cumbersome approach. The student's manual for the debugging course incorporates references to process knowledge concerning tracing, code reading, interviewing, and other skills. We ask students to flag those tips and procedures that are unfamiliar, or with which they feel awkward. At the course's end, students compile a list of those procedures, note ways of learning or practicing them, and discuss their plans with the class.

A second method is to debrief students after exercises concerning aspects of their performance that were below their expectations or that of their teammates.

Issue #2: Expertise requires practice. How can we help students learn skills that must be developed over the long term?

Though students may correctly identify the skills they need and study them briefly, attaining expert levels of speed and accuracy requires practice over time (Anderson, 1982; Newell and Rosenbloom, 1981) -- much more time than is available in a two- or three-day training course. The debugging course, for example, includes a short section on interviewing experts and customers for system information. We do not expect students to become significantly better interviewers during the course itself, despite the lecture, tapes, and an exercise. The practice is left to them. Learning high-level debugging strategies presents a similar challenge. What can be done to help students hone complex skills over the long haul?

A first step is simply to remind students that refining some skills is a long-term, even a career-long endeavor. When students expectations are realistic, the goals they set for themselves may be more easily achieved, they will be more likely to meet those goals, and they may feel encouraged to set and achieve other goals.

We have also found it useful to illustrate selected skills with videotapes of expert debuggers telling stories from their experience. Elaborated stories may be easier to recall than rules of thumb, in accordance with theories of elaborated and episodic memory, (Tulving, 1972; Schank, 1991; Bower, Black, and Turner, 1979). Story-based lessons may, thus, be more accessible on the job.

Finally, the debug course includes a take-away job aid that is designed to reinforce lessons over the long term. The job-aid consists of questions to be asked during debugging. It is intended to prime memory for concepts from the course. Such job-aids are potentially valuable in situations where skills are used infrequently.

In summary, then, teaching skills that develop over time may benefit from orienting students to the long term, providing lessons in a memorable manner (here, stories), and providing job-aids that will cue lessons concerning these skills.

Issue #3: Expertise requires strategic flexibility. How can we teach programming students the metacognitive monitoring and control skills that experts exhibit?

Experts exhibit a sensitivity to problem content and their own problem-solving process that allows them to shift among strategies fluidly and opportunistically. This finding has been demonstrated in fields as diverse as physics (Larkin, McDermott, Simon, and Simon, 1980), geometry (Anderson, 1985), and the sort of everyday affairs (errand-running) in which most adults presumably are expert (Hayes-Roth and Hayes-Roth, 1978). Protocol analysis of interviews with expert debuggers indicated that they exhibit such behaviors, as well (Riedl, Weitzenfeld, Klein, and Freeman, 1990). For example, experts are particularly adept in shifting between backward and forward search strategies during debugging. How can we teach students the self-monitoring and self-regulatory skills expert programmers use to control strategy shifts?

One approach is to provide a conceptual model of the cognitive processes that experts employ. We use just such a model in the debugging course. The model specifies that experts entering a new debugging assignment first clarify the bug symptoms and refresh their memory of the domain (this stage of the model is labelled "initializing"), then cycle between testing hypotheses ("interrogating") and incorporating ("integrating") their newfound knowledge into their existing understanding or representation of the system. When their knowledge of the system clearly explains the symptoms, the programmer has found the error.

We have found that employing this particular model of expert process has several benefits.

The integration phase of the model emphasizes the importance of examining both the local and global implications of new information that arises in tests, reading, and interviews. The focus on global implications may help students avoid fixating on local tests, a practice that experts assert often leads non-experts down long paths to dead ends.

The model also provides an instructional framework in which to illustrate that experts attend more carefully to choosing and planning (Glaser & Chi, 1988) their research than do non-experts. The benefit for experts, and for students who learn the lesson, is that they spend less time executing fruitless tests and less time analyzing the findings of worthwhile tests.

A second tactic for teaching metacognitive skills is to instruct students to attend to and act on cues that they often ignore. For example, in the debugging course, the instructor elicits from students stories of recent debugging episodes. Discussion focusses on periods in which the students felt that they thrashed aimlessly, but ignored that emotional cue to change strategies. The instructor validates these experiences for students, using videotaped statements by experts. The instructor also suggests appropriate responses to thrashing, such as seeking advice, describing the problem in writing, and representing the system graphically.

Issue #4: Expertise requires interpersonal skills. Given that technical profession-als often undervalue these skills, how can we teach them?

Popular opinion has it that programmers work with computers because they can't work well with people. This belief is clearly contradicted by the behavior of expert software debuggers, who frequently and readily call on colleagues and other experts during debugging episodes. Non-experts in this study tended to attempt to debug problems on their own. Experts are aware of this distinction between themselves and programmers to whom they are mentors, and they explicitly testified to the importance of interpersonal skills. This testimony, in conjunction with the underrepresentation of programmers in interpersonal skills courses within Bell Laboratories, suggests that non-experts simply undervalue interpersonal skills.

The first challenge in teaching social skills to technical professionals is convincing them that they should consider these skills important. The debugging course employs videotaped testimony by experts to convey this message.

The second challenge is to teach social skills in a manner that engenders respect from this particular audience. To this end, we teach interpersonal skills as if they were technical ones.

Many interviewing skills can be presented like technical tricks, at the expense of appearing somewhat Machiavellian. Among the interviewing skills handled this way in the debugging course are those for clarifying a source's statements: paraphrasing, asking devil's advocate questions, asking naive questions, and asking for repetition.

We also attempt to illustrate a resemblance between interviewing and the more technical practice of debugging generally: both benefit from planning. For example, students receive an interview-planning checklist and instruction in using it to consider, in advance of an interview, the character of the informant and how to approach them and the wording of complex questions.

Issue #5: How and when should software engineering courses employ hi-tech instructional tools?

Education for software engineering is generally conceived of as technical education. As such, it is often presented in terminal-equipped classrooms. This is not necessarily a judicious approach.

Expert debuggers, for example, are distinguished from non-experts by their facility with debugging strategies and interpersonal data-gathering skills. Neither benefits from on-line presentation.

Social skills are best taught in practice, and to practice them, a social setting is needed. For this reason, the debugging course is taught in a traditional classroom where students can exercise interpersonal skills with each other.

As we have previously mentioned, the challenge of teaching programming and debugging strategy in a corporate economy is to provide lessons that are valid across systems. On-line lessons are not feasible when there is no common computer language or system with which to conduct lessons.

In sum, on-line terminals are not useful for teaching expert software skills, as we have broadly defined them. Various video technologies, on the other hand, are valuable for such instruction.

The debugging course employs 40 videotape clips of experts individually discussing their experiences and debating in a group the applicability of various debugging techniques. Those video clips comprise a valuable complement to classroom lectures and exercises for several reasons.

The consensus voiced by recognized experts on videotape seems to lend validity to the assertions of the instructor. The effect is probably due to the authority of experts, but there may be some benefit in the elaboration of each message due to multiple sources.

In addition, videotape (or videodisc) is an ideal medium for story-telling. As mentioned above, stories are peculiarly memorable, and thus of potentially great value in teaching skills that are critical when needed, but need be recalled only rarely.

The shift in attention from lecture to video can enliven a class, and often catalyze discussion.

Finally, video is an inexpensive medium in the long run, and highly portable across audiences; it can support two languages on stereo tracks, if necessary, plus subtitles. Transcripts in the course materials are advantageous when the tapes may be difficult to understand, whether because of media quality or the technical complexity of the subject.

It can be difficult to create videotapes of expert storytelling that are adequate for classroom use. Experts are often novices when it comes to telling a tale for an audience, thus their stories tend to be overly long and circuitous, or brief and obtuse. We have learned two valuable lessons in this regard, which we feel may be of benefit to other developers:

* Story-telling benefits by rehearsal. Subjects should be given the opportunity to clarify their stories, simplify the terminology, and practice telling their tales before committing them to tape.

* Story-telling benefits from analysis. Stories told off-the-cuff often omit reference to cues (such as particular symptoms or test results), strategic options, and other matters that experts consider during performance. Professional

interviewers are skilled at helping   subjects identify the critical cues, decisions, criteria and criteria involved in an incident. In addition, a competent interviewer can help establish the flow of events and the type of language that may be clearest to the intended audience. Thus, it is particularly important in documenting the experiences of software experts, to provide a   professional interviewer with basic knowledge of the technical domain.

Issue #6: How can we tap the research opportunities in software education to further knowledge concerning software engineering?

Software engineering courses such as the expert debugging class provide research opportunities that may refine software engineering on several levels.

At the most specific level, software engineering courses in the professional environment offer the opportunity for exploratory research. The student population for the debugging course is typically far more experienced than subjects employed as experts in psychological studies. The students comprise a valuable asset. We frequently take the opportunity to survey students concerning common bugs, symptoms, and exercise scores that we suspect may correlate with aspects of their professional experience. This data is helping to direct our focus in larger research projects.

The effectiveness of a course is also an important subject for study. However, testing is a difficult matter when the effects of instruction (in strategic and metacognitive skills) are expected to materialize only after months of individual practice involving software systems unknown to the instructor.   A number of traditional metrics are available, including number of bugs found or number of lines coded over a long timespan following the course.   However, it is desirable to collect the same statistics for the student population before the course, and for a control group over the same time period. Practical matters make this difficult. We have temporarily settled for polling students immediately after the course concerning their satisfaction. We plan to poll students and supervisors after several months concerning the impact of the course on debugging practice.

Finally, courses that explore new territory in software engineering raise new questions and suggest solutions. These may be of value to the community of software educators. We have endeavored to communicate the issues we have faced in one such enterprise, and hope that our colleagues will do the same.

Summary

In sum, we have identified several educational questions that arise out of environmentally realistic research in software engineering. We have proposed solutions that illustrate how we can enlist students in customizing courses to meet their own needs, how we can convey procedural lessons that are memorable over time, how we can help boost students' metacognitive monitoring and control skills and how we can make interpersonal skills palatable to a technical audience. We have also provided some tips concerning media for software engineering education and identified several classes of research that can be conducted in software courses.

We realize that a great many other substantive questions have not yet been addressed, and that all of the answers we have proposed should be tested empirically and debated within the profession of software educators. We hope that this paper initiates inquiry and discussion of that sort.

Bibliography

Anderson, John R. 1982. Acquisition of Cognitive Skill. *Psychological Review*. 89(4), 369-406.

Anderson, John R. 1985. *Cognitive Psychology and Its Implications*. New York: W.H. Freeman and Co.

Atwood, M.E. and Ramsey, H.R. 1978. Cognitive structures in the comprehension and memory of computer programs; an investigation of computer program debugging. *Technical Report TR-78-A21, U.S.* Army Research Institute for the Behavioral and Social Sciences, Alexandria, VA. NTIS no. ADA060522.

Black, John with Kay, Dana S. and Soloway, Elliot M. 1987. Goal and plan knowledge representations: From stories to text editors and programs. *Interfacing Thought*. Boston: MIT Press.

Bower, Gordon H., J.B. Black, and T.J. Turner. 1979. Scripts in memory for text. *Cognitive Psychology*. 11, 177-220.

Brooks, Ruven. 1983. Towards a theory of the comprehension of computer programs. *International Journal of Man-Machine Studies*. 18, 543-554.

Chase, W.G. and Simon, H.A. 1973. Perception in Chess. *Cognitive Psychology*. 4(1), 55-81.

Chase, William G. and Ericsson, K. Anders. 1981. Skilled Memory. In John R. Anderson, *Cognitive Skills and Their Acquisition*. Hillsdale, NJ: Erlbaum.

Ehrlich, K. and Soloway, E. 1984. Empirical studies of programming knowledge. *IEEE Transactions on Software Engineering*. SE-10. 595-609.

Glaser, Robert and Chi, Michelene. 1988. Overview.In M. Chi; R. Glaser; and M. Farr (Eds) *The Nature of Expertise*. Hillsdale, N.J.: Lawrence Erlbaum Associates. xv-xxxvi.

Gould, J.D. and Drongowski, P. 1974. An exploratory study of computer program debugging. *Human Factors*. 16(3), 258-277.

Gould, John D. 1975. Some psychological evidence on how people debug computer programs. *International Journal of Man-Machine Studies*. 7, 151-82.

Hayes-Roth, B. and Hayes-Roth, F. 1978. Cognitive processes in planning. Rep. no. R-2366-ONR, Rand Corp., Santa Monica, Calif.

Larkin, J., McDermott, J., Simon, D.P., and Simon, H.A. 1980. Expert and novice performance in solving physics problems. *Science*. 208, 1335-1342.

Mayer, Richard E. 1981. The Psychology of How Novices Learn Computer Programming. *Computing Surveys*. 13(1), 121-141.

McKeithen, Katherine B.; Reitman J.S., Rueter, H.H.; and Hirtle, S.C. 1981. Knowledge organization and skill differences in computer programmers. *Cognitive Psychology*. 13, 307-325.

Newell, A. and Rosenbloom, P.S. 1981. Mechanisms of skill acquisition and the law of practice. In John R. Anderson, *Cognitive Skills and Their Acquisition*. Hillsdale, NJ: Erlbaum.

Pennington, Nancy. 1982. Cognitive components of expertise in computer programming: A review of the literature. Graduate School of Business, University of Chicago, Center for Decision Research.

Pennington, Nancy. 1987 Stimulus structures and mental representations in expert comprehension of computer programs. *Cognitive Psychology*. 19, 295-341.

Polson, Martha and Richardson, J. Jeffrey (eds.). 1988. *Foundations of Intelligent Tutoring Systems*. Hillsdale, N.J.: Lawrence Erlbaum Associates.

Riedl, T.R., Weitzenfeld, J.S., Klein, G.A., and Freeman, J.T. 1990. Application of a knowledge elicitation method to software debugging expertise. *Proceedings of Behavioral Sciences Days '90*. Proprietary, AT&T.

Rist, Robert S. 1986. Plans in programming: Definition, demonstration, and development. In Soloway, E. and Iyengar, S. *Empirical Studies of Programmers*. Norwood, N.J.: Ablex Publishing Co.

Robertson, S.P., Davis, E.F., Okabe, K. and Fitz-Randolf, D. 1990. Program comprehension beyond the line. In Diaper, D., Human-Computer Interaction. *The Proceedings of INTERACT '90*. Elsevier Science Publishers, B.V. (North-Holland).

Robertson, S.P. and Yu, Chiiung-Chen. 1990. Common cognitive representations of program code across tasks and languages. *International Journal of Man-Machine Studies*. **33**, 343-360.

Schank, Roger C. 1991. *Tell Me a Story*. NY: Charles Scribner's Sons.

Sheil, B.A. 1981. The psychological study of programming. *ACM Computing Surveys*. 13(1) 101-120.

Staszewski, James. 1988. Skilled memory and expert mental calculation. In M. Chi; R. Glaser; and M. Farr (Eds) *The Nature of Expertise*. Hillsdale, N.J.: Lawrence Erlbaum Associates.

Tulving, E. 1972. Episodic and semantic memory. In Tulving, E. and Donaldson, W. (eds), *Organization of Memory*. New York: Academic Press.

Weitzenfeld, J.S., Freeman, J.T., Riedl, T.R., and Klein, G.A., 1990. The critical decision method (CDM): A knowledge-mapping technique. *Proceedings of Behavioral Sciences Days '90*. Proprietary, AT&T.

Knowledge elicitation for software engineering expertise

Julian S. Weitzenfeld
Thomas R. Riedl
Jared T. Freeman
Software Quality Services
East Windsor, NJ

Gary A. Klein
Klein Associates, Yellow Springs OH

John Musa
AT&T Bell Laboratories, Murray Hill

ABSTRACT

Software engineers typically show considerable growth in abilities over the first 5-10 years on the job. We propose that knowledge elicitation methods, normally associated with the design of expert systems, can be used to design training to accelerate this growth of human expertise. This paper examines some of the issues that arise in using such methods to develop expertise-focused training as we confronted them in a study we conducted to produce materials for a course to accelerate the development of software system debugging skills.

INTRODUCTION

Knowledge elicitation is the body of methods that have evolved, primarily for providing material for knowledge-based automated systems, to discover the body of learned knowledge that distinguishes human experts from non-experts at some task[1]. In comparison with the methods typically used in needs assessments for curriculum and course design, it uses more cognitive modeling, more structured methods based upon cognitive models of human memory, and is more intrusive. Where there are clear differences in expertise, particularly where they are the result of years of on the job experience, there is good reason to believe that such a body of learned knowledge exists to be elicited and turned into training material. The goal of this training would be to accelerate the development of true expertise and to produce greater overall efficiency of the work force.

We believe that software development presents such an opportunity. We focused initially on debugging because debugging activities occupy 40% or more of the time of large numbers of developers[2]. Developer time, needless to say, is expensive. Moreover, anecdotal evidence suggests a long learning curve for developers -- a fairly steep curve for five or six years.

Currently, much of the course-based training provided for developers consists of facts that can be recorded (declarative knowledge) -- facts about services, systems, etc. -- or knowledge about how to use particular languages or tools. It is either derived from software development disciplines or is about the specific project environment. These forms of knowledge do not include judgmental abilities or efficient habits and practices

Another component of training is assignment to a mentor. Mentoring uses substantial amounts of time of the most skilled developers, but is very variable in quality, depends a good deal on the attitude of the mentee toward the mentoring process and toward the mentor, and is repetitive for the mentor. Although mentoring has the advantages of providing just-in-time information in the actual job environment, we believe that we can transfer expert knowledge to new developers more efficiently by encapsulating large parts of it in a standard package. Moreover, we can capture aspects of expertise that the mentors themselves may not have known about, and can draw together the expertise from several mentors.

In this paper, we wish to present an account of a study we conducted in 1990 at Bell Laboratories' Kelly Education and Training Center (KETC) to produce a course in expert debugging skill. We shall discuss some of the methodological issues concerning the application of knowledge elicitation methods to the expertise of software engineers.

CHALLENGES AND ISSUES

The first challenge this task presented to us was that there may not be a generic debugging expertise, the same across different computer languages, different systems, and different work environments. We had no way of telling before we began whether expertise was very situation-specific or not. One possible outcome of the study was an outline of topics that would have to be filled in with different training material for different environments, according to the languages, tools, and systems prevailing there.

We considered other issues about the feasibility of this approach. Even if there was a body of expertise to be grasped, we might not have been able to elicit it for any of several reasons. One was whether the technical nature of the subject matter would in fact prevent us from capturing the expertise in any reasonable time frame. This was not a basic research project -- we were committed to producing training within a year. We brought enough knowledge of software engineering to the project to realize that the expertise might be so technology-dependent that we might have difficulty capturing it.

We should review here our own expertise to provide context for our methodological discussion. Of the current authors, John Musa supported the project and monitored its progress, but was not involved in the actual data gathering effort. Three members of the course development team had some programming experience in C, the language common to our examples. Moreover, the project manager had several years experience teaching a team productivity course in Bell Laboratories and participated in software process assessments and similar projects, which gave him both anecdotal and statistical data about project environments. However, no member of the team had been a software developer at Bell Laboratories.

Our primary body of expertise was in cognitive psychology and behavioral data collection. We brought to the data a sensitivity, in particular, to the differences between experienced judgment and declarative knowledge. We also were in a position to recognize signs of skilled memory, metacognition, etc. when they appeared. (Skilled memory is extraordinary recall abilities developed over time in a particular area of expertise; metacognition is knowledge or thinking about one's own abilities and problem solving processes.) Our skills would be helpful in turning the data into instructional material, but the material itself would require technical concepts.

We had to consider the attitude of "techies" toward non-technical people. Although the project included people with programming background, we were primarily a group of cognitive psychologists. Would the technical informants be willing to stay with us over the time required? They might not have had the required communication skills or might have found it too frustrating to spend the required time with us.

The technical subject matter itself was a potential obstacle, particularly when we considered using the Critical Decision Method (CDM), in which the subject matter expert tells a story that exhibits his or her expertise. These were going to be the most difficult debugging cases, and that was reason to believe they would be communicated with difficulty. If we had to interrupt every few minutes for an explanation of terms, CDM would have presented a problem. Given enough time, this problem can be solved. The questions here were whether our informants would give us enough time and whether we could afford the time. Our resources were limited.

A further issue concerning the level of difficulty of the debugging problems was whether our informants would have retained enough information about past episodes to be useful. Although the research literature on human expertise and the experience of some of our team members suggested that the expert memory of our informants would match the complexity of the tasks, we had some concerns about the impact on memory of the combination of complexity and technical content.

Another concern we had was the tool-orientation of management and technical staff. There was a widespread presumption that the nature of debugging expertise lay primarily in knowing how to use on-line debugging tools. Our own goals in planning the study reflected this to some extent. An interesting thread to follow in this discussion is how our methods produced data that refocused our image of the course -- our set of subgoals for the course development, in problem solving terminology. Our over-riding goal was to discover what strategies, habits, and heuristics characterize the performance of the most proficient program debuggers in typical Bell Laboratories software projects. However, subordinate to that, we wished to discover:

1) What kinds of bugs are most accessible to expertise, what criteria can be used to identify them, and what the best strategies are for eliminating them.

2) Which debugging tools are most effective in Bell Laboratories' software environments and whether they are used differently by the most proficient debuggers than by lowerperforming staff.

3) Which kinds of bugs would produce the highest investment/payoff ratio for improving debugging performance. Although we found some data bearing on at least the first two of these subordinate goals, they were dominated by our informants' claim that this was not the highest priority material for a course. We changed our goals for this initial study appropriately. Our results, summarized in Riedl, et al. (1991), reflected this change of focus. The evidence that we did get bearing on the more technical issues suggested that the answers would vary more by site, kind of project, etc., than the skills on which we concentrated.

PHASE 1

The initial phase of a knowledge elicitation project is to get an overview of the task. What has to be done in the targeted task? What is provided initially to do it? In the case of a job function that underlies much of the work of an organization as large as Bell Laboratories, these factors may vary considerably. We conducted a survey to determine how variable they were.

The survey was distributed in two mailings to 120 supervisors of software groups, all of the groups that we could identify as primarily software development groups. Twenty-nine returned the forms. This was a nominal completion rate of 25%, but the actual response rate was higher because many supervisors targeted in the mailing had changed groups or left the company. The survey consisted of 42 open-ended questions. One set of questions was to help us identify experts to use as subject matter experts, and to determine whether their supervisors already had a good idea of what made them experts. A second set of questions focused on the debugging environment and task. A third set was to help us assess the size of the potential market for the course.

More than three fourths of the respondents were able to identify a subset of their staff as experts. All of the supervisors who were not able to do so came from projects smaller than 10,000 lines of code, which may have produced a ceiling effect. About 70% of the supervisors were of the opinion that debugging skill accompanies general programming ability. However, they proved quite uninformative about how to characterize the expertise. Most used speed and experience to identify their experts and a large proportion focused in their answers to one or another question on the "methodical approach" of their experts. In retrospect, we take this to be a reference to the fact that experts do more planning.

We found that about half of the projects that we could classify clearly as either maintenance or new development were maintenance projects. Although working modules were generally kept below 1,000 lines of code, the range of project size was immense, best measured on an exponential scale. Moreover, a substantial portion of the debuggers were in an environment in which there was no use of parallel processing technology and another substantial portion was in environments where there was some use of parallel processing technology. The variables all might have defined completely separate bodies of debugging expertise.

We also found variation in the definitions of the task. Almost half of the debuggers debug their own code exclusively, while almost half also debug code written by others. The amount of information accompanying a typical assignment ranged from almost none to "requirements, architecture document, related design documents, names of contacts and support of team."

The survey also provided an intimation of a fact made very salient in our interviews: most debugging is done in teams. Over 40% of our respondents supervised groups in which all debugging is done in teams, and in over 80% of the groups at least some debugging is done in teams. Supervisors also indicated in their responses that there were many ad hoc teams. Although the survey provided no data about the structure of these teams, the interviews we conducted later did.

At this point, we knew that there was a great deal of variation in the work environments, and that most of them were quite different from the environments in academic studies, and that much of the work was done in teams. We had no evidence yet that any special skill was necessary to work on an ad hoc debugging team. We did have reinforcement for our belief that commercial work environments differed from academic environments substantially in ways that could affect what counts as good work.

CRITICAL DECISION METHOD

Given that we knew that debugging tasks may take a substantial amount of time, and that the environments could not be reproduced in a laboratory, and, given the variation in environments, we wanted a research method that would allow us to survey a reasonable sample of real-world work environments and debugging tasks in a practical amount of time. Rather than define the debugging difficulties for our experts, we wanted to allow them to define the difficulties for us. One or the other of these considerations eliminated direct observation, thinking aloud protocols, and the use of artificial experimental material or situations.

We decided to use the Critical Decision Method [3]. CDM is a knowledge elicitation method in which subject matter experts are asked to identify relatively recent instances of work in which their expertise made a difference. They tell these stories several times, during which the interviewer uses cognitive probes (methodical questions) to identify decision points, alternatives, and the criteria used to make these decisions. Because the experts themselves identify the critical episodes, they determine the relevance of various aspects of their expertise. Because the stories are retrospective, episodes extending over days, weeks, or months can figure in the data, with attention focused on the critical decision points. Because the experts are merely telling the story and not introspecting or planning lessons, we look at what they did and not at what they think they should tell someone to do [4]. However, in commenting on their own stories, our informants did make quite clear to us what lessons they thought ought to be derived from them.

The importance of not relying on expert informants to tell you explicitly what you want to know without systematic probing (the raison d'etre of knowledge elicitation methods) can be illustrated by our interview with an expert whose account began "First I mused over the code a while." This "musing" proved to be a day and a half of examining printouts and planning strategy.

The first step in identifying expert debuggers was to identify target organizations for the course. One source of information was responses to our initial survey of supervisors. A second source was queries to a course enrollment database maintained by the education center (KETC). We queried for the organization numbers of students who had taken certain programming and software engineering courses in the previous 2-3 years. Hardcopy organization charts were a third source of information. In addition, extensive "networking" was undertaken to identify members of management in software organizations who represented likely prospects for identifying expert debuggers. Once we had identified appropriate groups, we enlisted their managers to identify and give us access to experts.

The criteria we provided for identifying the expert debuggers included: those to whom you refer others who are having difficulty debugging; those to whom you give the most complex problems; those who seem to solve debugging problems faster and more efficiently. We also indicated that we would prefer people who were or had been mentors because we believed that they would be better able to explain what they did. We shall describe below some incidental benefits that accrued from having mentors as subject matter experts (SMEs). It did, however, introduce a bias into our sample. It focused our attention on the needs of those who are assigned mentors, for one thing. Given our training demands, this was useful in getting our a course with a large potential market. It also introduced the possibility of a bias toward one style of expertise. In fact, our informants were aware of at least one other style and, in some cases, were quite explicit in the limited value of the non-communicating "Lone Ranger." We believe an interesting question remains to be explored here.

CDM interviews typically take about two hours. In two cases, we conducted follow-up interviews because we felt we had not exhausted the material in the first session. The interviews are very compressed information exchanges. We videotaped our interviews, and our initial analysis of each interview took twice as long as the original session. We also went back to the tapes later with specific questions in mind. We found it expensive and frustrating to try to get transcripts of the technical interviews. Typists were unfamiliar with the vocabulary and could not follow the sense of the conversations. Although we could clean up the transcripts ourselves afterwards, they were not as useful as research tools as our own notes of the sessions. The notes were our basic data source, but the tapes were critical supplements when detailed questions arose. We consider this information part of our acquired expertise in conducting these investigations, and would expect future studies to be more efficient as a result.

Because the interviews were relatively short, we were able to schedule interviews at three different sites, with both male and female developers, and on five different projects, including both large and relatively small projects. Interviews were scheduled in such a way as to allow us to monitor the results from the interviews for signs of qualitative differences in expertise. If we had found no variation in the first 6-8 interviews, we were prepared to stop. As it was, we found enough variation to lead us to continue. If we were planning a complete curriculum for developers, we would have sampled further. However, we found enough consistent material for a first course in debugging in the 15 interviews we conducted.

In addition, we conducted two interviews with developers identified as "more typical," i.e. less expert. (These interviews were interspersed with the others and the interviewers did not know whether the respondent had been identified as an expert or not.) Given the small sample and the fact that expertise is not a dichotomous variable, we were satisfied that there was an identifiable difference between those identified as experts and the others.

After the first few interviews, we realized that we needed a structured method for representing the decision making so that all the participants could work from a common frame. Accordingly, we used a flow charting procedure to reflect successive stages of the process of troubleshooting or debugging. The initial state listed the situation awareness when the problem was first identified -- the symptoms the nature of the system, background contextual information, and so forth, along with the initial hypotheses about the source of the problem. Along the top of the flow chart was a timeline to link the process to an objective temporal frame. Figure 1 is a simplified example of such a chart.

The interviews using the flow chart appeared more systematic and more efficient because it was easier to take the interviews on tangents knowing that these lines of inquiry could be abandoned whenever the interviewer wanted to return to another topic. The flow chart was thus a departure point -- an overview of the topics to be discussed -- and an organizing structure.

The interviews were conducted in the following way -- first an initial incident account was generated by the SME. Then a rough flow chart was generated, along the time line. Next, the flow chart was elaborated by using selected probes to investigate promising lines of inquiry. Finally, the SME was asked where in the process it was possible for someone with less experience to make mistakes. The entire flow chart was reviewed, with potential error pathways highlighted in red.

For several of the interviews, we conducted an additional segment to obtain concept maps. These are semantic linking relationships such as "instance of," "in order to," "causes," and so forth. Concept maps were obtained for three SMEs, and were fairly consistent, although the specific terminology differed from one SME to another. The value of the concept map is to portray the overall understanding of the task, to provide a perspective for the more detailed data collected using the Critical Decision Method. Since different experts use different terminology, these are not easily combined into a single map. This is a current issue in the knowledge elicitation literature[5].

ANALYSIS

The basic analytical and validation process for the CDM interviews was the same method used for expert systems: rapid prototyping and informant feedback. In this case, our initial analysis was done in the interview sessions, in which material was recorded on a white board as decision points, decision alternatives, background knowledge, etc. was elicited. The informants were invited to correct and add to this material. In addition, the interviewers would occasionally formulate their understanding of what was happening and propose it to the subject matter experts.

In the longer term, we circulated several documents to the original informants and to other experts for comment: an initial report of cumulative findings, the course requirements document, and the instructors' guide. Another major vehicle for additional feedback was a day-long focus group, which we shall describe below.

Day 0
* Calls fail 10% of time (1% is acceptable) under heavy call load with new call generator
* Was setting up the new eqt
* This is a bad debugging situation because:
* there are lots of calls and features: many events going on
* tracing interferes with system timing

Day 3
* Assign to developer
* He says code is ok (He should have studied interface code)
* I say this is not a trivial problem
* Mistrust his switch
* This developer has a tendency to try to turn problems back and ask lots of question.
* I kept the problem in mind.
* We met daily.
* He professed to have free time

Day 8
* He tests in lab
* No results
* I step in to get it done faster and to keep the system around for experimentation.

Day 14
* Hooked in all test equipment
* 5 messages found where four were expected
* Test equipment was on-screen display
* This bug didn't kill a call, but I believed it could if it occurred in any of 3 of 10-15 possible windows.
* Developer missed seeing it
* All events are processed serially in this system. Thus, the problem could not be caused by race conditions between problem subcomponents.

Day 15
* Test: Wrote code to save info in buffers
* Buffers are complex.
* often bugs in the diagnostics themselves
* Printf affects the stack (e.g., uninitialized variables). Thus printfs point to a class of faults.

Day 16
* Connection mgr joins in lab
* Set breakpoints
* Mgr sees 3 parties on call. I know there are 2. (5th msg is for a 3rd party)
* Read disk traces from the bottom to the top.

Day 16
* Saw two problems:
  * Request for 3 ports to connect and
  * Two of the three port names are almost identical
* Knew this code had been changed
* We have several versions of endport assignment routines
* I distrust this developer somewhat.

Day 16
* Review code that makes requests
* Reservation code was outdated.
* Must reserve time on 3 slots.

Day 16
* Discover that old version of reserve request routine was used in the code. Replace with new version.

Background
* System 75
* New protocol interface
* Note: 2 hours per day in the labs

We compiled lists that were directed in part by our need for teaching material and in part by theoretical concerns. Separate lists were maintained of tools used, rules of thumb, bodies of information mentioned, and judgmental capacities.

FOLLOW-UP SURVEY

We conducted a second brief survey after the interviews. CDM is an intensive method, not an overview method. The sampling of experts ensured that a variety of techniques and bodies of knowledge were brought to our attention, but we had no way of prioritizing them and no assessment of how general the use was. We sent a brief email survey to our subject matter experts to address these questions.

One section of the questionnaire listed various techniques that either surfaced in our CDM interviews or that were prominent in the "How to debug" literature. These included both general strategies such as backward analysis, and very specific techniques such as truth tables. We asked our informants to rate each of these on a scale of 0 to 4 for how often the method was used, how effective it was when used, and how much room for improvement there was among the developers in their environment. The scale points were not defined further. Because we had some suggestions that the experts read code differently from less expert developers, we asked a few open-ended questions to get their views about this.

Our email surveys allowed the respondents to answer directly in the email message that they received and then return it via email to our data analyst. It required minimum effort on the part of the respondents and came in the form of communication with which they felt comfortable. We had a high return rate and a quick turnaround.

The rating data was combined into an overall priority ranking for the various techniques and was used to set the agenda for our validation focus group. The qualitative questions elicited replies of varying degrees of helpfulness. They supported the interviews in confirming that our informants believed that they could keep relevant information more accessible in memory than less experienced developers, and suggested some deliberate actions they take when reading code carefully. However, there was neither a history of having done anything to develop these skills nor a uniform set of suggestions. The questionnaire established this as a fruitful area for further research and gave us a set of tips. (We turned to the cognitive psychology literature for help in identifying strategies for developing these skills.)

GROUP DISCUSSION

Our initial hope was to able to validate our findings with experimental research and/or survey data that would corroborate the differences between experts and non-experts that our informants believed to exist. Time and funding did not materialize. We still believe that such corroborating research, as well as more detailed knowledge elicitation in several focused areas, would be very fruitful. Our schedule for producing a course required that we depend upon the consensus of our informants, together with other experts, including more research-oriented programmers from KETC to confirm and expand our findings.

We selected a tightly scheduled day-long group discussion, bringing together SMEs from the various sites. We wrote a preliminary summary of our findings and sent copies to all participants before the meeting with a request for comments and corrections. Eight of the informants came, with their own groups paying their expenses. This is an indication both of the felt need for a course such as this and the respect for our project that had been generated by our earlier contacts. The group was enlarged by several experts from KETC (up to 3, not all of whom stayed for the entire session).

The morning session was entirely devoted to debugging techniques, according to the priorities established by our survey. However, our panel, with a strong consensus, made the point that learning the specific techniques was secondary to having an overall strategy. They clearly felt that the major problem with novice developers is not a failure of skills, but a failure to recognize when they are thrashing and/or having ways to break out of thrashing. This message redirected our planning for the course.

The afternoon consisted of two hour long topics, a break, and then two 45-minute sessions. The topics, in order, were: code reading, cognitive skills (memory, practiced skills), overall strategy, and interpersonal skills. The plan proved to have anticipated the natural flow of the discussion, and one session often segued into the next with minimal transition efforts from the facilitator. The participants clearly enjoyed the interaction, and themselves thrashed out what had appeared to be inconsistencies or site-specific differences in our data.

They also introduced material that had not surfaced in our CDM sessions because of the linear nature of the probes. Habits of assimilating the data, running it through one's mind, etc. turned up in the group. (A more curious fact turned up. It appears that many of our informants have mental imagery for code similar to "number forms"[6]. That is, vivid, idiosyncratic, sometimes metaphoric, images associated with the code. Informants could represent locations in the code to themselves with this imagery.) However, as with the number forms, there was no evidence of this imagery playing a functional role.)

Another advantage of the group discussion was that it allowed us to document with a video camera testimony from our subject matter experts about rules of thumb and advice that might be unwelcome to the less expert. As we discuss elsewhere, much of the cooperation we received was generated by a sense of frustration from our informants. In their roles as mentors, they felt they had an uphill battle in getting across certain concepts, and they welcomed the opportunity to offload some of that work and get reinforcements for the message. The three critical issues in this regard were the importance of preparing properly before coming for help, the importance of overall strategy, and the critical role of interpersonal skills.

The group discussion format, unlike the CDM interviews, allowed for statements that had been planned a little bit in advance and with an eye toward classroom use, and the vocabulary our experts used was naturally less situation-specific. In another paper, we shall address the question of using videotaped testimony in courses.

CONCLUSION

Knowledge elicitation for the design of expertise-based courses in feasible, enlightening, and potentially profitable. At least in the case of debugging skill, there is sufficient generic expertise to provide the basis for training[7]. However, such data collection requires at least as much planning and methodological expertise as in knowledge elicitation for designing expert systems. CDM interviews provided an excellent core method, allowing the experts to define their tasks and set priorities while not requiring as much time as direct observation. Survey methods can supplement CDM to provide information about variability in the task environments and validation for CDM findings. Face to face group discussions are another useful supplementary method, providing both validation and access to other kinds of information.

NOTES

1. McGraw, K. L. and Harbison-Briggs, K. 1989.

2. Dunn. 1984.

3. Klein, G. A., Calderwood, R. & MacGregor, D. 1989. CDM is a variant of the Critical Incident Technique developed by J. Flanagan (1954).

4. Ericsson, K. A. and Simon, H. A. 1980.

5. Shaw, M. L. G. and Gaines, B. R. 1989.

6. McKellar, P. 1957.

7. Freeman, J. Riedl, T., Weitzenfeld. J., and Musa, J. 1991.

BIBLIOGRAPHY

Ericsson, K. A., & Simon, H. A.. 1980. Verbal reports as data. *Psychological Review*. 87.3:215-251.

Flanagan. J. C. 1954. The critical incident technique. *Psychological Bulletin*. 51.4:327-358.

Freeman, J. T., Riedl, T. R., Weitzenfeld, J. S. & Musa, J. 1991. Instruction for Software Engineering Expertise.

Klein, G. A., Calderwood, R., & MacGregor, D. 1989. Critical Decision Method for eliciting knowledge. *IEEE Transactions on systems, man, and cybernetics*. 19:462-472.

McGraw, K. L. & Harbison-Briggs, K. 1989.
Knowledge Acquisition: Principles and Guidelines.
Englewood Cliffs, N.J: Prentice-Hall.

McKellar, P. 1957. *Imagination and thinking*. London: Cohen & West.

Shaw, M. L. G., & Gaines, B. R.. 1989. Comparing conceptual structures: consensus, conflict, correspondence and contrast. *Knowledge Acquisition*. 1:341-363.

Lecture Notes in Computer Science

For information about Vols. 1–454
please contact your bookseller or Springer-Verlag